PRAEGER LIBRARY OF U.S. GOVERNMENT DEPARTMENTS
AND AGENCIES

The Department of State

Consulting Editors

Ernest S. Griffith

Former University Professor and Dean Emeritus, School of International Service, American University; former Director, Legislative Reference Service, Library of Congress; and author of *The American System of Government; The Modern Government in Action;* and two volumes in *A History of American City Government: The Conspicuous Failure, 1870–1900;* and *The Progressive Years and Their Aftermath, 1900–1920*

Hugh Langdon Elsbree

Former Chairman, Department of Political Science, Dartmouth College; former Managing Editor, *American Political Science Review;* former Director, Legislative Reference Service, Library of Congress

THE U.S. GOVERNMENT today is a maze of departments and agencies engaged in a worldwide range of programs and activities. Some departments are as old as the government itself; others are newly created or have been expanded or redirected by recent legislation. The books in this series describe the origin, development, function, methods, and structure of specific departments or agencies and explain how far their activities extend and how they relate to other branches of the government and to the public. All are written by authors with firsthand knowledge of their subjects.

The *Praeger Library of U.S. Government Departments and Agencies* is the only comprehensive, detailed source of such information. A list of those titles already published appears at the back of this volume.
—THE EDITORS

The Department of State

Thomas S. Estes
and
E. Allan Lightner, Jr.

PRAEGER PUBLISHERS
New York

To

Ruth and Dottie

Published in the United States of America in 1976
by Praeger Publishers, Inc.
111 Fourth Avenue, New York, N.Y. 10003

© 1976 by Praeger Publishers, Inc.

Library of Congress Catalog Card Number: 73-21345

ISBN 0-275-55470-8

This book is No. 43 in the series
*Praeger Library of U.S. Government Departments
and Agencies*

Printed in the United States of America

Contents

*Organization charts face pages 66, 78, 108, 112, and
113. A section of photographs follows page 86.*

Preface

This book was to have been written by the late George V. Allen, a distinguished foreign service officer, twice an assistant secretary of State, four times an ambassador, and director of the U.S. Information Agency from 1957 to 1960. Ambassador Allen had completed only the introductory chapter on the early diplomatic history of the United States at the time of his death. We picked up where he left off.

During 1972, when our first draft was being written, President Richard M. Nixon and his assistant for National Security Affairs, Henry Kissinger, conducted most of the important diplomatic operations of the U.S. Government from the White House. The Secretary of State played a subordinate role. With the accession of Dr. Kissinger to the Cabinet position of Secretary of State in September, 1973, the focal point for the direction of American foreign policy was returned to the State Department. Almost at once the new Secretary became immersed in efforts to bring about a Middle East peace settlement. Then, because of the growing loss of public confidence in President Nixon, Secretary Kissinger found he was called upon to assume extraordinary authority in directing the whole course of U.S. diplomacy. The role of the Department and the entire decision-making process were, of course, affected by these developments, and it was evident that a revision, not just an updating, of this manuscript would be necessary. That task was completed in 1974 but before the fate of President Nixon and its effect upon American foreign policy were known. Several footnotes have been added at a late stage in the production of this book to bring factual statements up to date.

This book does not cover or take into account the subsequent changes in the top leadership and the changing relationships among those leaders and Congress. However, its co-authors hope that what it has to say about the State Department in the period up to mid-1974 will give readers a background for a better understanding of the Department's role after that date. In any case, we stress that the Department, to contribute its best, needs a strong Secretary of State who has the backing of the President and of a congressional majority, but that when these conditions do not exist it can cope, often effectively, through its bureaucracy with a large part of the government's business with foreign governments.

Our principal purpose was to describe what this U.S. diplomatic business consists of and how it is conducted by the various bureaus and agencies that are a part of the State Department itself or have a special relationship to it in the administration of foreign affairs. Our approach to our task has been to give a brief description of the Department's organization and its many functions and then to select a few functions or areas to describe in greater detail. If some readers feel that we have not covered adequately a subject of special interest to them, we are sorry; our need to be selective was caused by the complexity of our subject and the limitations of space; our choices undoubtedly reflect our own experience.

We take this opportunity to express our deep appreciation to the many former colleagues and other officers of the Department of State whom we consulted in the preparation of this book. We are most grateful for their cooperation, candor, patience, and friendly encouragement.

We cannot adequately express our gratitude to our editor, Lois O'Neill, without whose tireless editing and patient perseverance it it unlikely that this book would ever have been finished or published.

T.S.E.
E.A.L., Jr.

Washington, D.C.
February, 1976

I

Colonial to Constitutional Diplomacy, 1624–1789

BY GEORGE V. ALLEN*

The diplomatic history of the United States is usually considered to have begun when the Second Continental Congress created the Committee of Secret Correspondence on November 29, 1775, to initiate covert relations with foreign countries.

It would be a mistake, however, to suppose that the American colonists had had no prior experience in diplomacy. As early as 1624, Virginia had sent a representative to London to look after the settlement's interests, and by the end of the colonial era, some two hundred individuals had served the colonies as agents in what amounted to diplomatic assignments. In the early years, these agents were appointed as special emissaries to look after specific problems. Then, during the 1680's, Virginia instituted the practice

* This chapter is extracted from a draft manuscript that the late Ambassador Allen was writing at the time of his death. A career diplomat, George V. Allen entered the Foreign Service in 1930 as a vice-consul and later served as Ambassador to Iran, 1946–48; Ambassador to Yugoslavia, 1950–53; Ambassador to India and Nepal, 1953; and Ambassador to Greece, 1956–57. He was twice assistant secretary of State; director of the U.S. Information Agency, 1957–60; and director of the Foreign Service Institute.

of maintaining a regular agency in London, and other colonies followed—although the youngest, Georgia, could not bring itself to spend the few hundred pounds required to defray the expense of a permanent agency until 1763.

AGENTS IN LONDON

The essential task of the agent in London was quite similar to that of a diplomatic mission today. There were, however, important differences, which should not be overlooked. Ella Lonn, in *The Colonial Agents of the Southern Colonies* (University of North Carolina Press, 1945), comments that the agent was "a sort of ambassador or minister, from the colony to the Court of Great Britain," and that his job was "to interpret America to Great Britain and conversely to interpret Britain to the American colonies." But perhaps half of the colonial agents, all told, were British politicians, merchants, or lawyers, some of whom had never been to America. Such agents were usually chosen because of sympathy for the colonial point of view, or for their supposed influence among government circles in London. An outstanding instance, qualified in both respects, was Edmund Burke, a prominent member of Parliament who served effectively as agent of New York in London during the critical years before 1776, although, as a leading exponent of the Whig point of view, he carried little weight with the ultraconservative Cabinet of Lord North when the final issues between Crown and colonies arose. The same individual sometimes served as agent for more than one colony—the most notable being Benjamin Franklin, who represented Pennsylvania during most of the years from 1757 to 1775 and also acted as agent for New Jersey, Massachusetts, and Georgia from time to time. Eventually, Franklin came to be recognized as the principal spokesman for all of the colonies in matters of general interest.

The right to appoint and to instruct the agent led to bitter disputes between the governor and the legislative assembly in several colonies. Under the general pattern of colonial government, the governor and the governor's council were chosen in London, while the assembly was elected by the qualified voters of the colony. The assembly's control of the purse meant that it could insist on having an agent in London responsive to its views, but it could not prevent the governor and council from also appointing their own agent. Thus, there were sometimes two agents in London representing the same colony. The authorities in London found the agency system a useful one, since information about the colonies was frequently required and someone close at hand was needed to supply the facts and serve as a channel of communications. But inasmuch as the governor was responsible to London, his own agent usually reflected London's views, with the result that London was merely talking to itself when it discussed colonial matters with the governor's appointee. For this reason, the British authorities themselves sometimes insisted on the presence of an agent who represented the views of the assembly.

Where a single agent represented the colony, the elected assemblies insisted on their right to instruct the agents or at least to have the majority voice in drafting such instructions. The usual practice was the appointment of a committee of correspondence consisting of members of both the council and the assembly, with a majority from the assembly. The members of these committees, who were usually the ablest and most energetic personalities in the legislative chamber, became accustomed to carrying out one of the most important functions of the subsequent Department of State. It is not insignificant that Thomas Jefferson, the first Secretary of State, had been a leading member of the Committee of Correspondence of the Virginia House of Burgesses. Nor should it be forgotten that, when members of these colonial legislatures were elected to Congress, they naturally tended to continue taking an active part in the conduct of foreign relations (often to the annoyance of President Washington, who maintained that, under the Constitution, foreign affairs were his prerogative).

An important duty of the colonial agent was to promote the trade of the colony he represented, and often the agent's correspondence resembled that of a commercial attaché or economic counselor of a present-day embassy. As events developed, the agents' activities in this field were largely of a negative character, since they spent most of their time combating limitations on the freedom of the colonies to trade with foreign countries. North and South Carolina wanted permission to sell their rice and ship stores to France, Spain, and Portugal. New England merchants, anxious to buy sugar, molasses, and rum from the cheapest source, resented the British mercantilist policy that limited their trade to the British West Indies, when the French, Spanish, and Dutch islands offered these commodities at a considerably cheaper price.

But although the most pressing original reason for establishing the agencies was to deal with commercial matters, the agent's duties in time began to center on other aspects of foreign affairs. During the decades prior to 1763, the colonial agents were chiefly concerned with the defense of the colonies against French and Indian threats from Canada and along the Mississippi. The cost of defending the colonies from outside aggression had been deemed a responsibility of the British Crown, and London did not quarrel with this basic concept. Nevertheless, as the colonies became more populated and economically more viable, the British Government took the position that the colonies themselves should make more substantial contributions, particularly in manpower, to their defense. The colonists thought otherwise. France was making serious efforts to gain control of the Mississippi and thus link French Canada with New Orleans and the Caribbean, constructing a series of forts on the Ohio and other tributaries of the Mississippi and forming alliances with powerful Indian tribes. The agents in London were flooded with requests from their assemblies for troops, guns, and, above all, gunpowder, and instructions to them that Britain must build and man forts to keep in check both the French from Canada and the Spaniards from Florida grew more insistent. Disputes multiplied over billets for troops, the building of cantonments, and the provisioning of garrisons. Issuance of paper currency by the colonies to meet these costs became a source of much controversy. Agents needed to be informed about military strategy and finance as well as trade.

Thus it was that when peace terms with France were being prepared in 1763, Benjamin Franklin came to play a decisive role in influencing perhaps the most important long-term issue that arose—what to do about Canada.

As agent for Pennsylvania, Franklin was particularly aware of the trouble France had made in the Ohio region and in western Pennsylvania around Fort Duquesne (now Pittsburgh). If France retained Canada, her agents could continue to stir up the Indians against the English colonists not only in the Great Lakes and Mississippi-Ohio region but also in northern New York and New England. Franklin argued strongly for the expulsion of France from the North American continent and the West Indies.

Many influential people in London felt differently. Canada was a cold, difficult area to settle and produced little in trade products except furs. The French islands in the Caribbean, however, produced valuable sugar, rum, and molasses. Britain had seized both Guadeloupe and Canada. If France demanded the return of one or the other as the price of peace, why not give her back the frozen wastes of Canada, with the struggling, small settlement of French-speaking Catholics at Quebec, and retain Guadeloupe?

Franklin wrote and had published several pamphlets describing the future possibilities of Canada in English hands and the mischief the French could continue to make using Canada as a threat to all of Transappalachia. The decision was a close one, but Franklin's views prevailed and Britain kept Canada, returning Guadeloupe to France. (By a curious turn of fate, fourteen years later Britain used its Canadian base to launch its most dangerous attack against the rebellious colonies. If the troops under General "Gentleman Johnny" Burgoyne, driving toward Albany in 1777, and Lord Howe's forces, expected to come up from New York, had succeeded in splitting the colonies, France might not have been willing to risk an alliance with the colonies, and Britain might have defeated George Washington and his ill-equipped Continental Army. (Until the outcome of this campaign was sure, Franklin must have wondered whether he had been wise in helping to persuade Britain to keep Canada. Nevertheless, his was probably the most important intervention in British foreign policy by a colonial American.)

The expulsion of France from North America at the end of the

French and Indian War, although welcomed by the colonies, brought about a sudden and decided change in British policy toward the Americans. The war had been costly to the British Exchequer. Most authorities in London felt that, since a primary purpose of the fighting had been to protect colonial borders, the colonies should bear a part of the cost. Prior to 1763, the British Parliament had generally respected the claim of the colonies that any taxes levied within them should be voted by their assemblies. No serious challenge to this principle arose until the Stamp Act of 1765, when the British Cabinet openly and clearly, for the first time, took the position that its colonial subjects were, in fact, represented by the British Parliament and that London would impose taxes as it thought best.

Sentiment in all the American colonies against the Stamp Act was immediate and vociferous. Every colonial assembly instructed its agent in London to protest the Act in the strongest terms and to concert with the other agents in a joint effort to achieve repeal. Various agents had occasionally cooperated in matters of mutual interests, but usually they worked at cross-purposes, under the stress of intercolonial jealousies and disputes. The Stamp Act controversy was the first in which representatives of all thirteen colonies were specifically instructed to combine their efforts for a single major purpose.* Franklin acted as chief spokesman for the group.

Fortunately for the experiment the united effort of the agents, combined with demonstrations in the colonies and lobbying by supporters of the colonial point of view among British merchants and Whig politicians, was successful. The Stamp Act was repealed. This demonstration of the strength of the colonies acting in unison was clear for all to see, and the issue of taxation without representation became a rallying cry throughout the colonies. As the language used by the Americans (the Adamses and James Otis in particular) became more violent, the British authorities became

---

* One agent, Edward Montague, who represented Virginia, undertook to explain to the people back home the British reasoning that led to the Stamp Act. He was considered to have taken the part of Great Britain in the dispute and was soundly chastised in the Virginia legislature.

more intransigent. The agents who were Britishers found their tasks increasingly trying. Americans in London, including the more moderate ones like Franklin, began to despair.

In 1774, the colonies joined together to form the Continental Congress, which assumed responsibility for the conduct of the foreign relations of the colonies. The First Continental Congress, which met in Philadelphia, September 5 to October 26, 1774, drew up a petition to be presented to King George III, which may be said to constitute the first diplomatic document issued by the American colonies acting as a whole. The agents in London were requested to present the petition to the King. Some of them felt strongly that they should demand an audience with the King himself, in order to deliver the paper into his own hands. But Franklin, realizing that such a demand might meet with a rebuff from the King that would add such fuel to the flames of passion in America as to render further dialogue impossible, persuaded his colleagues to agree to present the document to the Earl of Dartmouth, the King's private secretary. In so doing, he succeeded, at least for the moment, in discharging the first duty of a diplomat—to keep the channels of communications open.

Until almost the last, Franklin was inclined to look hopefully toward the King and to blame the stubbornness of London on the King's ministers, particularly Lord North, the aristocratic Tory who took delight in treating Franklin with scorn. Franklin's references to the King were always polite, and his efforts over many years were to achieve self-government for the colonies without a final break from England. He envisaged a self-governing America as the prototype of a group of such entities, including Ireland and other colonies, as a sort of family of nations under the British Crown. Not until the petition of the First Continental Congress met with a categorical and sharp rebuff from the King himself did he lose hope. Then Franklin asked to be recalled, and in 1775 he returned to Philadelphia.

One of the less spectacular but significant duties of colonial agents was to send back to the colonies copies of newspapers, pamphlets, and other publications containing current news of commercial and political interest. The political writings of Burke and others in Britain were of particular value to colonial leaders (and thoughts expressed in such publications frequently found their way into the orations of Patrick Henry and the writings of Thomas Jefferson).

The agents also encouraged liberal-minded individuals to emigrate to the United States. Franklin himself encouraged one of the most facile minds in London, Thomas Paine, to try his fortune in America and gave him letters of introduction, which he presented on arrival in Philadelphia in November, 1774. Public agitation against British suppressions in Boston shortly caught Paine up in the revolutionary ferment. In early 1776, he brought out his famous pamphlet *Common Sense,* calling for full and complete independence. It swept through the colonies, cementing opinions and winning to the cause many who had been wavering.

The agency system existed for 152 years, 1624–1776.* The agent of longest service, Richard Partridge, who represented Rhode Island in London for forty-four consecutive years, set a record not surpassed by any American diplomat since that time, and equaled only by Jefferson Caffery, a member of the U.S. diplomatic service who began as a clerk in the American Legation in Venezuela in 1911 and retired as U.S. Ambassador to Egypt in 1955.

Among the important personages who served as colonial agents were William Byrd II, who represented Virginia at intervals between 1698 and 1725; Charles Pinckney, who represented South Carolina in London between 1753 and 1756; and Peyton Randolph, who served Virginia during the same period and returned to become, subsequently, President of the Continental Congress. But most important to the story of American diplomacy is the fact that two of the first three agents of the Continental Congress to assume activity in France, in 1776, were former colonial agents in London —Arthur Lee and Benjamin Franklin.

In a letter from London to his son William, on August 19, 1772, Franklin commented, "Several of the foreign ambassadors have assiduously cultivated my acquaintance, treating me as one of their

---

* In Georgia, it survived until 1779, and even the following year a former agent, Grey Elliott, wrote to the Georgia Commons House of Assembly offering his further services.

corps." Like good diplomats of every time and country, the ambassadors were prescient.

AMERICA'S FIRST DIPLOMAT

Benjamin Franklin has been called, with justification, not only the first American foreign service officer but also first information and cultural attaché, first science attaché, and the nation's first intelligence agent. Any study of the Department of State must give full consideration to the work of this remarkable individual who retired from his eminently successful career in diplomacy before the Department of State was created.

When Franklin returned to Philadelphia late in 1775, following almost two decades of service in London as agent for Pennsylvania and other colonies, he was promptly elected to the Second Continental Congress and became the leader of its most important group, the Committee of Secret Correspondence, whose chief tasks were to get as much help as possible from abroad and to find out what attitude foreign countries might take if the dispute with Britain culminated in an all-out break.

Shortly after Franklin became a member of the Committee, a secret agent of the French Government arrived in Philadelphia, purporting to be visiting for curiosity and pleasure but, in fact, to investigate the situation in North America at first hand. He made himself known to Franklin, who let him understand that the final decision of the colonies might depend on how much support could be counted on from foreign countries, especially France. The visitor in turn made it clear that France sympathized with the colonies but that French actions would depend on colonial determination to see the matter through. He also emphasized that their conversations must be kept confidential.

The Committee of Secret Correspondence promptly decided to appoint clandestine agents of its own, to test out sentiment in Europe and to carry out such activities as might be feasible. Arthur Lee, a Virginia lawyer living in London, was the first to be so designated, in a letter signed by Franklin on November 30,

1775. Lee met with little success in England since most persons there, no matter how favorably disposed toward the colonies, were reluctant to give aid and comfort to the rebellious Americans, who by this time had already slaughtered a large number of the King's soldiers at Bunker Hill.

The second agent selected by Franklin's group, Silas Deane, met with considerably greater success. Chosen to go to France, Deane left for Paris in the spring of 1776, with secret instructions, drafted by Franklin, to carry on such "commercial and political" business as might be entrusted to him. Deane reached Paris two days after the Declaration of Independence was adopted in Philadelphia, but knowledge of this important act did not reach Paris until a month later. Deane nevertheless was able to make significant and useful contacts immediately. The attitude of Frenchmen of all classes was favorable to the American cause, in considerable part because of the French desire to see Britain weakened and, if possible, humiliated. Britain's defeat of France only thirteen years previously still rankled, and the French nation hoped for an opportunity for revenge.

Franklin's instructions to Deane were drafted with no thought in mind that he himself might have to carry them out. But four months after the colonies declared themselves to be an independent nation, the Continental Congress insisted, in October, 1776, that Franklin become the first avowed U.S. representative abroad, naming him chief of a three-man commission to negotiate with France. The other commissioners were Lee, who had slipped away from London and was in Paris, and Deane. When Franklin arrived in Paris, in December, 1776, the guidelines under which he carried out his duties were largely those which he himself had addressed to Deane. Like officers who go abroad today after serving in the State Department, he soon discovered that accomplishing objectives in the field was more difficult than drawing them up at headquarters back home.

Although the French Government and people were both sympathetic to the young American nation, the official policy of King Louis XVI was to avoid any open acts of recognition or support that would give Britain an excuse to declare war anew and seize the remaining French colonies. In consequence, the French Foreign

Minister, Charles Gravier, Comte de Vergennes, issued orders that there were to be no formal conversations or official contacts with the representative of the rebellious American colonies. Franklin's awkward situation in no way deterred his efforts, however. Since the former colonies were now operating in the open, he did not have to disguise his purpose for being in Paris, even if his methods had to be circumspect. He immediately launched varied and imaginative propaganda efforts on behalf of the American cause. Essays and articles flowed from his pen, setting forth the grievances that had led to the break with Britain, the aims of the new republic, and the desire for friendship and trade with all countries. These writings were translated (later, after a few years in Paris, Franklin became proficient in French and wrote it fluently himself) and printed in pamphlet form. Franklin personally bought the press used for this purpose. It was set up in the basement of his home in Passy, a suburb of Paris, and since printing was his lifelong craft, he made the press a hobby as well as a tool of his mission, often setting the type himself and supervising the whole job. Finally, he and his secretary sent the propaganda broadsides to the chief opinion-makers in France. This entire operation, so similar to that carried on abroad today by the U.S. Information Service (USIS),* he began before he could undertake anything in the traditional field of diplomacy.

In addition to these information activities, Franklin also represented his country in the manner of a modern cultural attaché (in present-day American practice, a USIS officer attached to any embassy overseas). In this, a principal pursuit of his eight years in Paris, during the days of the great salons, he was without peer. Ladies of fashion rivaled each other in efforts to attract to their "at-homes" the most distinguished personages of the day, and he was lionized. Franklin, already seventy years of age when he reached Paris, had considered himself too old for the job when the Continental Congress asked him to take it. His oft-quoted remark was "I am old and good for nothing; but as the storekeepers say of

---

* For a full account of USIS activities abroad today, see *The United States Information Agency,* by John W. Henderson (Praeger Library of U.S. Government Departments and Agencies, No. 14), 1969.

their remnants of cloth, I am but a fag end, and you may have me for what you please to give." This modesty was characteristic, but at the time Franklin reached Paris, he was already world-famous. Moreover, he was in every way a Renaissance man, as much at home in the salons of Paris as in the frontier towns of Pennsylvania. Though dressed in homespun and without powdered wig, he soon dominated the most fashionable as well as the most intellectual establishments of the Paris of Louis XVI—setting future cultural officers a high standard to emulate.

Franklin also, of course, met often with French scientists and may be regarded as the precursor of present-day science attachés, who since 1951 have served in a number of U.S. embassies overseas as members of the ambassador's staff.* The responsibilities of these officers include maintaining contacts with leading foreign scientists and reporting to Washington on scientific developments where they are stationed. They also, when appropriate, exchange information with their foreign associates, in the interest of cross-fertilization and of breaking down barriers to international understanding. Franklin, noted for his writings and his experiments with electricity, had been in contact with European scientists for more than thirty years. He continued to keep in touch, and the reports he sent from Paris to the Philadelphia Philosophical Society and other scientific groups and personalities in the United States entitle him to be considered not only the first but probably also the most noted science attaché any nation has ever had.

But important as Franklin's information, cultural, and scientific activities were, they did not achieve the spectacular success of his clandestine operations during the first year of his assignment in Paris. His cloak-and-dagger style was much like and quite as effective as that later to be employed by Colonel "Wild Bill" Donovan, Allen Dulles, and other twentieth century American intelligence officers.

Prior to Franklin's arrival, Silas Deane had already made valu-

* The United States in late 1974 had twenty-three science attachés serving overseas in nineteen countries. Twenty-three nations, plus the Delegation Commission of European Communities and the Pan American Union, had forty-seven scientific personnel stationed in Washington.

able contact with Pierre de Beaumarchais, an important man-about-Paris, social figure, playwright, businessman, and intellectual. Like the Marquis de Lafayette and some other French aristocrats, Beaumarchais had been imbued with the liberal teachings of such philosophers as Voltaire and Rousseau and supported the American cause not only because it suited French national interests but for personal reasons as well; the Declaration of Independence, with its emphasis on human as well as national rights, was a magnificent propaganda document and had had a considerable impact on men like him throughout Europe.

Franklin took up the underground activities with enthusiasm. He joined Deane and Beaumarchais in the management of a spurious corporation, given the fictitious name of Hortalez et Companie, to serve as a cover for their operations. Through this dummy commercial firm, secret shipments of gunpowder and other critical commodities urgently needed by the Americans were sent across the Atlantic in neutral vessels, consigned to pretended purchasers in the West Indies. Thence they found their way into U.S. ports. Much of the money to buy them was furnished secretly by the King of France.

The French Government's reluctance to give formal recognition to the young American nation was due primarily to uncertainty about the ability of the Americans to resist the British forces. During the first year, the American Army met with more failures than successes. Lord Howe, the British commander, delivered several punishing blows against the Americans on Long Island and along the Hudson. British military strategy was to separate New England from the rest of American territory through occupation of a corridor along the Hudson, linking British forces in Canada with those in New York. This strategy became apparent even before Franklin left for Paris, and his most urgent requirement was to ship rifles, lead for bullets, flint, and above all, powder, not only for Washington's men but also for the various patriot groups along the important route from Canada.

The efforts of Franklin and Deane were more successful than anyone had reason to expect. O. W. Stephenson, in the *American Historical Review* of January, 1925, estimated that at least 90 per cent of the gunpowder used by the American forces during the first two and one-half years of the war was supplied by Europe, most of it through Hortalez et Companie, which at one time had fourteen ships under its control.

Moreover, gunpowder shipped to the American forces by the dummy corporation has been credited, specifically, with enabling the Green Mountain Boys under Ethan Allen, together with a regular force of Continental Army under General Horatio Gates and smaller groups of local militia, to win the first significant American victory of the Revolution—the Battle of Saratoga. Burgoyne's troops, which had been harassed for several months, were finally forced to surrender on October 17, 1777. Five thousand officers and men laid down their arms.

When news of the Battle of Saratoga reached Europe in December, 1777, it created a sensation all over the continent. Former skeptics changed their attitude toward American chances of survival. Vergennes sent word to Franklin that the French Government was now ready to grant recognition. He invited the American commissioners to come to the foreign office to discuss a treaty. At last the stage was set, very much through his own efforts, for Franklin to enter into regular diplomatic negotiations.

When the Americans arrived, Vergennes asked for their nation's priority needs. Franklin was ready. He pointed out that he and his associates, working with their French friends, had not found it difficult to buy and ship supplies. His problem was that they had run out of funds. The most pressing need, therefore, was for a loan; the Americans would be most grateful for an advance of a million gold sovereigns. Vergennes wanted to know what collateral they could put up as an assurance of repayment. The only acceptable guarantee that Franklin could offer was tobacco, and the loan was backed by 5,000 hogsheads of prime Virginia leaf as collateral. In this instance, Franklin might be regarded as yet another prototype —of today's U.S. Treasury attachés.

Franklin's first true diplomatic task, following upon the loan, was to negotiate two treaties with France. He accomplished both simultaneously and quickly. They were signed in Paris on February 6, 1778, or less than two months after negotiations started, and ratified by the Continental Congress on May 4, 1778, a few days after the arrival of the documents in Philadelphia.

The first was a standard treaty of amity and commerce such as existed between most sovereign states. It extended recognition to the United States as an independent nation, provided for normal commercial transactions between the two countries, and paved the way for each country to maintain diplomatic and consular establishments in the capital and principal cities of the other. Treaties with provisions of this kind (sometimes referred to as treaties of establishment) are generally the first to be negotiated between two countries that wish to enter into formal relations. Their negotiation, however, is often long drawn out and sometimes accomplished piecemeal. (The United States and the Union of Soviet Socialist Republics, for example, agreed to establish embassies in Moscow and Washington in 1933, but a consular treaty, although discussed from time to time over a period of thirty-one years, was not signed until June 1, 1964. Even then, consent to its ratification was delayed by the U.S. Senate for another three years. The Russians, in turn, delayed for another year. Not until June 13, 1968, at a White House ceremony, did President Johnson and the Soviet Ambassador finally exchange ratifications. The treaty came into effect thirty days thereafter.)

The second agreement that Franklin negotiated was a treaty of alliance. It provided for joint military actions against a potential common enemy (Great Britain) and was accompanied by an "Act Separate and Secret," which provided that, if Britain went to war with France, neither of the two allies would sign a separate peace. (It is interesting to note that Franklin's treaty of alliance with France was the only military alliance entered into by the United States for the first 173 years of the nation's existence. The North Atlantic Treaty creating NATO was the second.)

During the first two years of his sojourn in Paris, Franklin was merely the chief of the U.S. Commission, which included Silas Deane and Arthur Lee. Although he was the dominant member, the situation created a certain awkwardness. On September 14, 1778, the Continental Congress elected him sole U.S. diplomatic representative in France, with the title of Minister Plenipotentiary.

It is from this appointment that his designation as father of the U.S. Foreign Service derives.

The Constitution of the United States gives to the President the power to appoint "ambassadors, other public ministers, and consuls." However, the United States did not have ambassadors in its diplomatic service until 1893. The young republic regarded the title as pretentious and unsuited for a modest country, proud of its simple, democratic ideals. Moreover, the concept prevailed that ambassadors were exchanged only between emperors or great monarchs. Lesser nations, including the other republic of the day —the Swiss Confederation—exchanged ministers. Since the exchange of diplomatic representation was reciprocal, as it remains, Franklin agreed that the U.S. representative in Paris would carry the title of Minister Plenipotentiary, and Vergennes consented to send a diplomat of the same rank to Philadelphia.

The new Minister's credentials were in the form of a letter from the only executive the American nation had at the time—the President of the Continental Congress—addressed to the French monarch. Franklin presented it to King Louis XVI on March 23, 1779.

The first diplomatic credentials ever issued by the United States read very much the same as such letters do today. Whether addressed to a King or to a President, the salutation was, and is, "Great and Good Friend." The letter Franklin presented went on to say that the Congress of the United States had made choice of Benjamin Franklin of Pennsylvania, to reside near His Majesty's Government as representative of the United States in the capacity of Minister Plenipotentiary. The Congress requested His Majesty to put full faith and credence in whatever Franklin might have to say on its behalf. The phrase "full faith and credence" was the key, giving it the capacity of a "Letter of Credence," hallowed in diplomatic usage before and subsequently.*

The term "Plenipotentiary" meant that Franklin had full power to negotiate and sign treaties and to communicate information or

---

* Following the adoption of the Constitution in 1789, letters of credence have retained the same format but have been written in the first person. They are addressed by the President of the United States to the head of a foreign state, saying "I have made choice . . . ," etc.

proposals to the government of France on behalf of the United States on a continuing basis, as long as he held the position. His previous designation as commissioner had been for a specific *ad hoc* assignment, with limited powers. When he presented the letter of credence naming him Minister Plenipotentiary on March 23, 1779, the conduct of the foreign relations of the United States began in a formal and traditional sense.

Franklin continued to perform brilliantly in Paris for six more years, until at the age of seventy-nine he was finally permitted to come home. He was followed, in 1785, by Thomas Jefferson—who insisted that he had not replaced Franklin. No one could do that. Jefferson described himself as merely Franklin's successor.

A DEPARTMENT OF FOREIGN AFFAIRS

The Continental Congress operated for nearly seven years entirely through committees, including the Committee of Secret Correspondence, authorized in 1775. Following the Declaration of Independence, the word "Secret" was dropped, and on April 17, 1777, the name was changed to the Committee for Foreign Affairs. It was permitted a secretary of its own, and Thomas Paine, the pamphleteer, was the first named, at a salary of $70 a month.

During the period when foreign relations were handled by the Committee for Foreign Affairs (1777–81), the Continental Congress undertook a number of measures in an endeavor to elicit support from European countries. Most members of the Congress favored an all-out effort to persuade other nations to recognize U.S. independence, even though Franklin, in dispatches and letters from Paris, opposed the effort. He thought it undignified for the young country to beg for recognition, but the Congress appointed agents to go to Spain, Prussia, Russia, Tuscany, and the Netherlands for this purpose. They were also instructed to seek financial assistance.

None of these efforts succeeded. Spain would not even allow Arthur Lee, the intended agent, to reach Madrid, turning him back on the way. Lee was also commissioned to Prussia and was able to reach Berlin, where he became the first American diplomat to have his secret documents stolen—by an agent of the British Minister. His brother, William Lee, achieved the equally dubious distinction of committing the first significant U.S. diplomatic blunder. His commission was to the Austro-Hungarian Empire, which was then at war with Prussia. When William reached Vienna, he foolishly discussed publicly the U.S. efforts to enter into friendly relations with Prussia, thereby rendering it impossible either for him to make any headway with the Austrians or for his brother to gain recognition from the Prussians in Berlin. Francis Dana, sent to Saint Petersburg, reached that city but was subjected to constant rebuffs throughout his two-year stay there. Ralph Izard, named to Tuscany (the most important sovereign state on the Italian peninsula) got as far as Paris but did not even try to proceed further when he learned that the Duke of Tuscany would not receive him. In September, 1779, there was some hope that Spanish mediation might bring an end to the war, and Congress sent John Adams to Paris to aid Franklin in negotiating a peace treaty. The Spanish efforts failed, and Adams was sent to The Hague to seek recognition and aid, pending the arrival of Henry Laurens of South Carolina, who had been selected by Congress as the U.S. envoy to the Netherlands. Laurens was captured by the British en route, and Adams was instructed to remain in The Hague, where his efforts at first were unsuccessful, although they finally showed some promise.

The multiplication of American agents overseas resulted in an increased number of reports coming in from Paris and other European capitals to the Committee for Foreign Affairs in Philadelphia. These reports had to be handled, decisions taken, and replies dispatched. Energetic Tom Paine kept up with the tasks. Then, in 1779, Silas Deane was accused of having mismanaged the matter of French aid and of having profited from the business of Hortalez et Companie. A considerable controversy arose in the press and in Congress. Paine's journalistic proclivities were strong. He published some of the confidential documents that came into his hands and was dismissed from his position.* Without him, the Committee's

* The unauthorized release of similar documents has plagued the U.S. Government frequently since that time.

business was soon seriously neglected. A member, James Lovell, wrote to Arthur Lee on August 6, 1779, that

> there is really no such thing as a Committee of Foreign Affairs existing, no Secretary or Clerk, further than I persevere to be one and the other. The books and papers of that extinguished [sic] body lay yet on the table of Congress, or rather are locked up in the Secretary's private box.

Drastic action was necessary to improve the situation. Several members of the Continental Congress suggested the creation of a permanent executive department to handle foreign affairs, separate from the Congress itself but subject to congressional directive. Opposition to the establishment of any such executive body remained strong, however, even though the winter of 1777–78 had nearly seen the extinction of Washington's small force at Valley Forge, and Washington himself was in despair over his inability to elicit replies to his appeals to Congress for support. It was not until May, 1780, that Congress was willing even to appoint a special committee to examine what should be done about the Committee for Foreign Affairs. This special committee recommended that a "Department of Foreign Affairs" be established.

The use of the word "Department" was a significant victory for those who saw the necessity for an executive branch of the government, but another eight months passed before the Continental Congress took the necessary steps to create such a department. Finally, on January 10, 1781, it passed a resolution providing for an office to be established "forthwith" for the Department of Foreign Affairs, "to be kept always in the place where Congress shall reside" and also providing that "there shall be a secretary for the dispatch of business of the said office, to be styled 'Secretary of Foreign Affairs.' "

Although the legislative history of the resolution made it clear that Congress intended for this new "secretary" to be something more than a clerk, which had been Paine's position, another lapse of seven months occurred before Congress elected Robert R. Livingston, who had been a delegate from New York, to the new post. Livingston took his oath of office on October 20, 1781, the day after Cornwallis's surrender at Yorktown had ended the military phase of the American Revolution.

The Revolutionary War had been fought and won before tentative steps were taken toward establishing an executive branch of the government in Philadelphia. Even then, another four months passed before the enactment of regulations on February 22, 1782, referring to Livingston's position as "Secretary to the United States of America, for the Department of Foreign Affairs" in language that indicated there were to be other secretaries to the United States to direct other executive departments. Thus, Livingston became not only the first holder of the position known subsequently as Secretary of State, but also the first man in the new nation to hold an executive appointment of any kind.

With a staff of two under secretaries, a translator, and a clerk, Livingston established his office in a small brick house near the corner of Sixth and Chestnut streets in Philadelphia, a short distance from the seat of the Continental Congress. There he received reports from the American commissioners in Europe—and urged them to send more. In addition to directing his office and carrying on extensive correspondence with officials at home and abroad, he was expected to keep Congress closely informed of the state of U.S. relations with foreign countries. His public standing and talent brought prestige to his role, but he remained in office less than two years, resigning in June, 1783, in the midst of the negotiations in Paris of the peace treaty with Great Britain. Fortunately, Benjamin Franklin's ability and prestige were sufficient, together with the important assistance of John Adams and John Jay, to carry the negotiations through without additional instructions from America.

Following Livingston's resignation, the new department was without direction for almost a year. The text of the peace treaty, signed in Paris on September 3, 1783, arrived in Philadelphia several months after Livingston had resigned. As a tentative but emergency measure, the President of the Congress assumed temporary charge of the Department and submitted the treaty for ratification. The treaty was more favorable to the United States than most members of Congress expected, particularly as regarded the boundaries of the United States, and it was ratified promptly, on January 14, 1784.

Livingston's successor, John Jay, also of New York, was chosen on May 7, 1784. Jay was in Paris at the time. He had been sent to Spain as U.S. Minister in 1780, when Spain at last agreed to recognize the United States, but he had been able to accomplish almost nothing in Madrid due to differences over a number of issues, including, notably, the unwillingness of both the United States and France to agree to continue fighting until Spain achieved its chief war aim—Gibraltar. Moreover, the Royal Government in Madrid had never wanted to see the rebellious colonies succeed in obtaining independence; the ideas of independence and republicanism might spread to Spanish possessions in America.

In 1782, Jay had been instructed to join Franklin in Paris, to assist in the peace negotiations with Great Britain. He remained there until the treaty was ratified and even then was reluctant to return to the inhospitable atmosphere of Madrid. His selection as Secretary for Foreign Affairs enabled him to return to America instead.

During the five years Jay held the office (1784–89), it continued to carry, officially, the long and cumbersome title "Secretary to the United States of America, for the Department of Foreign Affairs," but it had been shortened by common usage to "Secretary for Foreign Affairs." Jay's tenure, throughout the remaining period of the Continental Congress and the adoption of the Constitution, was marked by continued effort to negotiate treaties with foreign countries to obtain recognition of the United States and the establishment of trade relations. During this period, American agents, commissioners, and ministers abroad were called on to perform consular as well as diplomatic functions. The dividing line between these duties was indistinct, as it remains to this day.

Much of the work of a consular officer involves assistance to his fellow countrymen (businessmen, missionaries, tourists, students, and others) residing in or visiting his consular district. The chief functions of a diplomat involve negotiating with foreign governments, reporting to his government on political, economic, cultural, and other matters, and representing the President and government of the United States in the country to which he is accredited. However, consular officers also report on these same subjects and represent the United States in their areas; consular posts may be thought of, in effect, as embassy branches (although in some places the American Consulate General is an independent entity, and its functions are as much diplomatic as consular).*

The 1778 treaty of alliance between the United States and France, which Franklin negotiated, provided that the two countries would exchange ministers and receive consular officers to reside in one another's ports and principal cities. The first consular official to be appointed by the United States was William Palfrey of Massachusetts, who was chosen by the Continental Congress on November 4, 1780, to reside "in France." Palfrey was lost at sea en route to his post and thus became the first U.S. consular or diplomatic officer to die under "heroic or tragic circumstances."†

In June, 1781, Thomas Barclay, an American merchant already living in France, was designated "vice consul in France" and four months later was promoted to Consul, in the place of Palfrey. Within a year, he was being referred to in Congress as Consul General—a record of promotions hardly equaled before or since.

When Jay became Secretary for Foreign Affairs in 1784, Barclay remained the only U.S. consular officer assigned abroad, although Congress had also appointed a merchant from New York living in Madeira to be "commercial agent" there "to assist the merchants and other citizens of the U.S. trading to the Island of Madeira and Porto Santo."

American trade with foreign countries did not expand as rapidly after independence as had been hoped. France and Spain maintained strict control over the trade of their colonies in the Western Hemisphere, and even the British islands of the Caribbean, which had previously been open to American ships, were now closed to

---

* For a full explanation of consular work, see *The Foreign Service of the United States,* by W. Wendell Blancké (Praeger Library of U.S. Government Departments and Agencies, No. 18), 1969.

† This is the manner in which the American Foreign Service Association describes the 113 officers whose names by 1974 had been inscribed on a bronze plaque that the Association installed in the lobby of the Department of State building in Washington in 1933. William Palfrey is first on the list. T.S.E.

the United States, a foreign country. However, since European powers had not extended their colonial domination over China and certain other parts of the Far East, American ships could trade there on an equal basis with all others. Canton, in South China, was becoming an important center for such trade, and American clipper ships soon began to find their way to the Orient. A flourishing commerce was established within a short time, and need arose for a consul in that faraway port to assist American sea captains and merchants in their dealings with the Chinese authorities and purveyors. Jay commissioned Samuel Shaw of Massachusetts to be American Consul at Canton in January, 1786, and Thomas Randall of Pennsylvania was appointed to assist him. No salaries were provided, but the men were glad to assume the positions for reasons of prestige. They were engaged in the China trade and were permitted to continue their private businesses.

The same year, Jay commissioned Consul Barclay as special agent to negotiate a treaty of peace and friendship with Morocco, the North African country thought most likely to be willing to enter into such an agreement. The Barbary states were preying on American commerce in the Mediterranean and demanding large tribute as the price of "protecting" American ships from piracy, but trade with Morocco, while difficult, was no more difficult for Americans than anyone else. Barclay was successful, and a treaty with Morocco was signed in July, 1786. Since there were no suitable Americans living in Morocco to serve as consuls or vice consuls, Barclay was asked to recommend responsible Europeans there to look after U.S. interests. He designated an Italian merchant in Tangier, who was already serving as consul for Venice and vice consul for Genoa, to serve also as consular agent for the United States, subject to ratification of the treaty and approval of the nomination by Congress. Jay sent the treaty and nomination to Congress with his recommendation for approval, and Congress acted favorably on July 23, 1787.

The establishment of an American Consulate in Canton in 1786 and at Tangier the following year were indications that the United States, as a new nation entering the international trade field, had to look for markets where it could. Jay thought that the United States should also establish a number of consular posts in Europe, but Congress was opposed to the expenditures involved and authorized American diplomatic officials there to perform such consular duties as might be required.

Thus, in the era prior to the adoption of the Constitution, the United States managed to get along with minimum expenditures for official representation overseas. Jay's staff in the Department of Foreign Affairs was limited to one assistant, a translator, and two clerks.

THE CONSTITUTIONAL CONVENTION

The weakness of the American Government under the Articles of Confederation was evident in many areas, but nowhere more glaringly than in the conduct of foreign affairs. Under the Confederation, the Continental Congress was supposedly in control of all matters having to do with the nation's foreign relations. In fact, each state levied its own import and export duties and enforced them in its own courts. Largely because of the inability of the Continental Congress to enforce any agreement that might be signed and ratified, Secretary for Foreign Affairs Jay and John Adams, the first U.S. Minister to Great Britain (1785–88), had been unable to negotiate a commercial treaty with the British authorities following the Treaty of Paris of 1783. Other countries were also reluctant to enter into a treaty of commerce with the United States.

During the Constitutional Convention of 1787, the participants quickly agreed that the thirteen states could not continue to pose as a single nation unless the Articles of Confederation were supplanted by a new framework of government. The alternative, thirteen separate nations, each entering into its own arrangement with foreign powers and vying with the others or working at cross-purposes over trade, boundaries, defense against the Indians, and a host of other foreign and domestic problems, was too depressing to contemplate. But it was the necessity for a united approach in foreign affairs that became the single most important consideration holding the Convention together. It was almost the only issue on which all could agree.

Important decisions had to be made regarding the manner in which foreign affairs would be handled. The concept of an executive branch of the government, distinct from the legislative, already existed in the embryonic Department of Foreign Affairs. As finally drafted, the Constitution made no specific mention of this or any other executive department, but in the words authorizing the President to "require the opinion, in writing, of the principal officer in each of the executive departments," it recognized that several would be created. The new Constitution was a compromise in almost every respect, and the checks and balances between the executive and legislative branches embodied in the document have seriously affected the conduct of the foreign relations of the United States throughout the nation's history.

During the preceding years 1776–89, the conduct of foreign relations had been the prerogative of the Continental Congress. In transferring the initiative and chief responsibility in this field to the executive, the founding fathers insisted that the legislative body retain a share in it, as a check on the executive. Thus, the President was given the power to "make treaties," but only "by and with the advice and consent of the Senate." (The awkwardness inherent in this provision was soon to become apparent. Washington, noting that he must obtain not only the "consent" of the Senate but the "advice" as well, construed the phrase to mean that he should consult it, as a body, during the negotiations. His first effort to do so resulted in such a tumult of advice that he left the Senate chamber in a huff, muttering that he would be damned if he would go there again. No President since Washington has formally sought the advice of the Senate as a whole during the negotiation of a treaty.)

WASHINGTON'S SECRETARY OF STATE

When Washington became President in 1789, he named Thomas Jefferson Secretary of State. Jefferson, however, was still in Paris, serving as U.S. Minister there. Pending his return, Washington asked Jay, who had been Secretary for Foreign Affairs for six years under the Continental Congress, to remain on as acting Secretary of State. In his previous position, Jay had been responsible to Congress. Now he was responsible to the President.

Under the new Constitution, the duties of the Secretary of State included not only advising the President on foreign policy and directing U.S. diplomats and consuls overseas; he was charged with certain domestic functions as well. The Secretary of State was made the custodian of the Great Seal, to be affixed to laws, commissions, and other domestic documents of the federal government as well as to treaties, commissions, and other documents relating to foreign affairs. He was also designated as the channel for communications between the federal government and the governors of the various states.

The duties of the Department of State in domestic matters, never very significant, have steadily declined and today are limited almost entirely to keeping the Great Seal of the United States, which is affixed to Presidential commissions and other documents as required. Secretaries of State witness the application of the Great Seal only on rare ceremonial occasions. (John Foster Dulles was the last one to do so, in 1957.)

John Jay's appointment indicated that President Washington thought his Secretary of State's principal duties would lie in the foreign rather than the domestic field. The tone for the office was thus set and has continued ever since.

II

The Department Develops

The first Congress assembled under the new Constitution in March, 1789, in New York accorded the same primacy to foreign affairs as had the Continental Congress. By the Act of July 27, 1789, it created the first executive agency of the government, designated the Department of Foreign Affairs and headed by a Secretary to the Department of Foreign Affairs.

In light of contemporary as well as historical events, it is worth noting that the affairs of this first department were to be conducted "in such manner as the President of the United States shall from time to time order or instruct." Washington soon made it clear, as have a number of his successors, that the Act merely reinforced the broad Constitutional powers of the President to take personal charge of foreign affairs and to accept the advice of the Secretary —or that of any other advisers—as circumstances dictated.

Congress had second thoughts, however, about a single department devoted solely to foreign affairs. Perhaps recalling that John Jay was carrying the entire burden of foreign relations with the help of a couple of clerks, as had Robert Livingston before him, it added a host of domestic duties in a new Act of September 15, 1789, at the same time changing the agency's name to the Department of State and designating its head Secretary of State. In contrast to the broadly defined duties of the Secretary in the foreign field, specific domestic duties were enumerated, and, except for those assigned to the Treasury and War departments, these included almost everything else necessary to ensure the functioning of the executive and, to a degree, the legislative branches. State established the first mint at Philadelphia, was responsible for keeping all official records, and took care of government printing. The Department also conducted the census and issued patents and copyrights. It had custody of the Great Seal, which was—and still is—affixed to civil commissions and state documents such as treaties. At one point, even the mail service was to be handled by the State Department, but this job was transferred to the Treasury.

In September, 1789, Congress authorized funds to staff and operate the new department, which in spite of the additional domestic duties, remained at approximately the same level—employing four to six people, including the Secretary. Jay continued his duties throughout the organizational period.

Although John Jay seemed the logical choice to head the new department, he preferred an appointment as Chief Justice of the Supreme Court to being named Secretary of State. President Washington then offered the post to Thomas Jefferson, who was serving as Minister to France, a position he wanted to keep. Nevertheless, Jefferson acceded to Washington's request and was commissioned on September 26, 1789, establishing for himself and his successors the ranking place in the President's Cabinet. When Jefferson returned to France to terminate his mission there, Jay carried on in his place until Jefferson finally assumed charge of the Department on March 22, 1790.

GETTING ORGANIZED

In the first dozen years of its existence, the Department increased its home staff slightly, from six to ten members. Their duties also increased. Domestic salaries by 1801 totaled $11,500, and the "Foreign Fund" was averaging $40,000 a year for the salaries and allowances of the five ministers and several consular officers in the overseas branch.

The first attempt to organize the Department of State is credited to John Quincy Adams, who, as Secretary in 1818, found "disorder and confusion" and more work than he or his small staff could handle, even though he reluctantly worked on Sundays. Adams defined work assignments and established effective operating procedures. Discipline was rigidly enforced, and a new accounting system was begun.

Eight years later, Secretary of State Henry Clay again tried to organize the Department. In a report to Congress, he pointed out that only eight of the fifteen categories of work performed by the Department related to foreign affairs; the other seven all involved domestic duties, which Clay felt could be better handled by a separate "home" department. Congress did not approve these recommendations, but it did add some personnel to the Department staff.

In June, 1833, the first major reorganization of the Department of State was instituted under the direction of Louis McLane. As chairman of the House Ways and Means Committee, he had received the suggestions of Henry Clay and succeeding secretaries for improvements in the administration of the Department. Now, as Secretary of State, he undertook to carry them out.

The reorganization proved particularly valuable, because it established clear lines of responsibility and specific duties for individuals, while allowing for flexibility to meet future changes. McLane established seven bureaus, whose duties reflect the dual nature of the Department's functions at that time—the Diplomatic Bureau; the Consular Bureau; the Home Bureau; the Bureau of Archives, Laws, and Commissions; the Disbursing and Superintending Bureau; the Translating and Miscellaneous Bureau; and the catch-all Bureau of Pardons, Remissions, Copyrights, and Library. This last bureau was later abolished, and its first three duties assigned to the Home Bureau and the Library to the Translating Bureau. Another Department unit, the Patent Office, was not affected by this reorganization, since it was administered separately.

Gradually, the numerous domestic functions were transferred to other departments. The 1850 census became the responsibility of the Department of the Interior, which, the previous year, had also taken over the Patent Office. Nevertheless, the work load continued to grow—with staff increases lagging behind. On the eve of the Civil War, the Department's personnel numbered just under thirty —including the Secretary—to handle the remaining domestic duties and the correspondence with 33 diplomatic missions and 480 consular posts.

During the Civil War the principal diplomatic goal of the United States was to prevent other countries from giving formal diplomatic recognition to the Confederacy, and in this Secretary of State William Seward and the members of the Department at home and abroad were completely successful.

As might be expected, there were a number of changes in State Department personnel, because of divided loyalties, but temporary clerks were hired, and the Department ran efficiently with no breaches of security.

THE 1870 REORGANIZATION AND CIVIL SERVICE

The Department structure that Secretary McLane instituted lasted nearly forty years. In 1870, however, Secretary of State Hamilton Fish, whose staff of clerks was reduced by Congress from forty-eight to thirty-one, was forced to reorganize the Department in a way that would enable this smaller force to carry the work load. Fish established nine bureaus, which were later consolidated into six by the Act of March 3, 1873: the First and Second Diplomatic bureaus, the First and Second Consular bureaus, the Bureau of Indexes and Archives and—inevitably—the Bureau of Accounts. Vestiges of the first four units can readily be identified in the geographic bureaus of today; the other two are still very much in evidence in the administrative area. With administration greatly improved, the Department, under the leadership of Secretary Fish, substantively participated in the settlement of every major diplomatic problem of the era; its prestige had never been higher and in July, 1875, seemed to be sealed by its move into its portion of the granite State, War, and Navy Building that still stands like the Rock of Gibraltar next to the White House on Pennsylvania Avenue.*

Under the spoils system, however, the ranks of the senior personnel of the Department's home service and diplomatic and consular services abroad underwent an almost clean sweep with every new President. Obviously, the continuity of State's work, like that of every other department of government, was hindered, and therefore as early as 1865 the movement for a career civil service had begun. The Civil Service Reform League, founded in 1881, brought together the several disparate forces that wanted to end the odious political procedure that called for "throwing the rascals out," when one political party defeated the party in power. Its efforts were successful, when, two years later, with public opinion influenced by President Garfield's assassination by a disappointed office-seeker, the Pendleton Act was passed. This "Magna Charta" of the civil service proposed to substitute merit for political influence in appointments to federal government positions and to protect employees from being assessed part of their salaries for party contributions.

The first major test of the new legislation followed the election of Grover Cleveland in 1884, the first Democratic President in twenty-eight years. His party demanded 100,000 jobs for the party faithful, but the new President regarded "public office as a public trust" and did not require his Secretary of State, Thomas Bayard, to replace any of the Department's personnel. Only the home service of the Department of State, however, benefited from the Pendleton Act. Part of the consular service later came under a type of merit system under an executive order issued by President Cleveland in 1895, but not for over a quarter of a century would the diplomatic branch of the Department enjoy similar job protection.

---

* This classic example of an era of government architecture regrettably vanished now houses the executive offices of the White House. The original space allocations can be identified by the insignia on the doorknobs.

1900–1920: YEARS OF GROWTH AND WAR

By the turn of the century, the threefold increase in foreign trade and the general increase in diplomatic activities once again surpassed the capacity of the Department's staff to cope with the work load. In 1909, additional funds were obtained, and the first complete reorganization of the Department since 1870 was undertaken in order to enable it to discharge its duties. New positions were created, functions were reassigned, and, of greatest importance, three new political-geographic divisions and a Division of Information were created. To handle the work, the staff list grew to 210 officers and other staff. Even that number of employees, however, was unable to deal with the new burdens added by World War I. At that time, the permanent staff increased to over 350, and more than 400 temporary employees were hired to carry on the Department's business. Even so, work was not current, and the salaries were too low to attract outstanding new officers. Many of the deficiencies that plagued the Department during World War I can undoubtedly be attributed to the political appointments made by Secretary William Jennings Bryan prior to his resignation. The situation was not improved by his successor's lack of influence with President Wilson.

Robert Lansing, the new Secretary of State, had little effect on foreign policy-making after the United States entered the war. Presumably, he acquiesced in the creation of a "Little State Department" in New York headed by President Wilson's adviser, Colonel Edward House, to plan for the peace. Thus, the Secretary and other State Department personnel played only a minor role in Paris during the negotiations leading to the Treaty of Versailles. The final break came during the President's illness. Secretary Lansing called on other members of the Cabinet to meet with him to carry on government business, and, after a number of such meetings, President Wilson accused Lansing of unconstitutionally assuming the authority of the President and asked for his resignation.

Between the Wars

Passage of the Rogers Act of 1924 brought important changes to the Department of State in the booming decade following World War I. Foreign Service officers would now be appointed and promoted solely on the basis of merit, providing them with a permanent career. In addition, and of nearly equal importance, the separate diplomatic and consular services were amalgamated, constituting a unified Foreign Service. It would take a generation to remove sensitivities caused by distinctions made between the allegedly higher-level, diplomatic, "Ivy League" officers and the so-called lower-level consular officers and to assure equal promotional opportunities for all. In the meantime, however, the Congress improved administration of the Act to ensure more equal treatment for all Foreign Service personnel, regardless of prior duty, through the Moses-Linthicum Act, which became effective July 1, 1931.

Throughout the decade, the lot—and the salaries—of the officers of the Department continued to improve. The Welch Act of 1928 raised the top Department staff members to a CAF-15 rank, which paid $9,000 a year, the highest civil service salary of that day. Other Department officers accordingly received increased salaries. President Herbert Hoover and Secretary of State Henry Stimson, moreover, were highly successful in persuading Congress to augment the Department's personnel and provide sufficient funds for efficient operation. The appropriations for the year 1930 were nearly double those of 1929—$2,364,273, for that era a relatively vast sum—and, incredible for any era, only $4,000 less than had been requested. These increases, of course, came to an abrupt halt in the Depression with the Economy Act of 1932. The salary cuts were restored, however, two years later, and in 1935, a few promotions were authorized, and the first new appointments were announced.

In 1936, the veteran administrator of the Department and the Foreign Service, Wilbur J. Carr, was made Minister to Czechoslovakia. He was replaced by a career Foreign Service officer, George S. Messersmith, who, with the support of Secretary of State Cordell Hull, began a reorganization designed to streamline the Department and increase its efficiency. A substantial number of Foreign Service officers were selected out (retired involuntarily), and some Department personnel were assigned to positions overseas to broaden their experience. Some divisions were consolidated and others formed. Three years later, the Reorganization Act of 1939 enabled Messersmith to consolidate the foreign services of the departments of Commerce and Agriculture with the Foreign Service of the United States.

WORLD WAR II AND ITS REPERCUSSIONS

The war in Europe increased the work load of the Department tremendously, and a Special Division was organized in 1939 to carry out some of the necessary tasks that grew out of the inescapable involvement of the neutral United States: responses to the flood of inquiries by American citizens concerning friends and relatives abroad; representation of those belligerents who had broken diplomatic relations with their enemies and had requested the United States to act in their behalf; the protection and repatriation of Americans caught in war zones; and other war-related activities.

After U.S. entry into the war, the traditional dichotomy between the military and civilian elements of the executive branch prevented the Department's participation in deliberations over the conduct of the war. Consequently, the Secretary of State was often unaware of major military plans that could—and did—have a profound effect on diplomatic relations then and after the war. Roosevelt was in most respects his own Secretary of State, and like President Wilson, preferred to depend on a personal adviser in the conduct of foreign affairs in wartime rather than on the Secretary of State. For example, he sent Harry Hopkins on secret missions concerning which neither the Secretary of State nor the ambassadors abroad had information.

Nevertheless, the Department took the initiative in providing economic assistance to Morocco when it seemed that the French officials there were prepared to exchange manganese and cobalt for petroleum products. This exchange made possible the subsequent arrangements with French resistance leaders for the invasion of North Africa, in which a Foreign Service officer, Robert D. Murphy, played a central role.

By 1943, it was obvious that a reorganization of the Department was again badly needed, and Under Secretary Edward R. Stettinius established a special group to plan the restructuring. The reorganization was accomplished in two stages, one on January 15, 1944, and the final plan on December 20, 1944, one month after Stettinius succeeded Cordell Hull as Secretary of State. The plan refined the concept of grouping similar operations together, continued the primacy of the political-geographic areas, and concentrated administrative matters under the jurisdiction of a qualified and experienced official, Julius C. Holmes, a former Foreign Service officer.

Secretary Stettinius played a major role in the preparations for the organizational meeting of the United Nations, held as scheduled in San Francisco, April 25–June 26, 1945, in spite of the recent death of President Roosevelt. It therefore came as a surprise to many that President Truman, at the conclusion of the San Francisco meeting, announced Stettinius's resignation as Secretary of State and his appointment as the U.S. Ambassador to the United Nations. The President also announced the appointment of James Byrnes as the new Secretary.

The reason for the change, according to Margaret Truman in her book, *Harry S. Truman,* was the President's concern that the person who would next assume the Presidency, if he should die while completing President Roosevelt's term, should have held elective office.* Stettinius had never been a candidate, while Byrnes had been elected as senator from South Carolina. The latter had

---

* At that time, the Secretary of State was next in the line of Presidential succession. In 1947, this was changed so that the Speaker of the House of Representatives and the President *pro tem* of the Senate follow the Vice-President.

also served as Supreme Court Justice and had held several offices in the executive branch, including one, in the informal description of the day, as "assistant President in charge of the war effort." Further, President Truman hoped that appointing Byrnes as Secretary of State would help to overcome the latter's disappointment that he had not been nominated for Vice-President at the 1944 Democratic Party Convention. This action has been described, however, as a miscalculation, because of Byrnes's poor opinion of Harry Truman.

On assuming office, Secretary Byrnes asked the Bureau of the Budget to study the organization of the Department, to the dismay of many of its personnel, who had still not recovered from the Stettinius reorganizations. In this instance, no action was taken on the Bureau's report, which recommended a form of amalgamation of the home and field services, more emphasis on leadership and administrative skills in staffing posts, and an in-service training program.

Another unpublished report prepared by two Foreign Service officers, Selden Chapin and Andrew Foster, also foresaw a merging of the two services over a period of time. The two men led a study group that drafted a bill, which was approved by Congress, for a reorganized Foreign Service. The Bureau of the Budget opposed the legislation, on the grounds that it would perpetuate an elitist overseas branch of the Department, and only the intervention of Secretary Byrnes prevented the bill, now known as the Foreign Service Act of 1946, from being vetoed. In his critical analysis of Foreign Service personnel administration, Charles W. Bray, III, stated that this Act, still the "Bible" for the Foreign Service, contained the "only really successful innovations in personnel administration since the Rogers Act of 1924" and stressed that it was drafted by Foreign Service professionals.

It soon became clear to some, however, that the Department's field service needed additional specialists on a permanent basis, if it was to cope with increased postwar responsibilities, particularly in economic matters. The Manpower Act of 1946 authorized the entry of 250 officers into the Foreign Service under Section 517 of the Foreign Service Act. Some senior staff of the Foreign Service, however, so opposed any form of exceptional entrance—that is, other than by examination and at the bottom level—that only 166 new officers were admitted. In retrospect, this limitation seems unfortunate, for many of these new officers were highly successful, and several rose to ambassadorial rank.

The participation of top professional personnel in the many postwar conferences helped to restore the morale of the Department and the Foreign Service, which had been adversely affected by the way in which President Roosevelt had ignored them during the war. General George C. Marshall succeeded Byrnes as Secretary of State in 1947, and while he was Secretary instituted the innovative and highly successful Marshall Plan for the rebuilding of postwar Europe. He made no major changes in the structure of the Department, but he greatly improved procedures and established the Policy Planning Staff. This most important unit was supposed to devote itself exclusively to long-range planning of future policy but it tended to become involved in current problems. In addition, Marshall established an Executive Secretariat, similar to one he had known at the Pentagon, to centralize document control and other services for the top-level staff.

In 1948, John E. Peurifoy, at that time the assistant secretary of State for Administration, directed and completed a study that proposed, among other things, that the Department set up a better chain of command with a broader delegation of authority and responsibility and amalgamate the separate offices that administered the Department in Washington as one organization and the Foreign Service as another. Peurifoy also had plans for integrating, within limits, the civil service personnel of the Department and those in the Foreign Service. Although his proposals were not put into effect, Peurifoy's ideas paved the way for the conclusions of the Hoover Commission study of the Department.

The Commission on Organization of the Executive Branch of the Government, chaired by former President Hoover, had been established by the Act of July 7, 1947, and its recommendations were to become the guidelines for most organizational changes that took place in succeeding decades. The commission took as its premise the emergence of the United States as a world power and the participation of numerous government departments and agencies in the administration of foreign affairs. Because the Department of State had only a small percentage of the funds and personnel of the government, the commission recommended that the Department not operate programs at home or abroad but confine itself to the traditional roles of negotiating, representing U.S. interests, and reporting on conditions in foreign countries.

In its *Report,* issued in 1949, the commission concluded that the Department should take responsibility for defining foreign policy objectives and for formulating and executing these in five bureaus —the four geographic bureaus and a fifth that would deal with international organizations whose functions extended beyond a single regional bureau's boundaries. Functional units for public affairs, legal services, congressional relations, and economic and social problems would service the line bureaus. One deputy under secretary would coordinate substantive policy matters, while another would handle administrative matters. An Operations Committee would meet daily to coordinate all of the Department's internal foreign affairs efforts and, presumably, the foreign relations activities of other departments and agencies overseas. The commission also recommended that the personnel of the civil service and Foreign Service systems (above certain administrative grades) be mandatorily amalgamated within a very few years, those in the new service being required to serve in the United States or abroad as needed. Finally, the Secretary's chain of command was to be clarified so that there would be no question of his responsibility for administering both the Department of State *and* the Foreign Service. (This meant the abolition of the command position of director general of the Foreign Service.)

Dean Acheson, who had been vice-chairman of the Hoover Commission, replaced the ailing General Marshall as Secretary of State in 1949. Under his direction, the deputy under secretary for Administration reorganized the line bureaus to give them the authority, responsibility, and resources recommended by the commission. They were supposed to follow uniform procedures to be established by the central administrative organizations of the Department. The director general of the Foreign Service was made a staff aide, and a single Office of Personnel was established. Contrary to Hoover Commission recommendations, however, the two services were not fully combined. The Office of Personnel still included two separate divisions, one for the administration of civil service and the other for Foreign Service personnel, and not until 1953 would the separate identifications be eliminated. Moreover, although Public Law 73 of May 26, 1949, gave the Secretary of State clear authority and responsibility for administering the Department and the Foreign Service, with certain delegations specified, the abolition of the Board of the Foreign Service was not to come for more than a decade. Even then, amalgamation of the two services was deferred pending further study.

Secretary Acheson had reservations about mandatory amalgamation and' appointed an Advisory Committee on Personnel chaired by James H. Rowe, Jr., a Washington attorney and another member of the Hoover Commission, to review the commission's recommendation. The other committee members included William E. DeCourcy, a Foreign Service officer then serving as ambassador to Haiti, and Robert Ramspeck, a former member of Congress who had also served as chairman of the U.S. Civil Service Commission. The group was to study the personnel problems existing between the Department and the Foreign Service and advise as to what extent amalgamation would solve them.

The Rowe Committee, as it was called, reported that the Department's responsibilities and primary role in the conduct of foreign affairs called for a large number of highly qualified people. Because the staff had to possess a wide variety of professional skills, the personnel system should "provide for closer integration of the home and field services, greater flexibility, better methods of recruitment and the means of relatively easy expansion and contraction." In effect, the committee exceeded the Hoover Commission recommendations and advised that everyone under the Secretary of State, not just those above certain levels, be in a single service outside the civil service.

In March, 1951, after more than six months' consideration of the Rowe Committee recommendations, a "Directive to Improve the Personnel Program of the Department of State and the Unified

Foreign Service of the United States" was sent to the director of personnel by the deputy under secretary for Administration. Basically, it provided a liberalized procedure over a three-year period for entry into the Foreign Service and an increased exchange of assignments between Department and Foreign Service officers. Future needs were to be estimated and related to recruitment of personnel, the kind of training they would receive, and the rate of promotion. Lateral entry (that is, entry at grades other than the lowest) was encouraged through revised and more liberal standards. Specialists, with particular reference to executive ability, would be given recognition, and dual service positions were to be identified for exchange purposes.

In spite of limited success in some aspects, the directive largely failed to meet its objectives, particularly with respect to lateral entry—2,150 candidates filed applications, but, by 1954, only 499 had been examined and only 25 appointed—and little or no recognition of the need for specialists was given in the examinations or the promotion precepts.

With the election of President Dwight D. Eisenhower in 1952, the Republicans gained their first victory in twenty-four years. John Foster Dulles, who in the previous administration had negotiated the peace treaty with Japan, became the new Secretary of State.

One of the new Administration's first actions was an economy drive, which halted the recruitment that was taking place under the 1951 directive. Appointment of junior officers for two years was also suspended, and the civil service and Foreign Service staffs were cut by nearly 20 per cent.

In the meantime, McCarthyism was gaining momentum, and highly publicized internal security investigations and dismissals of career officers seriously affected morale. Scott McLeod, a congressional assistant highly regarded by Senator Joseph McCarthy, was appointed as head of both the security and the personnel offices of the Department, and he presided over a "witch hunt" that intimidated even the top political leadership of the Department. Some of the most competent and loyal members of the Foreign Service, especially the "old China hands," were forced to leave the service during what was certainly one of the blackest periods in the Department's history.

Several steps were taken early in the Eisenhower Administration to dilute the principle of a single, united Foreign Service of the United States. The first step was Reorganization Plan No. 8, which in 1953 created the U.S. Information Agency (USIA), subject to State Department policy guidance. Information activities and personnel from the Department of State were transferred to the USIA and its overseas service, the USIS. A second step followed quickly with the re-establishment of a separate Foreign Agricultural Service by the Agricultural Act of 1954, and a new State-Agricultural agreement was negotiated. Arthur G. Jones, a respected member of the Foreign Service, in *The Evolution of Personnel Systems for U.S. Foreign Affairs,* noted that:

> This agreement closed another chapter in the history of the Foreign Service. The change might have been prevented were it not for political considerations and for the apparent inability of the two departments to work out a more effective *modus operandi* on personnel and administrative matters. Once the Administration had decided to support the idea of placing agricultural attachés outside of the regular Foreign Service but subject to the chief of mission, State Department officials who supported the concept of a unified Foreign Service could no longer officially oppose the separation. The creation of USIA and the Foreign Agricultural Service were steps away from the concept of a Foreign Service of the United States as laid down in the Rogers Act and reaffirmed in Reorganization Plan No. 2 of 1939 and the Foreign Service Act of 1946.

Efforts were also made to re-establish the separate foreign service of the Department of Commerce, but this was avoided partly because of an agreement between State and Commerce that provided for the appointment of businessmen as commercial attachés. However, the question of a separate foreign commerce service has arisen periodically and undoubtedly will continue to do so. Finally, certain significant changes were made in the administration of foreign aid during this period, notably the consolidation in a new, semi-autonomous Foreign Operations Administration (FOA) of numerous existing programs including the nonmilitary activities of the Mutual Security Agency, the Department's so-called Point Four (Marshall Plan) aid, and the Institute of Inter-American Affairs. Henceforth, the FOA was to operate all these programs, but the Secretary of State was to monitor and guide the development of policies and activities through the FOA director.

The philosophy behind all of these changes in the early 1950's reflected Secretary Dulles's wholehearted agreement with the Hoover Commission recommendation that the Department not be directly involved in program operations but instead confine itself to the more traditional tasks of formulating foreign policy and negotiating treaties. The Department's role was to ensure that the multiplicity of agencies now involved in foreign affairs spoke with one voice for the United States, particularly since President Eisenhower made it abundantly clear that the Secretary of State was his principal deputy in foreign affairs. The President also announced that each chief of mission abroad was the coordinator and director of the overseas activities of all federal agencies in his area.

WRISTONIZATION

Early in 1954, Secretary Dulles appointed a Public Committee on Personnel chaired by Henry M. Wriston, president of Brown University, to recommend measures to strengthen both the civil and Foreign services. In particular, the committee was to submit recommendations regarding personnel management, specifically with regard to the "amalgamation and interchangeability" of the Department and the field services. The committee worked quickly and in mid-May transmitted its recommendations to the Secretary, establishing something of a record for action.

The Wriston Committee stated that it was "impressed by the high standards of devotion and loyalty animating the men and women of the Department of State and the Foreign Service" and that it "does not hesitate to urge the American people to reinvest their confidence, without reservations, in the character and steadfastness of both the Department and its diplomatic arm." Nevertheless, its report was highly critical of the way the Foreign Service had been administered since the Act of 1946, citing low morale—McCarthy's internal security investigations were acknowledged to be an adverse factor—the failure to recruit at the bottom or provide for enough lateral entries, lack of specialists, and the deficiencies of the Foreign Service Institute. It recommended a single Foreign Service system for officer personnel of the Department and the Foreign Service who had comparable functions in some 3,700 positions—1,440 in the Department and 2,250 in the field. Other suggestions were made to correct the administrative shortcomings found by the committee. All the recommendations were to be put into effect as quickly as possible, preferably within two years.

The Secretary agreed with the Wriston report conclusions and with the need for urgent implementation. A crash program followed that was one of the reasons the Wristonization period was difficult, especially for the civil service personnel who rather quickly had to opt for the Foreign Service or face the prospect of a dead end in the Department. Most had never served outside of Washington and had no desire to do so. Many Foreign Service nonofficer personnel welcomed the opportunity for lateral integration into the officer corps, only to regret it within a few years when they, along with many of the integrated civil service personnel, failed to be selected for promotion and instead were selected out—that is, dismissed. The integration period was also a difficult one for the administrative officials, who were under strict instructions to complete the job within the severely limited timetable established by Dr. Wriston. In the long run, however, in spite of the many individual hardships (and there were many), the Foreign Service as a whole benefited from the fresh ideas of the Wristonees. A number of these, moreover, had highly successful careers and made significant contributions to American diplomacy.

Effective administration of the Department remained a problem. Soon after assuming office, Secretary Dulles had approved the employment of a management firm to recommend measures for increased efficiency and greater economy, particularly in view of the drastic reduction in personnel. The survey resulted in several logical recommendations as well as many others that were far less logical and that proposed dramatic economies at the expense of the effective conduct of foreign affairs. The Wriston Committee recommendations in this area called for "the prompt designation of a suitably qualified individual for the position of Deputy Under Secretary for Administration," a post that had been left vacant for some time. The report went on to state that "if stability is to be achieved, it can best be done through the wise choice of executives to fill the principal administrative and personnel positions under the Deputy Under Secretary for Administration."

Fortunately for the Department, it obtained the services of a competent and understanding businessman to fill the principal administrative position, even before the new deputy under secretary for Administration was selected. I. W. Carpenter, Jr., of Omaha, Nebraska, was appointed assistant secretary for Administration in 1954 and immediately set about becoming familiar with operations at home and abroad. He soon began a series of internal administrative programs and realignments that overcame the worst effects of the drastic reduction in force and the management firm's detrimental proposals. Even while doing so, Carpenter had to respond to a searching congressional investigation regarding those proposals, and he was, of course, under the pressure of knowing that a new deputy under secretary for Administration would soon examine his program.

As the new deputy under secretary, the Department wisely selected Loy W. Henderson, a career Foreign Service officer whose most recent assignment had been Ambassador to Iran. Henderson was respected on Capitol Hill and in the Foreign Service, and he enjoyed a reputation for fairness, integrity, and tough-mindedness. His efforts in behalf of State Department people who were unjustly accused in the McCarthy era had done much, in the opinion of many, to restore confidence in the Department's concern for its personnel, and this view was strengthened by the way in which Ambassador Henderson and Assistant Secretary Carpenter undertook to carry out the recommendations of the Wriston Committee with the minimum possible individual hardship, often intervening to allow more time or adjust proposed assignments in specific cases.

The two men complemented each other well in other administrative matters and were often successful in convincing congressional appropriation committees of the need to restore or provide funds for various personnel "fringe" benefits and physical improvements. They even convinced the Bureau of the Budget and the congressional committees of the benefits to be realized from the construction of a $57 million addition to the building State had inherited from the War Department, in order to consolidate most of the staff and special equipment in one building.

Assistant Secretary Carpenter resigned in 1958 and was succeeded by a former governor of New Hampshire, Lane Dwinell, whose many years of political experience in New Hampshire served him—and the Department—well, especially on the Hill.

At the close of the decade, the personnel of the Department at home and abroad had still not fully recovered from the ravages of McCarthyism and the hardships of Wristonization. Under the leadership of Ambassador Henderson, however, a large measure of stability had returned to the Department, which was operating with reasonable efficiency. Its personnel seemed to be generally optimistic about the future of American diplomacy and their own career prospects.

A NEW ERA

President John F. Kennedy abolished the Operations Coordinating Board of the National Security Council (NSC) and made it clear, in the words of the new Secretary of State, Dean Rusk, that he expected the Department to "take charge" and be responsible for coordinating policy *and* operations abroad. Among President Kennedy's major complaints about the Department was its slowness in responding to White House requests for information or in taking action on directives. The President himself had an insatiable thirst for information, and many middle-level officers of State (and other departments) more than once were startled to receive a telephone call directly from the President seeking more details about some problem.* It has been asserted that Kennedy was distrustful of the Foreign Service, yet there were many individual officers whom he liked and for whom he had the highest respect. A few critics have blamed the Department's seeming inability to "take charge" in foreign affairs on the lack of positive direction and leadership by Secretary Rusk. Others point out that the Secretary expected his subordinates, especially the regional assistant secretaries, to assume responsibility; he told them, in effect, that power gravitates to men who make decisions and live with the consequences, because others will move aside.

Roger Hilsman, who served under Secretary Rusk first as director of the Bureau of Intelligence and Research, and later as assistant secretary for Far Eastern Affairs, in *To Move a Nation* described the Secretary's concept of his job as follows:

> Thus the President, in Rusk's view, should give leadership in terms of over-all goals and objectives, in terms of grand policies. The Assistant Secretaries, concentrating on particular regions, should be the formulators and advocates of specific policies and the managers of the State Department. But the position of the Secretary of State he seemed to see as being above all this and apart from it, permitting the incumbent to sit alongside the President in judgment precisely because he was free of the restraints and commitments of representing a department.

Although others might not agree, this seemed to Hilsman "to be a perfectly logical and reasonable view, providing a meaningful and useful role around which a President can build an effective organizational arrangement." Nevertheless, Hilsman concluded, the "task of managing the whole range of security policy that he (the President) had intended to assign to the Department, he assumed himself. For although he had not sought to be his own Secretary of State, in the end he had no other choice."

* In 1963, Ambassador Estes experienced at first hand the President's insistence on being informed. In the course of reporting on programs at his embassy in Upper Volta during a routine Washington call on the President, a highly successful children's vaccination program was mentioned. With some impatience, the President asked why he hadn't heard about it. He directed that a complete report be ready for him on his return from the trip he was to begin within the half hour—to Texas.

Under Secretary Chester 'Bowles had considerable respect for the personnel of the Department, both its civil service employees and those in the Foreign Service. Nevertheless, after completing the staffing of top-level State Department and ambassadorial positions by career and noncareer personnel who could be expected to reflect the New Frontier spirit, he seemed to be at loose ends. In a major personnel shake-up and reorganization in November, 1961 (sometimes called the "Thanksgiving Day Massacre"), George Ball was moved up from deputy under secretary to replace Chester Bowles, who decided to accept an advisory role even though, as he wrote a decade later in *Promises to Keep,* a complete break with the Administration would have set him free to spell out publicly the weaknesses in our foreign policy and in our State Department organization. Three White House aides were transferred to State. The veteran W. Averell Harriman agreed to become the assistant secretary for Far Eastern Affairs (a move Bowles had recommended). This reorganization and transfusion of fresh (White House) blood constituted another attempt by the President to make the Department "take charge" of foreign affairs.

George Ball was a capable lawyer, completely attuned to President Kennedy's policies at home and abroad. A clear thinker, decisive, short-spoken, and a writer of cryptic and to-the-point memoranda, he provided the quick responses favored by the White House.

Among the White House advisers sent to the State Department was Walt W. Rostow, who became head of the Policy Planning Council. (See Chapter III.) Rostow's mission was to produce long-range foreign policy planning consistent with the President's concept of State's role. In one of the most significant internal actions taken to strengthen the Department's leadership role, Rostow developed the National Policy Papers—systematic plans setting forth specified goals for the complete spectrum of foreign affairs operations on a country-by-country basis.

Insofar as they were able, those in the administrative area also tried to improve matters, but they were outside the policy chain of command; their authority and responsibility were limited to logistic support (more often called "housekeeping") and did not extend to executive management. These circumstances undoubtedly contributed to their relatively short terms of service. Roger W. Jones, former chairman of the Civil Service Commission, had won the respect of the Kennedy talent scouts by his sage advice and cooperation in the search for top-level Department personnel and was appointed to the position of deputy under secretary just vacated by Ambassador Henderson, who finally was allowed to retire with the highest honors the nation could bestow, several years after the normal retirement age. In spite of his many years of experience in dealing with Washington bureaucracy, Jones stayed only two years.

He was replaced by William Orrick, Chief of the Antitrust Division in the Department of Justice—and a close friend of Attorney General Robert F. Kennedy, the President's brother. Armed with a "blank check" from the White House, he should have been able to exert some influence and strengthen State's role. Perhaps it was the complexities of the budget process or the treatment he got on Capitol Hill, but in any case, he remained at State only a few months before returning to private life.

Orrick was succeeded by William J. Crockett, a career Foreign Service officer, in 1963. Crockett, who was well regarded on the Hill, had been appointed as assistant secretary for Administration at the beginning of the Kennedy Administration, and he was wise to the ways of the Department. Within his own jurisdiction, Crockett met some success in implementing Herter Committee on Foreign Affairs Personnel recommendations for strengthening the Department's role in foreign affairs through far-reaching administrative measures. Those reforms that affected other areas failed, however, partly because he did not have the full support of the Department's hierarchy and partly because the problem could not be solved by administrative measures.

Arthur Schlesinger has written: "To the end, the Department remained a puzzle to the President. No one ran it; Rusk, Ball, and (Averell) Harriman constituted a loose triumvirate on the seventh floor and, passing things back and forth among themselves, managed to keep a few steps ahead of crisis."

Other observers point out that from his first day in office, President Kennedy gave his personal attention to even the smallest details of foreign policy. If the State Department puzzled the President, the President's relationship to it was also puzzling to the Department. Kennedy complained about the inadequacies of the State Department and virtually ignored the NSC mechanism that existed for interdepartmental coordination. He undertook the management of the series of crises with which he was faced, not because the State Department let him down, but because he relished being his own Secretary of State. Actually, any strong President would probably have insisted on acting as manager in the kind of crises Kennedy faced: Laos, Cuba, the Congo, Berlin, Indonesia, and Vietnam. His personal handling of these situations, with the assistance of the Attorney General and a small coterie of confidants, including Secretary Rusk, became his general pattern for noncrisis decision-making. This, according to observers, hindered the Department in its efforts to "take charge." Their views are supported by an exchange, reported by Schlesinger, between the President and Ambassador Charles Bohlen, one of the Foreign Service officers for whom Kennedy had the highest respect. Schlesinger writes that in response to a question by the President as to what was wrong with the Department, "Bohlen answered candidly, 'You are.' " The historian continues with Bohlen's explanation that, although the President wanted quick answers, the Department had to consider all the ramifications of a sensitive issue before it could respond in a responsible manner. The impasse continued until the President's tragic death.

Lyndon B. Johnson as President handled crises in much the same manner as his predecessor, but he attempted to give the State Department an opportunity to exercise more control of the overseas activities of the United States. Addressing a luncheon meeting of the American Foreign Service Association in March, 1966, General Maxwell D. Taylor, then a special consultant to President Johnson, reviewed the history of that part of National Security Action Memorandum (NSAM) 341 that deals with the authority and responsibility assigned to the Secretary—"to the full extent permitted by law"—for the control of overseas activities.

He recalled that at the request of President Johnson, he and a number of experienced State Department, Foreign Service, and other personnel had begun a study of government activities in the counterinsurgency field, but this was soon expanded into a study of crisis anticipation and crisis management (the lessons of the Cuban missile crisis) and the results were incorporated in NSAM 341. He was surprised to learn that the Secretary of State had no mandate for the management of interdepartmental business comparable to that of an ambassador's authority, which derived from the written directives of three Presidents. The general did not believe that the NSC, as it then functioned, filled the void and suggested giving the coordinating authority to the Secretary of State, rather than setting up a new White House organization under the President to conduct interdepartmental business abroad. The "simple way" would be to use the Department to discharge this additional Presidential function. General Taylor stressed "additional," because he did not see this coordinating action as "inherently or organizationally a State Department function."

The key element of NSAM 341, also issued in unclassified form as the Foreign Affairs Manual Circular No. 385 of March 4, 1966, read as follows:

> To assist the President in carrying out his responsibility in the conduct of Foreign Affairs, he has assigned to the Secretary of State authority and responsibility to the full extent permitted by law for the overall direction, coordination and supervision of interdepartmental activities of the United States Government overseas.

Military activities were exempted. Interdepartmental activities were defined, and mechanisms to assist the Secretary were established, headed by executive chairmen, who were given both the authority and responsibility for making decisions. These were called the Interdepartmental Regional Groups (IRG's), each chaired by a regional assistant secretary. (This organizational feature corresponded with Secretary Rusk's concept that the regional assistant secretaries should be primarily responsible for formulating and advocating policies—and for managing the Department.) There was also a Senior Interdepartmental Group (SIG) chaired by the under secretary of State. The SIG was to assist the Secretary in discharging those interdepartmental responsibilities that could not be dealt with at the IRG level; in other words, it was an appellate body, although it could take initiatives if desired. The permanent members of both groups were representatives of State, Defense, Joint Chiefs of Staff, Agency for International Development (AID), Central Intelligence Agency (CIA), and the USIA. Other agency representatives attended as required.

The then under secretary, George Ball, appeared to be interested in matters other than the SIG-IRG mechanism and took no positive action to make the new system work. He resigned several months later and was succeeded by Nicholas Katzenbach, who gave up his Cabinet post as Attorney General to become a sub-Cabinet officer in State. Faced with learning the intricacies of the State Department, Katzenbach gave the SIG-IRG mechanism a low priority, until after a bit of prodding from the White House. When he did begin to hold meetings of the SIG, Katzenbach soon appreciated the value of the procedure, but by then it was too late. With Richard M. Nixon's election to the Presidency, time had run out for the SIG-IRG mechanism, and the State Department's best opportunity in recent years to assume leadership in foreign affairs was lost—at least for the time being.

Meanwhile, a significant number of Department and Foreign Service personnel were becoming aware of the need for bureaucratic reform insofar as Department leadership was concerned, and also of the need for modernization of its internal procedures, with particular emphasis on the personnel system. They began to make their voices heard in the mid-1960's.

FOGGY BOTTOM FERMENT

Historians say that in northwest Washington, close to the present location of the Department of State, there once existed an unhealthful swamp from which emanated a dense fog that shrouded the area. In time it came to be known as "Foggy Bottom." Unkind contemporary commentators claim that the miasma persists in the neighborhood to this day, at least insofar as foreign policy is concerned. In the late 1960's and early 1970's, however, increasing friction of ideas generated by activist officers in the State Department sparked a flame of reform that has helped to dispel some of the fog.

Long before the terms were in common use, there were individual activists and "creative dissenters" who played the "adversary role," especially throughout World War II and the postwar years, in policies involving China, Korea, Vietnam, and other countries. Although the careers of several were wrecked during the McCarthy era, most of these critics survived and set ample precedents for the young activists of this era who became concerned with the course of American foreign policy, the continued dilution of the Foreign Service Act of 1946 to the point where there was no longer a *unified* Foreign Service of the United States, and the trend away from State Department leadership in foreign affairs. This concern surfaced, among other places, in the American Foreign Service Association (AFSA).

The American Foreign Service Association is an outgrowth of the separate professional organizations that existed prior to the 1924 amalgamation of the former diplomatic and consular services. Until World War II, the membership of the association was limited to Foreign Service officers, but it is now open to all personnel of the foreign affairs agencies, regardless of rank or status. In general, the association attempted to look after the welfare and interests of its members and enhance their professional standing, and, until the mid-1960's, the presiding officers and board members were usually senior officers of the Department, closely identified with its personnel policies and procedures. Thus, those policies were seldom questioned by the association.

In the mid-1960's, the board of directors of the AFSA gave much time and thought to the direction the Foreign Service and the association should take in the future. The 1966–67 board testified on Capitol Hill and wrote letters in support of legislation affecting personnel. It maintained close touch with the Department's management in the interests of its members, arranged for participation of the Junior Foreign Service Officers Organization

(JFSOO) on the board and in its committees, and purchased a building for the AFSA headquarters. It also established two *ad hoc* committees to study the future roles of the association and of the foreign affairs community. The Planning Committee report, which was submitted in June, 1967, assumed that AFSA should serve the entire foreign affairs community, and urged the association to take various initiatives to improve the professionalism of the people in the Foreign Service and be more aggressive in protecting their interests. The Committee on Career Principles, bolstered by four members of the Planning Committee, was more specific in its interim report proposals of what AFSA could do to further these objectives.

The view that AFSA leadership should be more dynamic in protecting the interests of its members was very quickly translated into action, when a group of young officers, the "Young Turks," agreed on a progressive platform and campaigned successfully in September, 1967, for election to the board of directors. Several members of the group were members of the outgoing board and of the Planning and Career Principles committees. They intended to play an active part in determining "what their careers should be and how the foreign affairs community should be organized." Thus began a fundamental reform of the personnel system. The Young Turks sparked the enthusiasm of the association's membership and won the support of officers of all ranks, if not of all officers. They set about to make their views and opinions known to all, especially to whatever administration would assume power in 1969.

Practically the first action of the Young Turks was to reconstitute the Career Principles Committee under Ambassador Graham Martin, who organized an in-depth study and, a year later, in 1968, produced a blueprint "for the foreign affairs establishment and a Foreign Service of the United States adequate to meet the needs of this nation in the 1970's." The report, *Toward a Modern Diplomacy,* called for the re-establishment of the "Foreign Service of the United States" to be managed as Congress intended; it recommended a new "openness" between the foreign affairs community and the mainstream of American life. In the policy-making process, it recommended that there be opportunities to provide the

Secretary and under secretaries with fresh ideas and perspectives that differ from established policy and, in addition to several organizational and personnel improvements, called for an investigation of the applicability of new technology to foreign affairs problems. The major necessary actions included "a decision by the new President to resist the temptation to organize his own White House foreign affairs office—rather, he should insist on the full implementation of NSAM 341 by the Department of State."

Lannon Walker, the thirty-one-year-old chairman of the Young Turks' board of directors, continued the pressure for change in a stimulating article in the January, 1969, issue of *Foreign Affairs* calling for an overhaul of the foreign affairs organization and restoration of a unified, single Foreign Service of the United States. Why should the new President concern himself with these problems? Walker asked. The answer was simple: He must ultimately rely on the professionals for the conduct of the nation's foreign affairs business. Then, with considerable prescience, Walker added:

> At the same time, he requires of those professionals and of the system they serve: (a) that they reserve the most important decisions for him, bringing problems to him before they become crises and providing him with the relevant facts and advice—the present system is not good enough in this respect; (b) that they be flexible, imaginative and efficient in using scarce national resources abroad—the present system is none of these things; and (c) that they produce from within their own ranks the best talent for the critical jobs—they do not now.

Walker concluded by stating that the new administration "must hear this signal from the professionals." Quite correctly, he stated that "reform cannot take place without Presidential commitment."

Thus, the Young Turks and the AFSA, spurred on by the junior officers and their informal but vocal JFSOO, brought into the open the ferment from below. They made known their nonparochial frustrations, doubts, and expectations concerning the nature and future of the nation's foreign relations, in which they held that the Department of State should have the dominant role. All that remained was the response of the next President and his Secretary of State.

However, prior to his election, Richard Nixon had stated that, in his opinion, the foreign policy successes of the Eisenhower period were partly attributable to the planning and review process carried out by the National Security Council (NSC). Therefore, Nixon said, he would restore the council to its pre-eminent position in national security planning. The President-elect, his Secretary of State, William P. Rogers, and his assistant for National Security Affairs, Henry Kissinger, were well prepared. New Presidential directives were issued through the NSC on January 20, 1969, Inauguration Day, which brought about profound changes in the NSC system (see Chapters IV and VI) and transferred the locus of power from the Department of State, where it had been lodged (though somewhat neglected) by President Johnson, back to the National Security Council in the White House. Under the direction of Kissinger, and until he became Secretary of State in late 1973, the NSC was to be the principal forum for consideration of national security policy issues requiring Presidential decisions.

TASK FORCES FOR REFORM

The changes in the NSC system constituted compelling reasons, in addition to those advanced by AFSA, for changes in Department of State procedures, if the NSC was to fulfill the "central and dynamic role" intended for it by President Nixon. Secretary Rogers believed that these changes could best be accomplished by the Department's own career professionals, men who knew its strengths and weaknesses and were, thus, best qualified to undertake a program of reform and modernization. He directed his new deputy under secretary for Administration (later Management), William B. Macomber, Jr., to organize and implement such a program.

Shortly before this, the Foreign Relations Committee of the U.S. Senate had passed a resolution to organize a bipartisan commission to examine all aspects of the foreign affairs establishment. Macomber persuaded the committee's chairman, Senator J. William Fulbright, to postpone implementing this resolution in order to give the Department's professionals a chance to get on with their own study. After a preliminary examination of the problems to be studied, Macomber explained his "Program for the Seventies" to the Department's personnel on January 14, 1970.

The action program he outlined was for management reform and modernization. Although "management has not been our bag," Macomber said, he felt sure that the high quality of the Department's personnel and the existing "ferment of change" in their ranks justified his confidence that the reform program could be developed from within the Department. Macomber explained that he believed "the personal influence of Secretaries of State and the institutional role played by the Department should not be confused," that the Department as an *institution* had not met the challenge for foreign affairs leadership as well as it should have, and that the time had come to fish or cut bait. "Either we produce the improvements necessary to meet the challenge or—this will be done for us."

Over 250 career professionals in Washington and some recalled from overseas assignments were assembled into thirteen task forces to review the structure and procedures of the Department and of the Foreign Service and to recommend improvements that would meet the challenge. They labored long and hard and before the year was out produced a report, *Diplomacy for the 70's,* which Secretary Rogers released on December 8, 1970. It contained over 500 recommendations for establishing modern management procedures and for an improved personnel administration. The AFSA called the report a courageous and imaginative first step by the Department to reform itself and described the diagnosis as presented in the report as unusually accurate. The task forces were aware that leadership supported by nothing more than "bureaucratic ego" could not endure and that it could not be conferred by directive; leadership could only be *earned* by competence. This, the task forces believed, would result from their proposed program.

The reform program that emerged was designed to provide the Department with a strengthened capacity for managing foreign affairs. The plan was frankly built on the principle that the Department should be the point at which the diverse special interests of the various agencies could be forged into national policy, under the direction of the President and consistent with the responsibility of the National Security Council. Some of the recommendations were acted on immediately; others were implemented to meet 90- or 180-day deadlines; still others awaited congressional action.

Among the reforms implemented was a new system to improve functional specialization in the Foreign Service—the so-called cone system, whereby applicants had to choose their areas of specialization before they had any Foreign Service experience. They were then given the entrance examination applicable to the cone selected: administrative, economic, consular, or political. The number of applicants admitted to the Service in each cone was supposed to be related to the number of job openings available. Officers competed for promotion within their cone.

The cone system helped supply the professional skills needed but at some sacrifice to the development of top-flight leadership for foreign affairs. Like many other reforms in the personnel system this one seemed to be remedying one set of inequities by creating a new set. As a result, there was much dissatisfaction with it. The Director General undertook a special study of the problem, and in mid-1974 several modifications in the system were adopted. The system was to become less rigid; officers would enter the Service with a skill designation, but would be able to change that designation if they wished while still in the junior grades. Advancing to mid-career (Class 5), they would have to reaffirm their cone, or special skill designation, but rigidities in assignments would be reduced and shifting to another cone would frequently be authorized. In the senior grades (Classes 2 and 1) the cone approach would be further relaxed. In fact, there was to be a very strong emphasis on broadening the viewpoints of specialists by assigning them to areas outside of their principal expertise.

One of the few task force recommendations disapproved by the Department advocated a single employees' association under Presidential Executive Order 11491. The Department initially sought exemption from that order, which encouraged departments to permit employee representation on the basis of security requirements. The AFSA and the AFL-CIO–chartered American Federation of Government Employees (AFGE) vigorously opposed the Department's position. With a new Executive Order 11636, tailored to the special requirements of the Department and the Foreign Service and supported by AFSA, the Department changed its position.

In accordance with the provisions of the new executive order, the AFSA and AFGE conducted election campaigns at home and abroad to become the sole representative of (initially) the Foreign Service of the Department and subsequently of AID and USIA. At the end of 1972, it was announced that AFSA had won the right to represent the Department's Foreign Service by a wide margin, and, in early 1973, it also won the right to represent the overseas personnel of AID and USIA, though by smaller margins. The AFGE, which already represented some domestic units, subsequently won several others. A significant number of Foreign Service personnel joined AFGE regardless of domestic or overseas organizational affiliation.

Earlier in this chapter reference was made to the Foreign Service Act of 1946. One of its several provisions differentiating the Foreign Service from the civil service required the Secretary of State to prescribe regulations under which officers who are not promoted within a certain period of time or who fail to meet a required standard of performance must be retired from the Service, with certain benefits. This provision, known as "selection out," became particularly controversial after 1971, when a Foreign Service officer committed suicide after having been selected out two years earlier. The AFGE sponsored a legal defense fund in the officer's name that financed a class-action suit by several Foreign Service officers of State and USIA. According to press reports they did not object to a selection-out system but claimed it was administered unfairly. In December, 1973, a Washington, D.C., district court judge ruled that the selection-out *procedure*, as prescribed by the regulations then in effect, was unconstitutional. He said that officers to be selected out were entitled to be informed of the facts before, not after, a final decision. The Department has since changed its procedures to meet the constitutionality test.

By 1974, improvements in the Department's internal management procedures seemed to be facilitating the task of officers concerned with substantive matters. It is hoped that the changes in the personnel system, reflecting more of the labor-management relationships now prevalent throughout the rest of government, may serve as an added inducement to those considering a diplomatic career. In June 1975, the Secretary announced in a welcoming address to the 119th Foreign Service Office class that he had established a Priorities Policy Group to provide a mechanism for linking resource-allocations decisions to policy decisions, as well as several personnel management improvements. These changes bear a striking resemblance to the Task Force recommendations.

ALTERNATIVES FOR REORGANIZATION

It should be noted that there were—and are—qualified and sincere observers who believe that the conduct of foreign policy would be greatly enhanced by a much smaller foreign affairs establishment. Some, including veterans of the Department and the Foreign Service, would prefer to see State divorced from the many specialized programs. They would devote the energies of a small corps of professionals solely to foreign policy considerations. To the extent that the overseas programs of other agencies meet broad Presidential foreign policy objectives, such programs should not, in their view, unduly concern the Department of State.

One experienced observer, Charles Maechling, Jr., who occupied a senior position in the Department during the 1960's, would limit State to the exercise of routine diplomatic and consular functions. He would, however, create a new superagency in the White House, a Foreign Affairs Council, consisting of "the heads of the principal departments and agencies of the foreign affairs establishment" and "chaired by the President's Special Assistant for Security Affairs, now elevated to the new Cabinet post of Secretary for National Security Affairs." A small staff secretariat of civilian and military personnel from every agency of government, supplemented by a rotating element of professionals from civilian life and from congressional staffs, would concentrate on national policy-planning, coordinating overseas programs and activities, recommending action, and allocating resources. With certain concurrent organizational changes, and assuming it were "skillfully managed," according to Maechling, the new system "would close the present gap between formation and programs execution."

In a 1970 article in *Foreign Affairs,* the late John Franklin Campbell, Jr., a brilliant young Foreign Service officer, proposed a 50 per cent reduction in the Department's personnel by 1976, with comparable cuts in other foreign affairs organizations, to give effect to what he perceived to be President Nixon's change in foreign policy. He wrote that, "If we are indeed at the end of a period of ideological confrontation and hope to nurture negotiation, then events are pushing toward a rediscovery of the need for traditional methods." Campbell held that any President would benefit from a strong and able State Department, since its "stock-in-trade is a kind of expert knowledge and judgment and international negotiating skill that has no other institutional home in Washington." The way to strengthen State, he maintained, was to cut it back in size "while at the same time giving it new executive authority over other agencies." Campbell also suggested a "Fifteen-Year Program" to improve career diplomacy, stressing high academic standards for entry, accelerated promotions to about 5 per cent of FSO's for meritorious work, and the development of "a separate cadre of men and women to control and manage the Washington machine" —a permanent home staff to provide continuity.

THE MURPHY COMMISSION

The Foreign Relations Authorization Act of 1972 (P.L. 92-352 of July 13, 1972) established the Commission on the Organization of the Government for the Conduct of Foreign Policy (see Appendix A) that Senator Fulbright had deferred two years earlier to give the State Department's own task forces an opportunity to make their recommendations. It was not until March, 1973, however, that the executive branch appointments were made. The members of the commission met in April and chose retired career ambassador Robert D. Murphy as chairman. Organizational and planning meetings followed, and the commission began formal hearings in September.

The findings and recommendations of this joint Presidential-congressional study commission* could have decisive influence on the way foreign affairs are handled by the U.S. Government in the future. The commission is looking into the impact of the changing world environment and the changing role of the United States to determine how the government can be organized "to provide a more effective system for the formulation and implementation of the nation's foreign policy." The organization and relationships of all executive departments and entities that are concerned with foreign policy, of the White House, and Congress are subject to review and appraisal.

* See Appendix B for a summary of the commission's findings and recommendations.

III

Present Organization

It has been said that the structure of the Department of State is more complicated than that of any industrial organization, regardless of size. The Department must maintain staffs and operate, to some degree, in virtually every country in the world. Its primary function is to promote the long-range security and well-being of the United States, which requires that it become involved in a wide variety of issues—most fairly routine but others extremely sensitive.

With some exceptions, discussed in other chapters, Presidents normally look first to the Secretary of State and Department of State personnel for advice in the formation and execution of foreign policy. The staff members determine and analyze facts relating to most U.S. overseas interests, make recommendations on policy and action, and with the assistance of personnel overseas and other government departments, take the necessary steps to implement approved policy. The Secretary of State and his key assistants at home and abroad consult with other nations (even those with which the United States does not have diplomatic relations), negotiate treaties and agreements with foreign governments, speak for the United States in the United Nations and in most of the fifty-six major international organizations in which the United States participates, and represent the United States at more than five hundred international conferences annually. Department personnel also have numerous duties required by law not necessarily related directly to diplomacy, such as the issuance of passports and visas, promotion of U.S. business abroad, protection of American citizens and seamen, and payment of Social Security and other annuities abroad.

To carry out these manifold and diverse functions, the Department has developed an organizational structure based in part on historical tradition and in part on practical and realistic functional needs of the day. Consequently, the structure reflects a mix of long-standing, well-understood methods of getting things done and many of the more modern management techniques, with the wide variety of functions performed primarily by civil service and Foreign Service personnel.

Chart I shows the present-day organization of the Department of State. However, a simple chart cannot reflect all of the statutory obligations of the Secretary of State and his staff; the individual bureau organization charts in following chapters help identify these. In many instances, functional statements can be useful for an understanding of how the Department operates, and chapters IV through IX supply such information in part. However, space does not permit the detailed analysis that would provide a thorough understanding of the interlocking responsibilities of the hundreds of people in the operational levels, and the reader is cautioned that charts, job descriptions, and functional statements, even taken together with supplementary descriptions of geographic area clarifications and other particulars, can never convey a full understanding of how the State Department *really* operates or of the ever shifting relationships among individuals in the bureaucratic hierarchy.* At best, this book can only set forth what underlies the daily changing realities of policy, power, and practices.

In the past twenty-five years, the Department has been reorganized again and again, generally on the theory that administrative reforms would provide the answer to the needs of modern diplomacy. The fact remains that the effectiveness of diplomacy

* John P. Leacacos's *Fires in the In-Basket* provides a lively account by a top-flight journalist of day-to-day problems of the Department and how they were handled in the pre-Nixon years.

bears little relation to such changes. Rather, it is the competency of persons assigned to jobs that in the end determines how effectively diplomacy, like anything else, is managed. Thus, although quite a few pages that follow are devoted to describing the duties of the top echelon of officers around the Secretary of State, the key thing to remember is that decision-makers are hand-picked by the Secretary to discharge certain responsibilities assigned by him. Their duties may not necessarily be as similar to those handled by predecessors in the same job slots as one might expect and very often include extra responsibilities that are not covered or even hinted at in the formal job description.

Basically, there are three major decision-making areas within the Department of State—or four, if the overseas missions as a group are included. At the top are the Secretary, the deputy secretary, three under secretaries, a deputy under secretary, and the State Department counselor. Next in the chain of command are the assistant secretaries of the regional (geographic) bureaus, who conduct U.S. relations with the countries in their respective regions, subject only to the direction of the Secretary. The functional bureaus constitute the third decision-making area. They have many statutory responsibilities, but they must coordinate (or "clear") with the appropriate regional bureaus whenever an issue might affect relations with a foreign country.

THE SENIOR MANAGEMENT TEAM

The Secretary and his principal officers are generally referred to in the Department as "the Seventh Floor" (as though their physical location were a kind of corporate heaven). This is the group that in the management reform program of 1970 (see Chapter II) was formally designated the Senior Management Team. The term has already fallen into some disuse, but by whatever name these senior officials are called, they constitute the center of decision-making— the power center of the Department of State.

The Secretary and the deputy secretary direct the activities of this "team," whose additional members are the three under secre-

DEPARTMENT OF STATE

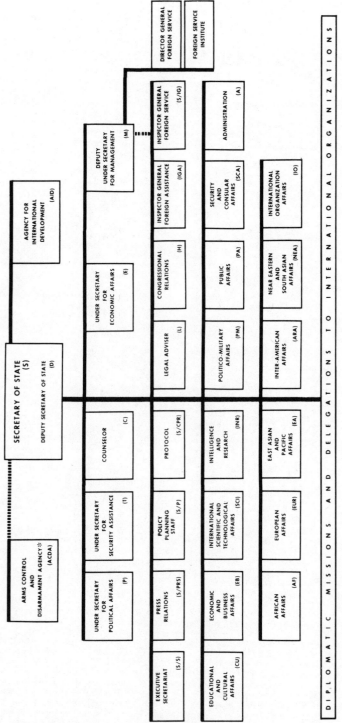

DIPLOMATIC MISSIONS AND DELEGATIONS TO INTERNATIONAL ORGANIZATIONS

* A separate agency with the director reporting directly to the Secretary and serving as principal adviser to the Secretary and the President on Arms Control and Disarmament.

taries for Political Affairs, Economic Affairs, and Security Assistance, the deputy under secretary for Management, and the counselor. As of the beginning of 1974 there were also three ambassadors at large reporting to the Secretary of State. They too had offices on the seventh floor. All these top officials are served by two staffs—the Executive Secretariat and the Policy Planning Council.

The Secretary of State

As head of the Department of State, the Secretary's functions are all-inclusive. He has numerous statutory responsibilities and in addition serves as the principal adviser to the President on foreign policies and for the supervision of U.S. activities abroad; he also has several clearly defined legal responsibilities, many of which are delegated to officials at the operating level.

In the administration of foreign assistance, for example, Section 622 (c) of the Foreign Assistance Act states, among other things, that nothing in the Act shall be construed to infringe upon the powers or functions of the Secretary of State, and, under the direction of the President,

> the Secretary of State shall be responsible for the continuous supervision and general direction of economic assistance and military assistance and sales programs. . . . to the end that such programs are effectively integrated both at home and abroad and the foreign policy of the United States is best served thereby.

The Secretary delegated operating authority for the economic assistance program to the Director of the Agency for International Development (AID) at the time that agency was organized (1954), and he delegated the important functions mentioned above under Section 622 (c) to the under secretary for Security Assistance in 1971. (See Chapter IV.)

The Secretary must also be concerned with the U.S. Information Agency (USIA). Section (c) (1) of the U.S. Information and Educational Exchange Act of 1948, as amended, states that

> the Secretary shall direct the policy and control the content of a program for use abroad, on official United States positions, including

interpretations of current events, identified as official positions by an exclusive descriptive label.

That section also requires that the Secretary provide the director of the agency full guidance concerning the foreign policy of the United States. (See Chapter IV.)

By Executive Order 11034 of June 25, 1962, he is charged with exercising "primary responsibility for government-wide leadership and policy guidance with regard to international educational and cultural affairs." Certain functions conferred on the President by the Mutual Educational and Cultural Exchange Act of 1961 are also delegated to the Secretary of State. The Secretary is to exercise those functions on behalf of the President "in order to assure appropriate coordination of programs," but he is to take "into account the statutory functions of the departments and other executive agencies concerned." (See Chapter V.)

According to the Arms Control and Disarmament Act of 1961, the Director of the Arms Control and Disarmament Agency (ACDA) functions under the direction of the Secretary and is the principal adviser to the Secretary and the President on arms control and disarmament matters. (See Chapter IV.)

Although the Peace Corps is part of the agency ACTION, the Secretary of State, through Executive Order 11603 of June 30, 1971, and Section 4 of the Peace Corps Act, has general responsibility for the effective integration of programs to best serve U.S. foreign policy. (See Chapter VI.) The Secretary in turn has delegated to other offices of the Department much of this responsibility.

Other laws, executive orders, or interdepartmental agreements provide the basis for a vast array of duties performed within the Department under the Secretary's direction. In practice, the degree of leadership and direction exercised by a Secretary depends on the extent of the authority he has been given by a President.

The Deputy Secretary

The deputy secretary of State (until 1972, under secretary of State) is the alter ego of the Secretary and his principal assistant in the supervision of all elements of the Department and the management of its planning, evaluation, and resource allocation. The deputy secretary also serves as chairman of the National Security Council (NSC) Under Secretaries' Committee, and generally supervises the Department's participation in the NSC system. (See Chapters IV and VI.) To facilitate the long, difficult preparation for and participation in meetings and conferences on the Law of the Sea, the deputy secretary headed up the NSC coordinating staff that was created for this purpose in 1973. An additional function stemming from the reform program is the deputy secretary's service as chairman of the Board of the Foreign Service.

The Under Secretary for Political Affairs

During the past twenty years, with only a few exceptions, the third-ranking position of under secretary for Political Affairs has been filled by a senior Foreign Service officer. Because of this, it has been recommended that this position be established legally as a kind of permanent under secretary and reserved exclusively for a senior Foreign Service officer. This, obviously, would provide continuity when Presidents change, but so far the recommendation has not been approved.

In addition to serving as acting secretary in the absence of both the Secretary and the deputy secretary, this officer assists them in the formulation and conduct of foreign policy and in carrying out their responsibilities for over-all direction, coordination, and supervision of interdepartmental activities. The under secretary for Political Affairs is the deputy secretary's stand-in on numerous committees of the NSC. He usually represents the Department in discussing matters of mutual interest with the top officials of the Defense Department and the Central Intelligence Agency (CIA). (See Chapters IV and VI.) Among his most important functions is to serve as arbiter between the bureaus when they are in disagreement. As the highest-ranking career officer, he is usually asked for his recommendations on principal career personnel appointments —a matter of considerable interest within the Department—and he also supervises the activities of several of the Secretary's special assistants.

The Under Secretary for Economic Affairs

The position of under secretary for Economic Affairs was elevated from the deputy level in 1972 in accordance with recommendations of the reform program task forces. As the title indicates, the officer is concerned with economic matters and is not involved with other operations of the Department. This under secretary serves as chairman of the Operations Group of the Council on International Economic Policy and as the alternate governor of the International Monetary Fund, the International Bank for Reconstruction and Development, the Inter-American Development Bank, and the Asian Development Bank. He is on the board of directors of the Overseas Private Investment Corporation.

The Under Secretary for Security Assistance

Following the recommendation of a Presidential task force, headed by Rudolph Peterson, that examined the entire foreign assistance program, the position of under secretary for Security Assistance was authorized by the Foreign Assistance Act of 1971 to perform, on behalf of the Secretary, those statutory functions conferred upon him by Section 622 (c) of the Foreign Assistance Act of 1961, as amended. The task force concluded that foreign assistance could be more effective in furthering U.S. foreign policy objectives if the Department provided better policy guidance, especially to the military assistance and related programs. Thus, policy guidance and coordination of military assistance programs with each other and with the economic assistance programs are the principal functions of the under secretary, together with supervision of the development of an integrated congressional presentation of these security programs. He must also give consideration to the defense requirements and financial situation of the recipient countries.

In addition, the under secretary for Security Assistance serves as executive chairman of the Interagency Security Assistance Program Review Committee, which has been established for the purpose of advising and assisting him. He is the principal State Department representative in all security assistance program activities and relationships with other agencies and with NSC groups and Congress. (See Chapters IV, VI, and VII.)

Besides a small personal staff, substantive staff support for the under secretary is provided by various bureaus of the Department —primarily by the Bureau of Politico-Military Affairs.

The Deputy Under Secretary for Management

A major recommendation of the reform program's task force was the transfer of two important bureaus, the Bureau of Administration and the Bureau of Security and Consular Affairs, together with the Inspector General Foreign Service, from the line supervision of the deputy under secretary for Management to the deputy secretary of State. This was done to give effect to the proposal that the deputy secretary should assist the Secretary in giving overall supervision and direction to "all" substantive and administrative elements. Furthermore, whereas the deputy under secretary formerly received his delegations of authority for managing the Department and the Foreign Service directly from the Secretary, he now receives them from the deputy secretary. He did, however, retain direct supervisory authority over the staff responsible for personnel policies and operations, headed by the director general of the Foreign Service; and he continued to share budget and fiscal responsibilities with the assistant secretary for Administration. Finally, the deputy under secretary also kept control over the Foreign Service Institute, where personnel of all agencies involved in foreign affairs may receive specialized training.*

Logical as it seemed to be to ask the deputy secretary to oversee both the substantive and administrative activities of the Department, in practice the deputy under secretary for Management has continued to operate very much as before as the supervisor of the entire administrative area.

---

* A new unit, Management Operations, was added in May 1975 and was expected to have a major role in tying together resources and policy.

The Counselor

The remaining principal officer of the Seventh Floor is the counselor, a special adviser on major problems of foreign relations, who handles international negotiations or other special assignments. Different secretaries of State use their counselors in very different ways, depending on the qualifications of the individuals. For example, the counselor who assumed his office in December, 1973, as a former close associate of Secretary Kissinger on the NSC, concentrates on many of the same problems he previously worked on there, such as European relations, the Strategic Arms Limitation Talks (SALT), and Mutual Balanced Force Reductions. In short, he is the person to whom the Secretary looks to ride herd on these and other assigned tasks.

The Executive Secretariat

As noted in Chapter II, the Executive Secretariat was established by General George Marshall when he became Secretary of State in 1947. At that time, a number of coordinating units were consolidated into one organization and headed by Carlisle H. Humelsine who, during the war years, had organized a similar unit in the Pentagon. Today, the head of the Executive Secretariat is the executive secretary of the Department and special assistant to the Secretary, whose rank is equal with that of an assistant secretary. Whatever goes up to the Secretary or to the under secretaries, or down to the regional or functional bureaus from the Secretary, passes through the hands of the executive secretary or his staff. He is the official channel for whatever documents pass between the Department and the White House, including National Security Study Memorandum requests; in many instances, moreover, he assigns responsibility for action within the Department on White House or other top-level directives and follows up to ensure that the action is completed within the allotted time. The executive secretary also has under his control the Operations Center, the around-the-clock monitor of the enormous communications flow coming into the Department. The center reacts to messages requiring immediate attention and sees to it that appropriate bureaus act on them. Also, in times of crises, the center houses within its confines special task forces set up on an *ad hoc* basis to cope with them.

In short, the executive secretary is the key man of the Seventh Floor complex for all administrative staff support. Since the reform program, the Executive Secretariat has served the office of the deputy under secretary for Management as well, ensuring that management is kept informed of substantive policies that may require human or material resources for implementation.

Policy Planning Staff

In addition to the Executive Secretariat, Secretary Marshall also established the Policy Planning Staff in May, 1947, to be "a long-range planning staff as an advisory group to coordinate State Department thinking." First director of the body was George Kennan, a Foreign Service officer who was later Ambassador to the Soviet Union and to Yugoslavia and who is now a distinguished historian at the Institute for Advanced Studies in Princeton, N.J. When Kennedy appointed Walt W. Rostow to head the group, in his time called the Policy Planning Council, the members tried to bring long-range perspective to the consideration of current problems. In 1969, the Council was reorganized to become the Planning and Coordinating Staff. In explaining the reorganization, then Under Secretary Elliot L. Richardson said that the Council had tended to be to insulated from the policy-making process and should be more directly plugged into decision-making. He believed that the reorganization would help to "manage the Department's input into the National Security Council system, as well as the follow-through from it."

The Planning and Coordinating Staff, as set up by Richardson, was responsible for policy planning—although that function gravitated increasingly to then National Security Adviser Henry Kissinger's White House staff. It coordinated the Department's work in the NSC committees and evaluated and allocated available resources on a country-by-country basis. The staff also was encouraged by Richardson to play a kind of devil's advocate role in reviewing policy papers and to come forward with alternative proposals. In general, the staff, which included professionals from outside the government, provided the Seventh Floor policy-makers with much valuable support in substantive, as distinct from administrative, matters.

When Dr. Kissinger was named Secretary of State in the latter part of 1973, he and the individuals who moved into Seventh Floor offices with him had a different concept as to the kind of support they needed. Deputy Secretary Kenneth Rush believed that the Seventh Floor had no business spending hours on resource allocation, which the bureaus more appropriately might handle. Only two officers seemed to be needed to coordinate staff work for the not-very-active NSC committees. Several staff members were assigned to work on energy matters, and two to work full time as speech writers.

The most important change that occurred had to do with policy planning, which, if it is to be effective, belongs close to the source of action and the power. Hence, it was natural for Kissinger to transfer the locus of policy planning back to the State Department when he took over. Former Foreign Service officer Winston Lord, a Kissinger protégé and member of his NSC staff, was made head of the Planning and Coordinating Staff. He breathed new life into its work, brought in some of the brightest, most competent people available, and restored the emphasis on policy planning. Coordination was left to the Executive Secretariat. In recognition of all this, the name was changed again in mid-February, 1974, to Policy Planning Staff. As has always been the case when this group has been headed by a person enjoying the full confidence of the Secretary, Winston Lord has often become involved in day-to-day crises; he has accompanied the Secretary on many of his trips abroad and in general has had less time for quiet deliberation than planners hope to enjoy. The Open Forum Panel, the vehicle through which all personnel can make their views on policy and programs known to the Secretary and his principals, was retained and continues to be a useful way to promote participation and innovations in foreign policy formulation. But the important thing from the Department's point of view was that policy planning was back; it was flourishing and being used by the Secretary and the Seventh

Floor. Indeed, it was once more functioning very much the way it did in Kennan's day.

THE OFFICE OF THE SECRETARY

The Secretary of State has several special advisers and independent organizational units attached to his own office that are not generally considered part of the Senior Management Team.

It has been customary for a President or Secretary of State to utilize the services of a high-level troubleshooter designated Ambassador at Large for special, often delicate assignments, such as heading the U.S. delegations to the SALT talks and to the meetings with Panama over the Panama Canal and participating in the Geneva Middle East conference. When not on such special assignments, these highly qualified veteran officials may be asked by the Secretary to follow up for him on certain problems or problem areas with the object of expediting action and, no doubt, relieving part of the work load on the Seventh Floor.

The Chief of Protocol is also part of the Secretary's office. He advises and assists the President, the Vice-President, the Secretary of State, and other high-ranking officials of the U.S. Government on matters pertaining to national and international protocol. These include the planning, preparation, and supervision of the ceremonial aspects of state visits by the heads of other nations or governments to this country; the presentation of Letters of Credence by foreign envoys to the President; state visits to other countries by the President; official travel abroad by the Vice-President, the Secretary of State, and other ranking officials; and the hospitality that they must extend or return on behalf of the government. The Chief of Protocol has a difficult task: Everything must go according to a strict time schedule but never seem rigidly organized. Moreover, the national customs and policies (dietary restrictions, religious views, friends and foes, status of women, and so on) must be known and observed, lest an unintentional discourtesy mar the successful achievement of the objectives of the occasion.

The Office of Press Relations, as its name implies, deals directly with the press. All matters relating to news policy and plans, press releases, and interviews are governed by this office. The daily noon briefing for the press is often an interesting event, with inquisitive, skilled reporters grilling the Department's "spokesman" and trying to extract more information than he is prepared (or authorized) to give. A substantial number of representatives of American and foreign, private and government media and media services, including Tass, the Soviet Government's news service, are accredited to the Department and have desk space in the press room of the Department of State. (See also Chapter VIII.)

Many problems that impinge on foreign relations are of interest to the Department even though they are not its direct responsibility. Included in this category are some of the new global problems that require international action. The Secretary has in recent years had a number of special assistants (including one designated to coordinate the combating of terrorism) to assist him in following these matters, to ensure the Department's cooperation and assistance, to coordinate actions between bureaus and departments, and often to participate as the Department's representative in international conferences.

The heads of two other very important organizations—the Inspector General, Foreign Service, and the Inspector General of Foreign Assistance—also report directly to the Secretary, even though they are physically outside his Office.

Inspector General, Foreign Service

The Inspector General, Foreign Service, serves under the direct supervision of the Secretary and deputy secretary even though he receives day-to-day guidance from the deputy under secretary for Management. The Inspector General and his staff provide independent evaluation of the programs, organization, administration, and personnel of the Department and the missions and consular offices abroad. Since the reform program, the inspectors have also been evaluating effectiveness of policies.

The Inspector General's staff develops, maintains, and distributes a guidance manual of management principles and supervises a Methods and Systems Staff that develops new analytical techniques and data systems for the Department.

Inspector General of Foreign Assistance

The Inspector General of Foreign Assistance is responsible to the Secretary for the effectiveness of U.S. economic and military assistance programs, and for Public Law 480 (Food for Freedom) activities. The Inspector General's office conducts inspections of these programs, makes recommendations to the head of the agency concerned, and follows up to determine what action has been taken.

AFFILIATED AGENCIES

The Agency for International Development and the Arms Control and Disarmament Agency, two extremely important organizations that maintain special relationships with the State Department, are discussed in Chapter IV.

THE GEOGRAPHIC BUREAUS

The five geographic bureaus—the Bureau of European Affairs, the Bureau of East Asian and Pacific Affairs, the Bureau of Near Eastern and South Asian Affairs, the Bureau of African Affairs, and the Bureau of Inter-American Affairs—constitute the Department of State's second decision-making area. All the bureaus are organized in substantially the same manner, except for the Bureau of Inter-American Affairs, which is integrated with the Bureau for Latin America of AID. In this case, the assistant secretary of State for Inter-American Affairs also serves as the U.S. coordinator for Latin America (AID), and most of the bureau offices are organized and function jointly with their AID counterparts, who are located elsewhere.

The assistant secretaries are really the heart of the Department's operations. The heads of the geographic bureaus are among the most trusted and senior officers of the Department and Foreign Service, for they are responsible for the general conduct of U.S. foreign relations, including the Foreign Service establishments (embassies and consular offices), within their respective geographic regions. By Presidential directive, they assist the Secretary in providing over-all direction, coordination, and supervision of interdepartmental activities in their areas of responsibility.

The heads of all other bureaus coordinate their major overseas programs, activities, or proposals with them. They must also be particularly watchful for indications of developing crises and ensure that appropriate and timely action is initiated; their level is the first at which the United States could be committed to a course of action abroad.

The assistant secretaries in the geographic bureaus have under them deputy assistant secretaries who are, with few exceptions, senior Foreign Service officers. A senior deputy serves as the *alter ego* of the assistant secretary, and one or two other deputies have special functional or regional responsibilities. Since the assistant secretaries and their deputies cannot handle the day-to-day activities and problems of every country in their region, they are assisted by country directors or office directors who are in charge of one or, usually, several countries in the area. Their duties include providing general instructions and guidance for the operations of the U.S. Foreign Service establishments in their country or countries, ensuring assistance to the ambassadors both within the Department and governmentwide, and in general supporting the diplomatic missions in every possible way. They also maintain contact in Washington with the diplomatic missions of the country or countries that they are responsible for. (See Chapter IV for more detail on the functioning of the geographic bureaus.)

THE FUNCTIONAL BUREAUS

The functional bureaus described below carry out many Department activities not generally known to the public at large. They

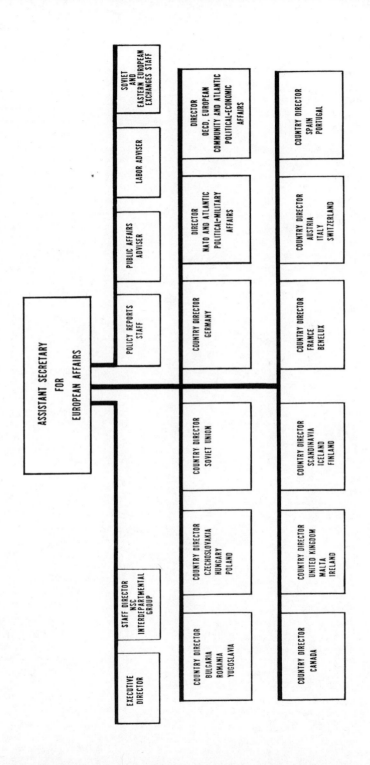

constitute the third major decision-making area of the Department.

Congressional Relations

The assistant secretary for Congressional Relations supervises and coordinates all legislative and nonlegislative relationships (except budget, fiscal, and operational administrative matters) between the Department and the Congress. He directs the presentation of the Department's legislative program and provides advice and information to the other areas of State on congressional matters. One of the main functions of this office is to assure that immediate and responsible replies are made to the thousands of letters the Department receives each year from senators and representatives. (See Chapter VII for further details.)

Legal Adviser

The legal adviser, whose rank is the equivalent of an assistant secretary, provides legal advice to the Secretary, the deputy secretary, and other top-level officers on all domestic and international problems arising in the course of the Department's activities. He participates in international conferences related to legal issues. He also represents the United States in international litigation and assists the Justice Department in domestic litigation that involves the Department. As a member of the International Law Commission, the legal adviser is responsible for U.S. activities in the field of unification and codification of public and private international law.

Politico-Military Affairs

Until the end of World War II, there was little coordination or collaboration between the Department of State and the military establishment. Although individual Foreign Service officers played useful roles as political advisers at several military headquarters, State was largely ignored by the White House and the military during the war, and only gradually was the need for increased cooperation in the postwar world recognized. Only a few years ago, politico-military matters were largely handled in the State Department by a deputy under secretary for Political Affairs assisted by a relatively small staff. The present organization indicates the manifold duties that now fall in this area.

The director of the Bureau of Politico-Military Affairs, with a rank equivalent to an assistant secretary, advises the Secretary of State on issues and policy problems arising in the areas where defense and foreign policy intersect. He serves as the principal channel of liaison and contact between the departments of State and Defense, discussing with State Department officials the views and positions advanced by Defense on politico-military problems under consideration within the NSC. He also chairs and provides leadership in the NSC Political-Military Interdepartmental Group (IG).

The director, working closely with the under secretary for Security Assistance, provides policy guidance and coordination to the military assistance and sales programs that are operated by the Defense Department. He also controls the commercial export of arms. Moreover, he has responsibility for the State-Defense Exchange Program (the exchange of civilian and military officers between the two departments), the assignment of Foreign Service officers to the military academies and war colleges, and the assignment of political advisers to the major military commands.

Oceans and International Environmental and Scientific Affairs

The international and global problems resulting from scientific and technological activity have required more and more of the Department's attention. For many years the Department's interests were handled by the Bureau of International Scientific and Technological Affairs (SCI) under a director of assistant secretary rank. SCI was organized into four offices: the Office of General Scientific Affairs, Office of Space and Atmospheric Affairs, Office of Atomic Energy Affairs (peaceful uses), and the Office of Environmental Affairs. The director advised the Secretary on these matters as they related to foreign policy; he provided foreign policy guidance, where appropriate, to governmental and nongovernmental scientific and technological agencies; he also directed the program that assigns scientific attachés to U.S. diplomatic missions abroad.

In accordance with Public Law 93-126 of October 18, 1973, the Department brought together the handling of oceans, environmental, scientific, and technological problems into a new bureau under an assistant secretary to give greater weight to State's increasing involvement in the foreign relations aspects of those problems. The new Bureau of Oceans and International Environmental and Scientific Affairs (OES) absorbed the former Bureau of International Scientific and Technological Affairs and the offices of the coordinator of Ocean Affairs and special assistant for Wildlife and Fisheries, special assistant for Population Matters, and special assistant for Environmental Affairs. Its main functions are to develop appropriate U.S. policies in the areas of its responsibility, to be the central point of contact on such matters with other U.S. Government agencies, and to provide foreign policy guidance and coordination for the international programs. The Bureau represents the Department in international committees, conferences, and negotiations and helps develop U.S. positions and strategy for such negotiations. Frequently, OES heads the U.S. delegations at international conferences.

Intelligence and Research

The director of Intelligence and Research, whose rank equals that of an assistant secretary, heads the Department's program of policy-oriented research and analysis. He is chairman of the Foreign Affairs Research Subcommittee of the NSC/Under Secretary's Committee and he represents the Department on the U.S. Intelligence Board and other interdepartmental intelligence groups and committees. The director is also responsible for coordinating the overt intelligence reporting activities of the Department in the field and serves as the Department's liaison with other agencies on intelligence matters, including those concerning defense attachés, the administration of the Foreign Agent Registration Act, and procurement of foreign maps and publications. He coordinates the Department's participation in the National Intelligence Survey program. The bureau has several geographic offices corresponding, in general, with the area divisions within the five geographic bureaus. Each of these is responsible for conducting policy-oriented research and analysis and preparing reports and estimates of situations for use in foreign policy formulation. There is also an Office of Strategic and Functional Research concerned with scientific, economic, social, demographic, and geographic problems abroad. The Office of Current Intelligence Indications, as its title suggests, deals with the world situation in the light of current intelligence derived from interdepartmental sources, civilian or military. The Office of External Research maintains liaison with universities, foundations, and institutions, as well as with other government agencies, for the purpose of clearing and coordinating contractual and private social science research projects in foreign areas. Essentially, it backstops the NSC research program mentioned above.

International Organization Affairs

The assistant secretary for International Organization Affairs furnishes guidance and support for U.S. participation in international organizations, notably the United Nations, and conferences and acts as the channel between the federal government and such organizations. An Office of United Nations Political Affairs handles policy and security matters relating to the United Nations and prepares for U.S. participation in the Security Council, the Trusteeship Council, and the General Assembly. There are a coordinator for Multilateral Development Programs and individual agency directors for specialized agencies concerned with human rights, health, labor, population matters, freedom of information, and so on. One office copes with the financial problems involved in participation in international organizations; another coordinates and provides administrative support for U.S. attendance at international conferences; still another recruits highly qualified U.S. citizens for employment in international organizations (each participating nation is entitled to have a reasonable number of its citizens employed). (See also Chapter IX.)

Public Affairs

The assistant secretary for Public Affairs directs the development and execution of Department-wide public information policy, plans, and programs, except for those relating to news, which are the responsibility of the Office of Press Relations. The assistant secretary coordinates government-wide foreign policy information activities, and his bureau conducts the Department's work-study program in which many college students have participated.

Chapter VIII is devoted to a fuller discussion of the Department's efforts to inform the public. Organizationally, these activities are handled by

the *Office of Policy and Plans*, which coordinates public affairs guidance on foreign policy within the Department, and, with other agencies, reviews and guides public statements (including manuscripts for publication), prepares analyses of public opinion, and develops plans for public information;

the *Office of Media Services*, which makes available information *services* (not news) concerning foreign policy and operations of the Department to the radio, television, magazines, the feature press, editors, journalists, educators, book publishers, and authors;

the *Office of Public Services*, which offers person-to-person information services to the general public and almost any civic, educational, or other group interested in foreign affairs. It arranges speaking engagements for Department officials, supports the Scholar-Diplomat Seminars (in which over 390 teachers of political science, history, and economics have participated so far) and helps to encourage the teaching of international affairs in secondary schools; and

the *Historical Office*, which prepares the official record of United States diplomacy, a series of volumes entitled *Foreign Relations of the United States*, by 1974 up to the year 1949.

Security and Consular Affairs

The administrator of the Bureau of Security and Consular Affairs, with statutory rank equivalent to an assistant secretary, administers and enforces the provisions of the Immigration and

Nationality Act as well as all other immigration and nationality laws relating to the powers, duties, and functions of diplomatic and consular officers of the United States, except where those responsibilities are conferred by law directly on consular officers. Thus, the functions of the bureau include among others the issuance of passports and related services, the issuance of visas for foreign nationals, protection of American citizens and interests abroad, representation of interests of foreign governments in third countries, and the determination of nationality of persons claiming U.S. citizenship but who were not born in the United States. The director also maintains liaison with and coordinates U.S. activities relating to the American Red Cross, the International Committee of the Red Cross, and the League of Red Cross Societies.

Anyone who has traveled abroad will be familiar with passport application procedures of the Passport Office, whether making application in this country or to a consular office abroad. The service is largely routine but can involve difficult decisions when controversial cases arise, as when an applicant refuses to take the oath of allegiance to the United States.

Although the consular officer has certain statutory responsibilities, the Visa Office administers the laws that govern the granting of visas and establishes the policies for approval of visa applications by aliens. Incidentally, a visa does not guarantee entry into the United States—it is only a permit to apply for entry; the Immigration and Naturalization Service decides whether the holder of a visa is legally entitled to enter the United States. The issuance or refusal of a visa may also catch the attention of the press. A recent visa case that was given some press attention concerned the refusal of a visa to a Syrian delegate to the United Nations and his wife, who, according to press reports, were linked to terrorist activities and therefore considered security risks while in the United States.

Educational and Cultural Affairs

The assistant secretary for Educational and Cultural Affairs directs the development and operation of programs contemplated by the Mutual Education and Cultural Exchange Act of 1961. This bureau administers programs and operations involved in awarding grants to Americans to visit other countries in the interest of interpreting and demonstrating U.S. achievements, policies, and institutions; sponsors cultural presentations that send American performing artists and athletes on tour abroad; and conducts foreign international visitor programs in the United States. Chapter V presents a detailed treatment of typical educational and cultural exchanges.

Economic and Business Affairs

The new name of this bureau, formerly the Bureau of Economic Affairs, indicates the emphasis being given by State to the promotion of commercial activities abroad. American exporters and importers have long pressed for more attention to their problems. Although a spokesman for one business group observed that its members really didn't care what agency promoted American business abroad, just as long as it was done effectively (to many businessmen, this simply means having commercial attachés who specialize in business and industrial promotion and who promptly report opportunities abroad for American firms), in 1972 a bill introduced in Congress by Senator Warren Magnuson went so far as to propose stripping State of most of its economic functions. Under this bill, which the Department vigorously opposed, all trade activities and field commercial reporting would have been transferred to the Department of Commerce. (See Chapter VI.)

Since the time the Magnuson bill was introduced, the assistant secretary for Economic and Business Affairs and his boss, the under secretary for Economic Affairs, have devoted much time to improving the Department's services to businessmen. At the end of 1973 a six-month study by the Office of Management and Budget was released that recommended that the Department retain responsibility for economic and commercial affairs abroad. President Nixon approved the recommendation, and the pressure for this drastic organizational change abated. However, the problem is a perennial one and can reappear at any time.

The main responsibilities of the assistant secretary are to formulate and implement approved policies regarding interregional foreign economic matters, negotiate agreements, and assist the office of the Special Representative for Trade Negotiations in carrying out agreements under the Trade Expansion Act of 1962. He is also responsible for Department representation in public lending institutions (World Bank, Export-Import Bank, international development banks), serves as deputy administrator for the Mutual Defense Assistance Control Act (Battle Act), and clears the assignments of officers to economic positions in U.S. embassies and consular offices.

The assistant secretary is aided by a deputy assistant secretary for International Trade Policy (international trade, general commercial policy, trade agreements, and East-West trade); another deputy is in charge of Transportation and Communications (aviation and maritime); still another handles International Finance and Development—a field in which the Treasury Department has a very special interest and desire to exert great control. The fourth deputy is responsible for International Resources and Food Policy (commodities, tropical products, industrial and strategic materials, fibers and textiles, fuels and energy). The remaining deputy deals with Commercial Affairs and Business Activities; it is his office that is being greatly strengthened in the effort to improve the Department's services.

Bureau of Administration

The assistant secretary for Administration is responsible for the preparation of budget estimates and allocation of congressional appropriations to the Secretary or the Department, although he shares supervision of the Budget and Finance Staff with the deputy under secretary for Management and substitutes for him when that officer is absent. He establishes program priorities for budgetary purposes and supervises the use of appropriated funds in accordance with congressional limitations, program objectives, and policies of the President and the Secretary.

The first State Department building (1781–83), at 13 South Sixth
Street, Philadelphia.

The State Department building, approximately 1865.

The State Department building today. This is the C Street, or diplomatic, entrance.

Meetings of international organizations, as well as conferences of business executives, educators, and news-media representatives, are held in this international conference room in the State Department building.

A 24-hour watch on world events is kept in the Department of State's Operations Center, where special task forces operate during international crises.

Secretary of State Henry Kissinger and Foreign Ministry Secretary Licenciado Emilio O. Rabasa arrive in Mexico City, February 20, 1974, for a foreign ministers' conference.

His deputy assistant secretary for Budget and Finance heads the office responsible for these matters in the bureau. The deputy for Operations provides audiovisual (graphics) services; automated data processing; library, interpretation, and translation services; publishing and reproduction; records (files); supply and transportation; overseas allowances; the allocation of space; and provision of furnishings and equipment. The deputy for Communications is responsible for the safest and fastest electrical transmission of classified and unclassified messages and for diplomatic pouch services between the Department and its missions and consular offices all over the world. The deputy assistant secretary for Security is charged with personnel security as well as the technical security of all buildings occupied by Department personnel at home and abroad. Finally, the director of the Office of Foreign Buildings is responsible for the acquisition and maintenance of embassies, consular offices, and residences used by Foreign Service personnel.

Director General of the Foreign Service

The director general of the Foreign Service (not to be confused with the inspector general, Foreign Service) advises and assists the deputy under secretary for Management in the formulation and implementation of policies for the administration of the Department and the Foreign Service. He* coordinates and directs the operating elements responsible for the personnel programs of the Department and the Foreign Service; this involves the career counseling and assignments of Foreign Service personnel, Civil Service staffing, recruitment of both Foreign Service and Civil Service personnel, and the provision of medical services for Foreign Service personnel. The director general also serves as chairman of the Board of Examiners for the Foreign Service.

The deputy director general and director of Personnel develops and implements the personnel policies and programs of the Department and the Foreign Service. Aided by a special assistant for

* Presently, she. Ambassador Carol Laise was named to the post on January 7, 1975.

Labor-Management Relations, he represents the Department in labor-management relations and is responsible for continuing liaison and consultation with labor, professional and other employee organizations. He also supervises the Newsletter and Information Staff, which keep Department and Foreign Service personnel informed of matters of direct interest to them, primarily through the monthly *Newsletter*.

The deputy director of Personnel directs several staffs that counsel personnel with regard to their career development and make appropriate assignments. There are also deputy directors of Personnel for Recruitment and Employment; for Management; and for Policy, Classification, and Evaluation.

The deputy assistant secretary for Medical Services is an important element of the director general's office. He is concerned with the physical examinations given to personnel before their assignment to the field and on their return. He is also responsible for those doctors stationed abroad, sometimes covering several posts, and registered nurses assigned to a large number of posts where medical services may be below American standards.

Foreign Service Institute

The Foreign Service Institute is responsible for training and instruction of Foreign Service and other Department of State personnel as well as personnel of other government departments and agencies involved in foreign affairs. Appropriate orientation and language training are also provided to family members of those officers and government employees in anticipation of their assignments abroad.

The Institute includes the Senior Seminar in Foreign Policy, the highest-level and final training for senior officers; a Foreign Affairs Executive Seminar; the School of Professional Studies; the School of Languages; and the Center for Area and Country Studies. Under the auspices of the Institute, a substantial number of selected personnel take university and college courses to improve their usefulness to the Department and the Foreign Service.*

* See footnote on page 71 about a new unit, Management Operations.

FIELD RELATIONSHIPS

The embassies and consular offices, located in every foreign country with which the United States has diplomatic relations, are the eyes and ears of the Department of State. Staffed by the Foreign Service of the United States, these offices in general look after American interests abroad.* The services they provide and duties they carry out, as well as the relationships of the Foreign Service and overseas embassies to other agencies of the U.S. Government, are described in the following chapters.

Embassies, headed by an ambassador accredited by the President of the United States to the chief of state of the foreign nation, are located in the capitals of all countries with which diplomatic relations are maintained. Diplomatic missions are also assigned to the United Nations headquarters in New York and to other international organizations. In general, embassies handle the daily diplomatic business that goes on between governments—matters relating to almost any field of mutual interest from fishing rights to wheat sales to treaty negotiations.

An embassy usually has a consular section to protect American citizens, promote American trade, assist businessmen, issue visas, and provide other services. Independent consular offices (both consulates general and consulates, in order of rank) can be found in important cities outside the capital. These offices represent the United States in the consular district, keep the embassies informed of local matters, and assist numerous U.S. civilian departments and agencies that may have particular interests in the area.

Embassies carry on a major reporting service, keeping the Department of State and other agencies informed of political and economic developments in the host countries. Specialized information usually goes directly to the responsible bureau within the Department or to the agency requesting the information. Thus the Department of Agriculture, for example, although it has its own Agricultural Foreign Service personnel in some major countries,

---

* For a full account of how the Foreign Service itself is organized and operates, see W. Wendell Blancké, *The Foreign Service of the United States* (Praeger Library of U.S. Government Departments and Agencies, No. 18), 1969.

depends on Foreign Service officers in other countries, and especially in consulates located in agricultural districts, to provide desired information.

In unusual circumstances, Foreign Service personnel are stationed in countries with which the United States does not have formal diplomatic relations (and vice versa). In those cases, another nation takes charge of U.S. property in that nation, and State Department personnel there are considered part of the embassy staff of the protecting power. Thus, somewhat normal relationships, which may or may not exclude business or trade, may still be conducted. Neither Algeria nor Egypt, for example, had diplomatic relations with the United States from 1967 to 1972, but U.S. Foreign Service personnel were stationed in the capitals of both countries, and a great deal of business was carried on between those two countries and the United States. Diplomatic relations were re-established with Egypt late in 1973.

RESOLUTION OF DIFFERENCES

No lines or boxes on organization charts, no words in functional statements, no specific directives explain quite how conflicting positions taken by two or more offices regarding an overseas policy or action of the United States are resolved—if indeed they are.

When the difference of opinion or aim is between the offices of a single geographic bureau, it is up to the assistant secretary of that bureau to resolve the issue and come up with a bureau position. If a difference affects countries in two or more geographic bureaus and the assistant secretaries responsible for the bureaus involved cannot resolve it, then the matter will be taken to the appropriate under secretary—generally to the under secretary for Political Affairs or Economic Affairs. When necessary—and this occurs infrequently—differences are taken to the deputy secretary or to the Secretary.

Decisions are often reached through the discussion of alternative courses of action in either informal or formal meetings. Each protagonist will argue his case. Dissenting opinion can be transmitted with complete protection for the dissenter through official channels directly to appropriate senior officials of the Department, and through the device of the Open Forum, where suggestions, constructive criticism, and dissent may be voiced with full assurance of being both heard and considered. On the most important issues, final decisions can only, of course, be made by the Secretary or by the President, to whom the Secretary may wish to present several options arrived at by Department personnel playing "adversary roles" in reviewing policy papers.

IV

Policy Making and Makers

During much of the nation's history, certain fundamental principles and aspirations have guided the direction of foreign policy. These are part of the American heritage and reflect its innate idealism and optimism. Despite American involvement in three major wars and several minor ones, despite specific acts that seem to contradict the fact, the United States has remained devoted to three goals— peace, democracy, and international well-being. It has been dedicated to a peaceful, prosperous, and cooperative international society not only as an ideal but also because only in such an international environment can the nation and its people find security and freedom.

It is difficult to separate foreign policy goals from foreign policy itself. By their very nature, foreign policy *goals* do not change appreciably over the years. But foreign *policies*—government-planned courses of action taken to carry out the fundamental principles and aspirations of the American people—do change. Throughout much of the nation's early history, indeed until well into the twentieth century, isolationism was, in a sense, both a goal and a policy of aloofness from European "entanglements." A basic change in this goal and its supporting policies came with World War I. But before and after that, specific policies that are worth noting here have included:

the *Monroe Doctrine* of 1823, originally a unilateral U.S. policy to prevent European powers from intervening in the Western Hemisphere that evolved after World War II into a multilateral Pan American defense doctrine, backed by the Rio Pact of 1947;

the *Open Door Policy,* a policy of cooperation with the great European powers to protect U.S. trade with China, that lapsed when the Chinese Communists took power in 1948–49;

the *Truman Doctrine* of 1947, which called for American support "to free peoples who are resisting attempted subjugation by armed minorities or by outside pressures" and was the basis for much of U.S. action during the Cold War, and the related policy of the containment of communism; and

the *Nixon Doctrine,* which was introduced in 1969 as a new policy but is basically an updating of containment and under which the United States is pledged to fulfill treaty commitments while at the same time being more restrained in its actions abroad (concurrently, allies are expected to undertake greater responsibilities of leadership and to share the burdens of assistance to developing countries). The heart of the concept is "Negotiation, not confrontation."*

The *peaceful settlement of disputes,* a policy of trying to avoid the use of force, which has long been a fundamental, underlying U.S. policy goal, calls for discussion, negotiation, or arbitration whenever possible. This policy remains as valid today as ever before, despite inconsistencies in its application over the years.

American foreign policies are made in Washington, but they are, for the most part, carried out abroad. Much of their effectiveness depends on the way this is done. Our man on the spot in the foreign country concerned, the American Ambassador, has to do most of the persuading, and he has a very difficult job because he is trying to influence another sovereign country to cooperate in a course of action that his own government designed to serve American national interests. Since the U.S. Government does not have any territorial claims on other countries' territories and sees its best interests served by conditions favorable to the peaceful development of all nations, it is sometimes difficult for Americans to understand why foreign governments do not always go along or are often suspicious of U.S. motives—and why the Department of

---

* *U.S. Foreign Policy for the 1970's,* February 7, 1972.

State and its Foreign Service frequently appear to fail to convince other nations to adopt policies that seem to be in their interests as well as our own.

WHAT MAKES POLICIES CHANGE

Foreign policies, whether basic or minor, change because of external happenings or changes at home. Often changes are forced by some threat from outside. Policies that do not help progress toward a basic objective must be altered or discarded. If the government is not responsive to such a need, the public is capable of making itself heard—not necessarily always with wisdom. U.S. entry into the Spanish-American War, for example, was largely the result of popular pressures within the United States; no responsible official or legislator wanted a war with Spain. Conversely, the decision to disengage from the war in Vietnam was heavily influenced by the public, and present policy is, to a great extent, an answer to the public's demand that the United States play a less active role in the affairs of other nations.

There are occasions when the temper of the times at home and relationships with the community of nations can give rise to a "great debate" or national reappraisal of the fundamental premises of American foreign policy. Since the people have the final word in determining basic policies, such public reappraisals can cause fundamental changes.

At the end of World War II there was a deep popular hope of achieving an international order through the United Nations, making obsolete the system of power politics that had led to two world wars in a generation. By early 1947 it had become clear to most Americans that this hope was ill-founded. The question of the proper course to pursue was debated for many months, but the American people recognized the unpalatable reality that the only way to safeguard their own security and ultimately achieve a system of peace in the world was to be willing to wield American power in a world unfortunately still ruled by power. The United States supports the United Nations, but under the containment policy, has resorted to the use of military force and threat of force to hold in check what have appeared to be dangerous extensions of Soviet or other communist power.

When administrations change, sometimes as a result of foreign policy issues, the incoming President may find that his promised new policies are no great improvement on the old. The responsibility of power is sobering, and an opposition party taking office soon finds that it acts out of national rather than partisan interest in making foreign policy decisions. At such a time, changes are not lightly made and, when they are, probably reflect external events, shifting international power relationships, and domestic pressures.

Of course, there have existed important partisan foreign policies in the nation's history. For years, the Democratic Party stood for low tariff and the Republican Party for high tariff. Yet on most foreign policy issues, from the Connally Resolution of 1943, which paved the way for the United Nations, to the Truman Doctrine in 1947, to the Gulf of Tonkin Resolution in 1964, which only later became controversial, there has been remarkable support from both political parties. The Vietnam War proved an exception, since it became a highly partisan issue, although the Congress did not divide along strictly party lines on it.

Sometimes a foreign policy started by one administration will be adopted and carried on enthusiastically by its successor. Thus Franklin Roosevelt, for instance, accepted the new neighborly relationships with Latin America put into effect by President Herbert Hoover and Secretary of State Henry Stimson and went on to highly publicize it as the Good Neighbor Policy. More often, however, inherited programs and policies are disavowed. The People-to-People Program, which had been identified with President Eisenhower, was given little government support when Kennedy took office in 1961. Similarly, Kennedy's Alliance for Progress went out of the limelight when the Nixon Administration took over.

Inherited policies that *are* acceptable to both parties, like the Open Door Policy, remain active as long as the reason for their existence remains valid. Policies that outlive their usefulness are scrapped. The official attitude of the United States toward China since 1948 is a case in point. It was a partisan issue in the 1952 Presidential campaign, but later American policy supporting the Nationalist Chinese Government and ostracizing Communist China was given bipartisan support. This hard-line approach became increasingly outmoded, and, when President Nixon abruptly shifted policy in the fall of 1971, his new approach was hailed by both political parties and the overwhelming majority of the American people.

Each new administration must learn for itself many of the lessons that the outgoing administration had also learned through experience. Its newly appointed decision-making officials must absorb a great deal very fast about what is going on in foreign affairs, the status of current policies and programs, and much background information. Yet while preparing themselves for foreign policy responsibility, they must simultaneously start making decisions and directing operations—often having to react immediately to new crises in the world. Of course, during this period some programs are bound to stall, foreign governments may postpone high-level meetings, and mistakes born of inexperience, such as the Kennedy Administration's Bay of Pigs fiasco in 1961, can occur. During these transition periods any continuity that does exist is provided by Department of State career officials and by the other departments and agencies whose bureaucracies continue to handle the day-to-day business of diplomacy.

Although the functioning of the various parts of the State Department must fluctuate from year to year—sometimes from month to month—certain of the functions are lasting and specific. These, like the Department's ongoing relationships with other government agencies and outside groups (see Chapter VI), can be described. The purpose of this chapter is to look generally at the Department's principal functions as they are or have been carried out by its leaders, bureaus, and offices. Later chapters examine in closer detail one functional area—the cultural and exchange program (Chapter V) and relationships with Congress, the people of the United States, and international organizations. (Chapters VII–IX).

THE ROLE OF THE PRESIDENT

The President, whose gravest responsibility is to preserve the security of the nation, is the central figure in determining U.S. foreign policy. He has the final say, and this is clearly illustrated in the dramatic crisis situations that make newspaper headlines, especially those—like the Berlin crisis in 1961, the Cuban missile crisis in 1962, the U.S. involvement in Vietnam—that threaten world war. But the President dominates foreign policy even when there is no crisis. He is empowered to negotiate treaties and agreements, to recognize new states and governments, to declare policy, to nominate or appoint diplomatic officials, and to exercise authority as granted him in various statutes.

The White House is in constant communication with other nations of the world. A stream of foreign visitors—chiefs of state, special emissaries, foreign ministers—have appointments with the President throughout his term of office, and he exchanges letters, messages, even telephone conversations, with chiefs of state and heads of government in other nations. The President's public comments—speeches, statements, and press conferences—as well as words he is rumored to have said about international affairs, are transmitted abroad and studied carefully by other governments.

During the twentieth century, the Presidential task of foreign policy making has grown enormously complicated. President Washington had only three departments to administer. Jefferson needed to communicate with only a few ministers in a few European capitals. Most early American Presidents and secretaries of State had all the knowledge and experience they needed to make decisions. In fact, four of the first six American presidents were former secretaries of State, and five of the six were skilled diplomatists even before taking office as chief executive. There was marked separation between domestic policies and international affairs, and Congress, although it possessed Constitutional powers in the latter area, rarely exercised them. This is no longer true. Today, the President needs a worldwide network of communications and manpower to make and execute foreign policy, and he needs an efficient bureaucracy to direct and coordinate these activities.

Through the nineteenth and into the early years of the twentieth century, it was widely accepted that the Secretary of State and his staff could adequately perform this function. Of late, however, several Presidents have appointed special foreign policy advisers, who, with a small staff, have served as the focal point in the White House for dealing with foreign policy problems. These special assistants have generally functioned in an advisory role and have had little to do with active diplomacy—Woodrow Wilson's Colonel House in World War I, Franklin D. Roosevelt's Harry Hopkins in World War II, and Richard Nixon's Henry Kissinger being notable exceptions.

The National Security Council

The Department of State did not take complete charge of foreign affairs in the early 1960's in spite of President John F. Kennedy's stated wish that it do so. The President himself handled the series of crises that developed, thus establishing a pattern for handling most important foreign policy issues from the White House rather than the Seventh Floor. Later, President Lyndon B. Johnson by directive formally delegated authority and responsibility to the Secretary of State as his "agent" for "the over-all direction, co-ordination, and supervision" of foreign affairs, and established within the National Security Council the so-called SIG/IRG system (see Chapter II, page 52) to implement his directives. The Nixon Administration continued the Secretary's delegation of authority, but the National Security Council mechanism, as utilized by President Johnson, was strengthened, so that the locus of power was taken almost entirely from State and returned to the White House. Most major policy matters were handled by the President and his National Security Adviser, the Middle East being an example of the several exceptions. A number of Foreign Service officers served on the NSC staff and others were called in as their special expertise was needed, but generally speaking, the Department was not directly involved in such crucial events as the historic visits to China and Russia and the negotiation of a cease-fire in Vietnam.

Throughout the first Nixon Administration, the Department of State continued to coordinate and direct the government's non-military overseas activities for which it had statutory or other authority, but it did not have control over the most important and dramatic activities that captured headlines.

The principal mechanism for the exercise of Presidential control of foreign affairs centered from 1969 onward to 1973 in the National Security Council in the Executive Office of the President, directed by the knowledgeable and able Dr. Henry Kissinger as assistant for National Security Affairs. Dr. Kissinger became the President's close confidant, crisis manager, supernegotiator, and diplomatic troubleshooter. With a staff of over one hundred people, Kissinger's office came to ride herd on the numerous agencies that make up the foreign affairs community, the State Department among them, through the formal mechanism of the rejuvenated NSC. The Peking and Moscow summit meetings and the secret negotiations for a Vietnam settlement as managed by Dr. Kissinger added to the aura of the White House as the diplomatic center of the nation—to a great extent at the expense of the Secretary of State and the State Department.

Every President since 1947, when it was created, has shaped the National Security Council to his own wishes. Former General Dwight D. Eisenhower used it as a kind of military staff, which, after much discussion and paper work, eventually submitted agreed-on policy recommendations to the President. According to Dean Acheson in *Present at the Creation,* President Truman found the newly established organization satisfied his "passion for orderly procedures," but "it was kept small; aides and brief carriers were excluded, a practice—unfortunately not continued—that made free and frank debate possible." Yet Truman relied so heavily on his Secretary of State that during the Truman years decision making on the big issues was mainly handled by Truman and Acheson, generally outside of the NSC. Secretary Dulles, like Acheson, frequently tended to bypass the NSC. He did so on some very important issues.

President Kennedy disliked receiving watered-down recommendations and so abolished some of the influential NSC boards and staff positions, returning their responsibilities to the executive departments. In his administration, NSC meetings were held only sporadically. Especially during crises, Kennedy depended on a few top advisers, plus special task forces and *ad hoc* committees hastily organized to deal with the problem. However, he found the NSC a convenient mechanism for informing his Cabinet-level officials of the policy line he intended to take on important matters. President Johnson, like his predecessor, preferred informal consultations with a few trusted advisers to the formality of the NSC. Most of the important decisions on the Vietnam War, for example, were taken at his regular Tuesday luncheons, which were attended by the Secretary of State, the Secretary of Defense, the special assistant for National Security Affairs, the White House press secretary, and often the Central Intelligence Agency (CIA) director, and the chairman of the Joint Chiefs of Staff (JCS). However, unlike Kennedy, Johnson had the NSC meet regularly, usually twice a month, for purely formal meetings and tried to delegate actual decision-making authority to the interdepartmental committee structure that he set up in 1966, with senior State Department officers having authority to make decisions on matters not requiring Presidential consideration.

One of President Nixon's first official acts as President was to "reaffirm the role of the National Security Council as the principal forum for Presidential review, coordination, and control of U.S. Government activity in the fields of national security and foreign affairs." In order to control all major foreign policy decisions himself, he thereupon absorbed the SIG/IRG system into the NSC structure.

The President has always chaired the NSC, which consists of the Vice-President and the secretaries of State and Defense. Others who attend regular meetings are the director of the Central Intelligence Agency (CIA), the chairman of the Joint Chiefs of Staff (JSC), and of course, the assistant for National Security Affairs. In addition, the Attorney General, the Secretary of the Treasury, and the deputy secretary of State frequently attend.

The heart of the NSC system today is an intricate committee structure—committees stacked at many levels. The first-tier committees, with the exception of the Under Secretaries' Committee described below, are all chaired by the versatile Dr. Kissinger. Membership differs, but the deputy secretary of State, deputy secretary of Defense, the CIA chief, and the JCS chairman belong to all key committees and groups. Their job is to review the policy studies and recommendations that come from below before they are submitted to the President for his consideration. Studies are generally levied by the NSC staff, but they can also be suggested by the Department of State and other agencies.

The Senior Review Group (SRG) handles the great majority of policy issues that are brought to the President through the NSC for his decision. Other committees and groups are the Verification Panel, which provides technical analyses on arms control issues; the Intelligence Committee, which advises the President on the adequacy of intelligence; and the hush-hush "Committee of Forty." The Intelligence Committee has not been especially active, but the Committee of Forty meets to consider delicate operations of the intelligence agencies (see also Chapter VI). The Under Secretaries' Committee, chaired by the deputy secretary of State, is supposed to follow through on policy decisions to see that they are carried out. It reports to the Secretary of State because the Secretary is responsible for supervising interdepartmental activities of the U.S. Government overseas, with the exception of the military forces, and its Research Subcommittee brings together the research people in the government.

With crises occurring so frequently in the world today, an important crisis-management group functioning under the NSC and called the Washington Special Action Group (WSAG) has become increasingly active. In April, 1972, for instance, when a massive North Vietnamese offensive got under way, the WSAG held meetings in the White House Situation Room to devise plans for handling the emergency. Henry Kissinger continues to chair this committee in his capacity as National Security Adviser, supported by an interagency task force based in the State Department. The Department itself is usually represented in WSAG by the under secretary for Political Affairs.

The entire NSC system is supported by a competent staff recruited from many agencies of the government. Among the staff's duties are the preparation of National Security Study Memoranda (NSSM), which assign studies to various departments, and of the National Security Decision Memoranda (NSDM), which record Presidential decisions. The input of the NSC staff in these policy studies would be hard to document but it can be considerable. Staff members work directly under, and draw on the reflected power of, their boss, the assistant for National Security Affairs, and can be very influential among the senior bureaucrats of the various departments. This was especially true from 1969 to 1973. Since that time, with Henry Kissinger wearing two hats as National Security Adviser and Secretary of State, both he and the President from 1973 onward have tended to bypass the NSC, and even the work of its various committees slowed down by the long absences from Washington of their peripatetic chairman. Yet the mechanism is there, providing a system of Presidential oversight that would have to be created if it were not already in being. As has been demonstrated, the system is flexible enough to adjust to the changing requirements of a succession of Presidents, secretaries of State, and Presidential advisers.

The Secretary of State and His Department

A vast and varied field of problems commands the attention of every Secretary of State. At one end of the spectrum, he can be preoccupied with finding ways to end the arms race and with matters of American security. At the other, he may be called on to rescue individual Americans in trouble abroad. In recent years, the flow of dangerous and illicit drugs into the United States from foreign sources has been still another of his concerns. Problems regarding tariffs, import quotas, immigration laws, and the granting of passports to Americans traveling abroad can all come to the Secretary's desk. And because some domestic problems may directly affect relations with another country, the Secretary of State must be particularly aware of the interrelationships and take them into account in his conduct of foreign relations.

During the long period of American isolationism—basically until World War II—the Secretary of State, with the Department of State at home and the Foreign Service abroad, conducted U.S. foreign relations with only occasional assists from other government departments. The last thirty years, however, have seen Presidential advisers and many government agencies—notably the Defense, Commerce, and Treasury departments—become deeply involved in foreign policy. Consequently, a Secretary of State does not necessarily now call the tune; his influence, now as always, depends on the degree of confidence the President has in him, the degree of authority the President delegates to him, and the degree of confidence Congress and the public have in him.

John F. Kennedy had a strong personal interest in foreign affairs and consulted many advisers in and out of government. He relied on Secretary of State Rusk but he also turned to his brother, Attorney General Robert Kennedy, and to his White House National Security Adviser, McGeorge Bundy. Lyndon Johnson had a somewhat similar approach. He was not comfortable with a structured system and often used a personal group of advisers when deciding critical matters. He depended more and more on Secretary Rusk, but he also relied on his White House assistants, first McGeorge Bundy and later Walt W. Rostow. President Nixon, as already noted, quickly centered control of the most important foreign policy matters in the White House, leaving the Secretary of State to handle the bulk of the routine, less dramatic workload. This situation changed when Dr. Kissinger in 1973, while retaining his White House duties, also became Secretary of State and thus responsible for all foreign policy matters, under the President of course. In these altered circumstances, the State Department again began to participate in many of the important areas from which it had been more or less excluded in recent years.

The Secretary of State is not only the President's senior foreign policy adviser. He directs the Department of State itself and its widespread overseas elements, which include representatives of other U.S. Government agencies who serve in many countries abroad under the American ambassadors.

It has been estimated that State has a leading role in more than 90 per cent of the business of conducting U.S. foreign relations. Much of this work load is routine—the quiet carrying on of U.S. relations with individual countries, and in international organizations and multinational conferences. The Department participates in countless interchanges that involve international trade, finance, science, culture, ideas, and people. It has been estimated that only about 15 per cent of the Department's work falls into the exceptional, nonroutine category, and only a small percentage of that is critical. Although there are important special problem exceptions, the Department even during the time William P. Rogers was Nixon's Secretary of State played the principal part in handling U.S. foreign relations with the Middle East, Latin America, Africa, and Europe. It was also very active in the multilateral organizations and in foreign economic policy.

Whether facing a crisis or a more normal day at the office, secretaries of State are on the go from morning to night. The Secretary's day begins early at his home, scanning newspapers, listening to radio or TV newscasts, reading summaries of telegrams from posts abroad, and catching up on recent happenings. This briefing session is continued for a while at the office, where classified material is available as well. Kissinger, who is also the President's National Security Adviser, usually starts his official day at his office in the White House executive building where he also goes over things with his NSC staff—that is, when he is in Washington.

In the Department the Secretary sees several key officials whose problems require his attention. His press relations assistant suggests several thorny questions that the Department may be asked to comment on. The deputy secretary checks out his proposed handling of a controversial matter coming up in an interdepartmental meeting. The Secretary brings together a few of his Seventh Floor confidants to hear their differing points of view prior to deciding what will become the Department's, and ultimately probably the Government's, position. He may be on the phone a good deal, talking to Department officers, to the Secretary of Defense, to an NSC staff member and, using his direct line, to the President himself—deciding what step to take next, who is to do what, the timing of actions on all kinds of subjects from matters of substance to those of protocol. Then there are the callers, a stream of visitors that may include U.S. congressmen, foreign ambassadors, and representatives of American organizations, associations, and institutions. The Secretary may be called to the White House or he may call the President for an appointment to discuss an urgent foreign policy development requiring Presidential decision. Other members of the NSC may or may not be present. Because he has to maintain close working relations with Congress, he is often called to testify before congressional committees. Secretaries of State have learned to give high priority to their appearances on the Hill.

Somehow the Secretary must find time before he leaves the office to read and sign the letters that await his signature. He does not personally have to sign outgoing telegrams except those that are sent in the first person, but many memoranda to the President are likely to be drafted by the Secretary. In the case of Dr. Kissinger, the same has been true of messages covering some of his *tète a tète* talks abroad.

A Secretary's official day is likely to include attending or hosting an official lunch and/or dinner in connection with hospitality for a visiting foreign dignitary. Or he may have a quiet lunch at a gourmet restaurant with an influential senator. These occasions provide opportunities not only for exchanges of ideas and information, but for establishing personal relationships that can be of inestimable value in the future.

After dinner on his way home in his official car the Secretary is likely to be joined by an officer from the Department's Operations Center (See Chapter III) with last-minute information on the current crisis.

The Geographic Bureaus

The heart of the Department's executive direction and policy formulation rests in the five geographic bureaus: for Europe; East Asia and the Pacific; the Middle East and South Asia; Africa; and Latin America. The assistant secretaries in charge of each run the line commands to U.S. embassies abroad—the main channel for receiving reports and communicating instructions, which are sent in the name of the Secretary but are often initiated and dispatched by the assistant secretary on his own responsibility. It is for the assistant secretary to decide when to obtain the approval of someone higher up in the Department hierarchy and when to clear the message with other State Department bureaus or other government departments whose interests may be affected or whose personnel may be asked to participate in the action. In the latter instances, the action office has probably called a meeting to discuss the issues with all interested agencies. After agreeing on the course of action to be taken, clearing telegraphed instructions is fairly routine. Sometimes clearances are obtained "in substance," which usually means by a telephone call giving the gist, but not the complete text, of the message.

If the problem involves security (as in the outbreak of hostilities), or if it seriously affects trade or American investments abroad (as when American firms are expropriated), or otherwise seems especially important, the assistant secretary checks in with an under secretary, the deputy secretary, or possibly the Secretary of State himself for guidance on the action to be taken. In some cases he might find that his superiors wish to handle the problem themselves.

More often than not, before the assistant secretary is brought into the picture, action on the subject will be started by the country director or desk officer responsible for handling relations with the country involved. The desk officer is likely to be in frequent, often telephone, contact with the U.S. Embassy's deputy chief of mission or the chief of section in the country involved. The desk officer works closely with his office director, who similarly handles problems involving several countries and must touch base with interested people in other bureaus and departments in developing what will become an instruction to the U.S. Ambassador affected. It is surprising how many organizations and individuals have a legitimate interest in any given international problem. By the time the desk officer drafts the message of instruction to show the assistant secretary, he wants to have the approval of, let us say, two other State Department bureaus and the departments of

Commerce, Treasury, and Defense. Often the list is much longer. An able desk officer knows more about the country he is dealing with than anyone else. And he knows how to cut through or skirt the red tape of bureaucratic Washington and come up with an agreed position in time to send out instructions that are prompt enough to be useful. He takes part in policy formulation by being in on it from the beginning, in day-to-day action matters. He also produces the initial drafts of papers for the assistant secretary, including top-level NSC studies.

The staff members of the geographic bureaus tend to sympathize with the policies of the countries they work with—up to a point, that is. Hence rivalries and policy differences can occur between rival desk officers handling relations with, for example, Israel and Egypt, India and Pakistan, or Turkey, Greece, and Cyprus.

Because many problems cut across single-country lines and involve entire regions and often regional organizations, the geographic bureaus include functional specialists, such as an economist, legal adviser, public affairs officer, and military affairs officer, on their staffs. These advisers often function as part of one of the regional offices that each geographic bureau generally has for economic and/or political and security affairs. The European Bureau, with two regional offices, one to look after NATO matters and the other to oversee European economic affairs, is a good example. The Bureau of Inter-American Affairs has a regional office for regional economic policy in addition to its mission to the OAS.*

The Functional Bureaus

The functional bureaus in the Department deal with matters that concern several or all geographic areas. Several of these bureaus are, therefore, organized on geographic lines, others are not.

---

* For a good account of the assistant secretary–country desk chain of command, see W. Wendell Blancké, *The Foreign Service of the United States* (Praeger Library of U.S. Government Departments and Agencies, No. 18), Chapter III.

The *Bureau of Public Affairs* (P) and the *Bureau of Educational and Cultural Affairs* (CU) both work closely with the U.S. Information Agency (USIA), which is concerned with the nation's image abroad. The P Bureau is also engaged in explaining policy to the American public through publications, conferences, seminars, and lectures. Neither of these bureaus is concerned with foreign policy formulation as such, although the assistant secretary of State for CU has an influential role in developing policies that guide the programs he operates, such as educational and cultural exchanges, and the assistant secretary for P and the Secretary's special assistant for press relations advise the Secretary on probable domestic and foreign reaction to proposed policies and actions. (The working of both these bureaus is described in greater detail in Chapters V and VIII.)

The new and specialized field of multilateral diplomacy occupies the attention of the *Bureau of International Organization Affairs* (IO). It coordinates official U.S. policies and positions to be taken in numerous international organizations, meetings, and conferences, and guides representatives at the U.S. Mission to the U.N. in New York. The IO Bureau works closely with every other bureau in the Department and keeps in touch with other governments, foreign embassies, and outside organizations. It is a little Department of State. (Chapter IX deals for the most part with the area of IO's responsibilities.)

What role intelligence reports play in the shaping of foreign policy is a much debated subject, but the selection of material and the slant of the discussion of alternative courses of action undoubtedly have an influence on the decision makers. The Department's *Bureau of Intelligence and Research* (INR) prepares reports and analyses of world situations for State. Its twice-daily summaries are on the Secretary's desk early in the morning and again after lunch. The director of INR is a member of the CIA-chaired U.S. Intelligence Board, which issues the prestigious National Intelligence Estimates. As in other areas, the extent of the director's influence on his superiors in the Department and in the NSC depends on the individual and the confidence he enjoys.

Foreign economic policy-making comes under the jurisdiction

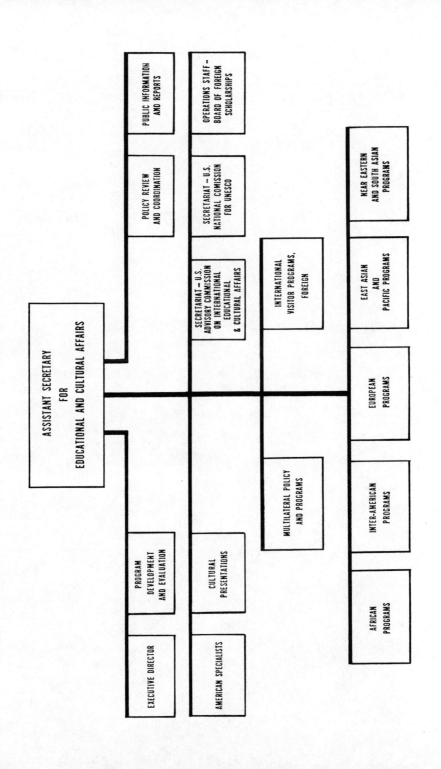

of the fourth-ranking officer of the Department, the under secretary of State for Economic Affairs. The *Bureau of Economic and Business Affairs* (EB), under an assistant secretary, is his principal organ for handling a wide range of international economic problems. These include such matters as balance of payments, trade agreements, transportation and communications questions, international investment policy, and expropriation. The EB Bureau defends U.S. economic interests not only against foreign competition but also against narrow, protectionist interests in the United States when these conflict with the broad national view. To be effective in achieving the right mix between domestic and foreign interests, the EB Bureau is involved in the activities of practically all the other bureaus of the Department and of many interdepartmental committees. It participates in a high percentage of the daily Department decisions because economic considerations play such a large role in the conduct of foreign relations. The bureau produces policy studies for the NSC Senior Review Group on such subjects as trade policy with China, and it also represents the Department in numerous bilateral negotiations with foreign governments on subjects as varied as sugar quotas, textile imports, shipping problems, and civil aviation. It is equally involved in multilateral negotiations, as in the General Agreement on Tariffs and Trade.

Because the Treasury, Agriculture, Commerce, and Interior departments have the basic economic responsibilities in finance, agriculture, business promotion, and oil, respectively, the EB Bureau must be in constant contact with them in order to try to see that the full scope of foreign policy considerations is taken into account. (See Chapter VI.) Yet in recent years some of the most important policies have been made without consulting the State Department. For example, a very strong Secretary of the Treasury, with White House backing, masterminded the dramatic new economic program of August 15, 1971. Although domestic infiltration was the prime target, the means of control involved changes in international financial, monetary, and trade policies and affected U.S. relations with other countries. Nevertheless, the State Department was ignored. State's role in trade policy and tariff negotiations also became less influential than it once was, having given place to Commerce Department and White House influence. The State Department succeeded in regaining some of its authority in the international economic area after changes were made in the top Treasury leadership in 1974 and after a strong assistant secretary of State for Economic and Business Affairs backed by Secretary Kissinger took over the Department's economic leadership.

Politico-Military Affairs

With today's heavy emphasis on national security, the State Department must obviously keep in close contact with the Pentagon. Foreign policy is broader than security policy, embracing many goals that have little or no security aspect. National Security policy, on the other hand, cannot be soundly conceived without consideration of its foreign policy, a point that has not always been well understood. During World War II President Roosevelt paid little attention to his Secretary of State or to the Department of State. Top U.S. military people were so involved in fighting the war that they, too, gave little thought to the political consequences of military strategy. But much water has passed under the bridge since those days. The need for the closest collaboration at many levels between the military and civilian policy planners is now better recognized.

Within the Department politico-military problems are dealt with by the Bureau of Politico-Military Affairs (PM), whose experts often play a key role in formulating policies having to do with such problems as Soviet penetration in the Middle East and South Asia, reduction of forces in Europe, military bases abroad, military assistance programs, limitation of defensive and offensive nuclear weapons, the return of Okinawa to Japan, and review of the defense budget. Some of these are long-term, continuing questions, and the policies that emerge go through the thorough, but slow-moving, machinery of the NSC system, beginning with discussions and drafting in the IG chaired by PM's director.

The PM Bureau is deeply concerned with policies and strategies relating to disarmament and works very closely with the Arms Control and Disarmament Agency (ACDA) (see page 113). The number two man at the Strategic Arms Limitations Talks (SALT), as well as two other members of the U.S. delegation have been from PM. In Washington, the bureau tries to keep tabs on everything the military is doing in the strategic arms area to make sure it is consistent with SALT. In fact, the State Department through PM tries to see that the military strategy, defense programs, and international security policy are generally consistent with U.S. foreign policy. This entails reviewing the defense budget (through an NSC committee) and commenting on basic policy papers, such as the Pentagon's strategic balance-and-disposition-of-forces studies and the annual report of the Secretary of Defense to Congress.

With large numbers of American forces stationed abroad, international incidents involving them are a constant danger. Foreign Service officers with experience in PM are therefore assigned to the geographic bureaus and to many U.S. embassies abroad; they work closely with military personnel to assist, for example, in negotiating with the host country a status of forces agreement, which would clarify the jurisdiction of local courts over American soldiers accused of crimes. Or they might be involved in getting permission of a foreign country for military training maneuvers on its territory, for naval ship movements off its shores, for visits of naval ships, or for overflight rights.

The PM Bureau is also charged with planning the U.S. military assistance program, administered by the International Security Affairs (ISA) section of the Defense Department, to ensure its integration into national foreign policy objectives. Since May 1972, a high-powered under secretary has been on the job to strengthen the Department's guidance of foreign security assistance programs. Both PM and the under secretary work closely with ISA in developing policy on the operations of the military program, which in fiscal year 1972 provided grant military assistance of over half a billion dollars to forty-seven countries, gave credits of the same amount to nineteen countries, and arranged for cash sales of over $3 billion. The perennial problem of determining which countries get how much stirs up differences between PM, which plays an adversary role, and the client-oriented geographic bureaus. Differences also exist between State and the Pentagon, and, when it comes to the appropriation of funds, between the executive and Congress. However, PM and ISA are often in agreement, each having difficulty with its own geographic elements.

Other PM Bureau activities deal with atomic energy and outer space operations that involve relations with other countries (nuclear-powered ships going into foreign ports, for example) and with control of munitions exports through a licensing system.

The director of PM chairs NSC's Interdepartmental Politico-Military Group, which has produced important studies, including one on United States–France military relations and a report on chemical-biological warfare that became the basis of later Presidential decisions.

AFFILIATED AGENCIES

Under the responsibility of the Secretary of State but administered as autonomous agencies are the organizations that deal with economic assistance and arms control and disarmament.

Agency for International Development

The Agency for International Development (AID), authorized by Executive Order 10973 of November 3, 1973, was basically a slightly reorganized version of a succession of earlier structures to carry on foreign assistance programs—the Marshall Plan's Point Four, the Mutual Security Agency (MSA), and the Foreign Operations Administration (FOA). AID is organized on functional lines, much like the Department of State itself, and working relations between the respective State and AID bureaus are reasonably close. In the case of Latin America, where the Alliance for Progress was given high priority by the Kennedy Administration, the State and AID Latin American bureaus were completely integrated. In general, the mechanism for formal coordination is through the established interagency system, including NSC committees.

AGENCY FOR INTERNATIONAL DEVELOPMENT

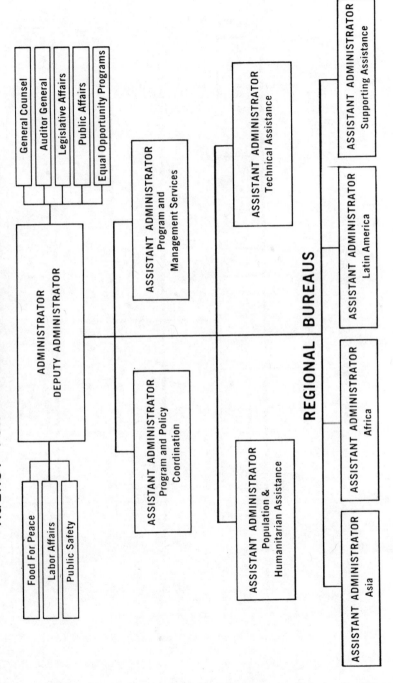

ADMINISTRATOR
DEPUTY ADMINISTRATOR

- General Counsel
- Auditor General
- Legislative Affairs
- Public Affairs
- Equal Opportunity Programs

- Food For Peace
- Labor Affairs
- Public Safety

ASSISTANT ADMINISTRATOR
Program and Policy Coordination

ASSISTANT ADMINISTRATOR
Program and Management Services

ASSISTANT ADMINISTRATOR
Population & Humanitarian Assistance

ASSISTANT ADMINISTRATOR
Technical Assistance

REGIONAL BUREAUS

ASSISTANT ADMINISTRATOR
Asia

ASSISTANT ADMINISTRATOR
Africa

ASSISTANT ADMINISTRATOR
Latin America

ASSISTANT ADMINISTRATOR
Supporting Assistance

UNITED STATES ARMS CONTROL AND DISARMAMENT AGENCY

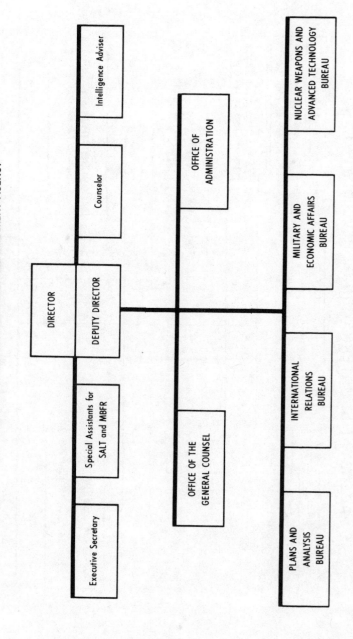

Determining who gets economic assistance, how much, and what kind is a complicated procedure in which AID, State, and the U.S. embassies abroad are the main participants. Departmental officers have tended to see economic assistance as a useful tool of diplomacy, using justifications that may be more political than economic. AID officers, understandably, have tended to give greater weight to the economic benefits of the assistance. Although it has always been recognized that there are benefits that cannot be quantified in dollars and cents, it has also been appreciated that rather tangible results are needed to sway Congress's Appropriations committees.

The AID assistance programs were revamped to conform to an in-depth study of military and economic assistance submitted by the Peterson Task Force in 1970. In general, the revised scheme, as put into effect, emphasizes more responsibility for the developing countries in planning programs; technical assistance concentrated in priority areas like agriculture, environment, population, and health; greater use of private sources of assistance; reduction of personnel; and closer coordination with the assistance programs of other countries and of multilateral institutions.

A Presidential proposal for drastic reorganization of AID, made to Congress early in 1971, had not been acted on as of 1974. This lack of action is undoubtedly related to congressional dissatisfaction with assistance programs as reflected in the increasing difficulty of obtaining funds from Congress for these programs.

Arms Control and Disarmament Agency

The United States Arms Control and Disarmament Agency (ACDA) was established by Congress in the Arms Control and Disarmament Act of 1961. The Act provided that the Director of ACDA would be "principal adviser to the Secretary of State and the President on arms control and disarmament matters" and, while reporting directly to the Secretary, he would have "primary responsibility within the Government" for such matters. The Director of ACDA ranks with the deputy secretary of State; the deputy director of ACDA ranks with the deputy under secretaries. ACDA is the main source of expertise on arms control and disarmament, but it also plays an important direct role in negotiations. The Department, specifically the Secretary, has the last word on policy. Nevertheless, ACDA, which does not like to be considered just another organizational element within State, has fought—quite successfully—to maintain an independent identity and position.

ACDA played a primary role in SALT negotiations, which began in November, 1969, and which eventually produced two initial agreements in May, 1972—a treaty limiting antiballistic missile systems and an interim agreement placing restrictions on strategic offensive arms. The agency also did much to bring about the Limited Test Ban Treaty (1963), the Nuclear Nonproliferation Treaty (1970), the Seabed Arms Control Treaty (1971), and the Biological Weapons Convention (1972).

ACDA has been headed by several strong directors, such as Ambassador Gerald Smith who also headed the SALT Delegation. Since his resignation in January, 1973, almost the entire top leadership of ACDA has been changed, and the Agency was without a head for several months. A chief of the U.S. delegation to SALT II was appointed early in 1973 but he did not have the dual role of also heading ACDA. For a time it seemed that the Agency was in the process of being downgraded. However, the new team proved to be an able one and the separation of the duties of the head of the SALT delegation from those of the Director of ACDA turned out to be a much more satisfactory arrangement than the previous one. (In fact, it has occurred to some observers that it is an example that the Secretary of State himself might well follow.) In any case, ACDA director Fred Iklé can direct his bureau in Washington and oversee many important arms control and disarmament functions, including SALT. He himself is an active participant in many of these activities. For example, he is a member of the NSC Verification Panel and its working group, where policies are coordinated. He chairs the interagency backstopping committees that guide the SALT II negotiations in Geneva and the negotiations on Mutual and Balanced Force Reductions (MBFR) in Vienna. He is the U.S. cochairman of the United Nations's prestigious Conference of the Committee on Disarmament (CCD) in

Geneva and he has been especially busy preparing for and participating in the review conference on nuclear proliferation, one of the most difficult and important conferences in this field.

FIELD POST CONTRIBUTIONS TO FOREIGN POLICY

The reports and policy recommendations from U.S. posts abroad are important elements in the Department's development of foreign policy. The United States has almost 300 embassies, legations, consular posts, and special missions in some 115 foreign countries. Every day 10,000 communications—more than 2,000 of them telegrams requiring urgent attention—are exchanged between them and the Department of State in Washington.

An American Ambassador is the President's personal representative in a foreign country, and he is responsible for all U.S. Government activities in that country. This means keeping an eye on programs that are operated by various official American agencies and assuring himself that they conform with U.S. policy objectives. When the host country requests economic and military aid programs, cultural exchanges, or training for its public administrators and police, for example, the ambassador must make recommendations and establish priorities. He has to consider the availability of U.S. resources as well as national policy objectives and the relation of U.S. programs to those of other countries and of multilateral institutions like the United Nations that may already be extant in that country. Interagency rivalries of both the United States and the host country complicate the ambassador's problem in determining which activities to recommend. Yet he must never lose sight of the totality of American interests in the country. His final judgment can solve a problem on the spot or strongly influence Washington decisions, if the problem is referred there.

The ambassador is assisted by his staff and on interagency matters may consult his country team, made up of heads of the departments in his mission—political, economic, administrative, aid, military, information, and so on. This advisory group can play a useful role. The ambassador may submit to it the policy plans that the directors of information, cultural, and assistance programs develop each year. On the basis of the country team's comments, he makes his recommendations or simply approves. The forum is also useful in providing the ambassador's top staff an opportunity to share ideas and information with the ambassador; the habit of consultation can produce a team spirit that is invaluable; it is a made-to-order executive organ for the assignment of tasks and systematic follow-up; and, in times of emergency, can readily be transformed into an operations center.

The ambassador's policy recommendations embrace a much wider field than interagency programs, of course. His State Department–Foreign Service staff keep in touch with all possible elements in the country that can provide information about what is going on; they identify trends, analyze developments, and then report in flash telegrams or longer "think pieces" their appraisal of the situation, with recommendations as to the appropriate American action or attitude. Policy can change on the basis of such field reporting and of prompt action taken in the field in the absence of specific instructions.

V

Educational and Cultural Exchange: A Closer Look

Rana Khrishnamoorty of India, aged twenty-two, tall, slender and erect in his new Western-style suit, arrived in Ithaca, New York, after a long two-day flight from his home in Madras. He was met by the Foreign Student Adviser of Cornell University, where Khrishnamoorty would spend the next nine months studying engineering at the graduate school. Several hundred miles west, in the teeming city of Chicago, ten medical students from Germany had already enrolled in Rush Medical School. Helga Ernsthof and Kurt Weigert, both from Munich, had traveled to Chicago together and were already graduate physicians from the University of Munich, but their American study would give them valuable knowledge in their field of specialization—heart surgery. Simultaneously, in Munich, Professor Charles Hanes of Colby College, Waterville, Maine, was unpacking his family in a small apartment not far from the Technical Institute, where he was scheduled to study and lecture for the next academic year. In Warsaw, Poland, to the north, the New Orleans Dixiecats had not yet arrived but were scheduled to perform within the week at the annual jazz festival. A group of Russian engineers in Moscow were already beginning an intensive refresher course in English, preparatory to their departure the following spring for a tour of automobile factories in Detroit and

River Rouge. And Harry Carter, writer and lecturer, passport in hand and typewriter in his luggage, would shortly be boarding a Pan American plane for Africa, where he expected to travel for at least three months, lecturing in various cities and conferring with African writers.

These examples are typical of what goes on under the State Department's educational and cultural exchange program, one of the activities chosen for a closer look at Departmental functioning. The objective behind this government-sponsored interchange is to help improve international understanding among individuals in a way that will help to forge strong ties among nations.

Through the program, which is run by the Department's Bureau of Educational and Cultural Affairs (CU), thousands of foreigners —friendly, neutral, and unfriendly—are given a personal experience in the United States each year. They have an opportunity to learn firsthand something about the character of Americans, and the way of life, ideals, problems, and varied institutions in the United States.

Under the same program Americans travel abroad, to study, conduct research, or lecture. They bring back not only greater competence in their own fields but also greater knowledge of foreign cultures and understanding of other peoples. In the past quarter-century over forty thousand Americans have been sent abroad through the bureau and over one hundred thousand people have come to the United States. Many have been top leaders and professionals in varied fields, but the great majority have been part of the academic program—students and teachers. In addition to academic exchanges and exchanges of top-level leaders and professionals, the CU Bureau has an active program that sends American performing artists and athletes on foreign tours.

It wasn't until the 1930's that the U.S. Government launched its first cultural exchange and technical assistance programs. The early activities were in Latin America and came mainly as a response to similar programs initiated by the European totalitarian powers in that area. What was begun on a small scale then was the forerunner of the sizable exchange programs that the State Department has been operating since 1946 under the authority of the Fulbright Act of that year and subsequent legislation.

The Fulbright Act, named for sponsor Senator J. William Fulbright, and hailed as a far-sighted, statesmanlike, and generous gesture, by authorizing the expenditure for educational exchange purposes of foreign currencies that had accumulated during World War II in many foreign countries to the credit of the U.S. Government, also solved part of the tough dollar-exchange problem resulting from the inability of the debtor nations to convert their own currencies to dollars. Other sponsors of the educational exchange program were the late Senators H. Alexander Smith and Karl Mundt.

Today, exchanges are conducted with 126 countries as compared with 22 countries under the 1946 Fulbright Act that began it all. The program has expanded as new, developing countries with vast educational and training needs have come into being. Exchanges with the Soviet Union began in 1958. None of the activities would be possible without substantial assistance from the many private educational and cultural institutions, foundations, and business and professional groups that collaborate with the program and from the foreign governments and private institutions abroad that also assist. In many instances the U.S. Government contribution is merely seed money or money for transportation. Private citizens, generally through organized committees, play important parts in selecting participants, giving advice, and providing orientation and hospitality.

Since the government-sponsored exchange programs assist only a fraction of the total number of foreign students and visitors who come to the United States, the programs can be justified only if they are highly selective. Accordingly, great effort is made to seek out those individuals who will be most likely to contribute to the objectives of the program.

It is impossible to quantify the results of the cultural and exchange programs since their beginning, but the sustained reputation of the program, the increased willingness of foreign governments and of institutions at home and abroad to share in the costs, as well as the large number of outstanding applicants every year testify to the value that many people in many countries place on these exchanges.

One of the strengths of the program is that it has tried to help foreign visitors see what they want to see, talk with people and groups they wish to talk with, study and observe what they have come here to do—without shielding them from the realities of American life. The theory behind the program has always been understanding rather than approval. A few hard-bitten visitors return home with new material to bolster previously held anti-Americanism, but these are the exception. There is no question that the program makes a positive contribution toward still distant goals.

Cultural relations have demonstrated their usefulness as a tool of diplomacy in many ways. In diplomatic crises, when other relations have become impossible, even when diplomatic relations have been severed, cultural ties can still be maintained—as in Egypt and Algeria after 1967. It may be that Sudan's renewal of diplomatic relations with the United States in July, 1972, was influenced in some degree by the continuation of cultural relations during the five-year break. The Department has contracted with a private agency—the American Friends of the Middle East—to handle many of the services generally performed by its own embassies in carrying out educational exchanges in Arab countries.

One American Ambassador to a Middle Eastern country reported a rather dramatic manifestation of the effectiveness of educational exchange in 1964, when the United States was being attacked almost daily in the local press as an imperialist and Zionist-inspired nation. The American Embassy had little opportunity to counter such attacks. The most that could be hoped for was to maintain, if possible, a reservoir of the good will that many Arabs as individuals felt for Americans. It was against this background that an American Fulbright professor, to the astonishment of the Ambassador, was awarded one of the Arab nation's highest decorations for his services at the university at a luncheon in his honor attended by the Prime Minister, the minister of education, the minister of health, and other government officials, as well as the rector and vice-rector of the university.

The cultural exchanges that have been taking place with the Soviet Union since 1958 have survived all the periods of political stress that have occurred between the two countries in the intervening years. However, by far the most dramatic illustration of cultural activities surmounting political obstacles was the private visit of the American Ping-Pong team to China in 1971, which helped to pave the way for President Nixon's subsequent visit.

There are of course problems, in addition to the occasional bolstering of anti-American feelings already noted. One perennial problem has to do with ensuring that foreign students return home after they complete their American studies. However desirable they might be as permanent residents, the fact is that students who have been subsidized by this program are expected to return to their own countries. Completing their studies in the United States is only the first part of their obligation; the second part is for them to return home and share the benefits of their experience with their fellow citizens. Accordingly, CU is actively concerned to see that this obligation is fulfilled; all foreign students are required to leave the United States when their studies are completed and their student (J) visas expire.

There is no record of the number of foreign students who later return as immigrants, although there are some individuals who do this. Those who decide that they want to make their home in the United States cannot apply for immigration visas until two years have elapsed after their departure. An exception to this procedure is provided for those students who can demonstrate that their lives would be endangered by a return to their home countries or that American spouses would not be accepted. Under either circumstance, students may obtain a waiver and change their status to that of immigrant without waiting two years or leaving the United States. The number of waivers granted is, however, less than 2 per cent of the total number of foreign exchange visitors who come to the United States under CU's program each year.

Because foreign countries are anxious to have their nationals return home after studying in the United States, CU finds most foreign embassies in Washington cooperative in establishing contact with their students at American institutions. Many send out newsletters to inform students of job opportunities at home and to give other information designed to keep them in touch and to encourage them to return after they finish their American studies.

LEADERS AND SPECIALISTS

In the early days of cultural exchange the greatest emphasis was on the so-called Leader Grant Program, which invited foreign political and labor leaders, journalists, community leaders, and other influential individuals for American tours. This was the time, in the 1950's when the emerging postwar leadership in Germany and Japan was especially eager to learn all it could about the United States. Americans in turn were eager to oblige. Today it is an extraordinary experience to travel in these countries and to meet everywhere, in every profession, friendly Germans and Japanese who look back with nostalgia on their experiences in the United States.*

The Leader Grant Program is still very active. In 1972, over two thousand foreigners visited the United States on leader grants and over the past two and a half decades more than forty-two thousand have come to the United States. As of July, 1971, fourteen chiefs of state and prime ministers then in office had visited the United States at some time under leader grants. There were also 247 Cabinet ministers from various countries, including 128 from Africa, and 12 of the 15 members of the West German Cabinet. Numerous chief justices, university presidents, labor leaders, editors and publishers, and leaders in many professional fields are also on the long list of leader-grant recipients.

* In Berlin in the early 1960's, when Ambassador Lightner was the officer in charge of the American mission, the Columbus Society—a group of former exchange visitors who had personally discovered America—held an annual get-together. It was a big social gathering to which several Americans living in Berlin were always invited. The high point of the evening was a series of satirical skits depicting an exchange visitor's arrival in the United States, language difficulties, contacts with customs officials, bell-hops, taxi drivers, and hosts, and an amusing series of adjustment problems. The whole thing was clever, penetrating, and friendly, and the Americans came away with renewed faith in the value of the cultural exchange program.

A conscious effort is made to identify future decision-makers early, before they have arrived in high positions, as well as to select leaders from fields other than politics. Communicators, using the word in the broadest sense, are especially sought out, people who influence the education and thinking of established leaders. Selection of these visitors is made by our embassies abroad. Recently, efforts have been made to choose people concerned with mutual problems—an Asian agriculture minister studying the U.S. agricultural system, Japanese governors meeting American politicians at state and federal levels, a Sudanese studying U.S. oceanographic institutes preparatory to founding such an institute in his own country. Meeting their American counterparts and discussing common problems helps many visitors form ties that continue long afterward. On arrival, leader grantees are given every assistance to help them accomplish what they have in mind and to visit any part of the United States they wish. In line with the objective of furthering their understanding, these visitors are encouraged to spend most of their time outside Washington and with private Americans. The absence of "hard-sell" propaganda for the United States or its policies and the home hospitality provided to these visitors seem to be especially appreciated.

The Leader Program also sends abroad each year approximately 100 American "specialists," all of whom are authorities in their fields. They visit one or more countries for short periods. American novelists, playwrights, architects, economists, and Nobel Prize winners in nuclear physics have all given luster to this program.

Finally, special educational visits to the United States are worked out for selected groups of young people who are student leaders or have already launched their professional careers. For example, in 1970, the University of California at Los Angeles, with State Department funding, arranged for just such a group of Brazilian students to tour the United States. Before they began their tour, they had a four-week series of lecture-seminars on the United States, and during this time they lived with UCLA students in a university dormitory, attending lectures and concerts, visiting law courts and law libraries and a jet propulsion laboratory, and talking with labor officials and with student leaders at the university. In Washington, they attended Senate hearings, met with congressmen, a Supreme Court justice, members of the Peace Corps, and other government officials and at the same time did the usual tourist rounds. Their U.S. tour also featured a visit to Puerto Rico so that they could observe what that Latin-oriented area had done toward self-development.

Programs for young professionals have been going on for fifteen years. Most of the participants now hold important jobs in their home countries. Some have helped to introduce new programs in the field of social work, like "Head Start" in Germany and a children's village in India.

THE ACADEMIC PROGRAM

Although the Leader Program may have been given more emphasis at the start, the heart of the exchange program has always been the exchange of scholars, lecturers, teachers, and graduate students. This group accounts for over 60 per cent of all exchange visits directly sponsored by the State Department. Since 1949, over 100,000 people have been exchanged in the academic program.

In the years since the program began, lecturers and research scholars have increasingly sought opportunities for study abroad, and over 1,000 are exchanged each year. In 1971, five times as many American scholars applied as there were grants available. The selection is handled for the Department by private scholarly bodies. American educators have helped build up departments of American studies in several foreign universities, while scholars from other countries have helped to create area studies programs in U.S. universities. Sometimes collaboration between colleagues on a common project can be fostered through exchange programs. As one example, American professors from Indiana University worked to help set up a program in business administration at the University of Ljubljana in Yugoslavia in 1971, and at the same time Yugoslav graduate students and young faculty members were studying at Indiana University, preparing to replace their American colleagues at Ljubljana.

Usually graduate students represent about one half of all the academic exchangees. Many of these graduate students subsequently rise rapidly to positions of leadership in their home universities and in the wider areas of politics, government administration, and diplomacy.

Teachers are the third component of the academic exchange program. Sometimes they take part in a direct, two-way exchange in which an American teacher merely changes places with one from another country. Group visits and study tours are also arranged, during which teachers may study schools and school systems or take part in specialized seminars, such as one in languages or in social studies.

Academic exchanges are supervised for the Department by a Board of Foreign Scholarships, made up of prominent U.S. educators and public representatives appointed by the President. The board selects all grantees through recommendations of screening committees of private individuals and organizations. This function is carried out in other countries through individual binational commissions. In August, 1971, the Board of Foreign Scholarships submitted a report, "Educational Exchange in the Seventies," which recommended updating several features of the academic exchange program. It reiterated the desirability of continuing to focus on quality at the graduate level, but it suggested that increasing numbers of exchangees from the nonacademic professions be included along with the academicians; it also recommended that exchange activities should concentrate on a few subjects at a time and that participants from various fields and at various professional levels be brought together to work in collaboration with one another. Such teams should be made up on a multinational or regional basis where appropriate, the Board felt. Logistics problems for such multinational programs are enormous, but a planning committee of the Fulbright Commission is already tackling them.

Assistance to Foreign Students Outside the Academic Program

There are about 145,000 foreign students in the United States at the present time, and more than 90 per cent of them come to study without U.S. government financial assistance. Of these, a significant number return home to become leaders in their own universities or governments or in professional life. The State Department and U.S. private agencies have become increasingly interested in trying to assist these potential leaders to get off to a good start in the United States. Special services for such foreign students concentrate on the major problems experienced both by students themselves and by the American institutions that receive them: the need for counseling students overseas on their choice of college here; the difficulty American institutions have in judging credentials of foreign students; adequate reception and orientation facilities for incoming foreign students; ways to help students learn about American society and the American people beyond the campus. Counseling is provided by many private agencies as well as by the State Department in offices located in key locations abroad.

Meeting new arrivals and making them feel at home is an important service handled by a voluntary organization supported by the State Department. First impressions can be very important. For strangers in a strange land, a smiling American inquiring, "Are you Mr. Varga (or Mikoshi or Aduba)?" is a welcome sight. The welcomer, usually wearing an armband identifying him or her as a foreign student adviser, is a member of the International Student Service, which guides the newcomer through the complexities of immigration and customs, checks on tickets and hotel reservations, helps change money, collects baggage, finds a taxi.

Because language is a problem for many foreign students, even though language requirements for study grants have been stiffened in recent years, intensive English-language courses are given to some foreign students who need such training before they start their graduate studies. Other subjects included in the orientation classes help introduce the American environment. Unfortunately, these courses, which the State Department encourages, reach a relatively small number of students, about 600 to 700 a year, but the value of training like this is recognized, and increasing numbers of colleges and universities now offer their own intensive English-language and other orientation courses. They also provide advisers to assist foreign students throughout the year. The advisers are organized nationally and run a field service program supported by the State Department.

Part of the foreign student's experience is, of course, with American communities and individual American families. Inviting a student to dinner used to be the common method of establishing contact. Today the idea is to interest him or her in the community with a view to sharing in mutual problems. Foreign students at the University of Chicago are participating in a program to get high school dropouts to go back to school. Others work in ghetto welfare and recreation programs or visit old people in nursing homes or fellow students in hospitals. Local schools in many places also invite foreign students to teach the history and culture of their own countries.

To open other horizons, the State Department has helped several private groups organize regional seminars during vacation periods at which foreign students meet outstanding Americans and discuss a wide range of topics centering on the current American scene, and it encourages and assists foreign students to travel within the United States during their school vacations.

Although the CU program for privately funded foreign students is mainly at the graduate level or higher, exceptionally gifted foreign high school students also have a chance to visit the United States under several privately sponsored programs. The teenagers live with American host families for a year, go to local high schools, and join in community, school, and family activities. The Department of State provides some assistance, but the host families make the main contribution. In 1971, some 4,500 young people came here under these largely private programs.

CULTURAL PRESENTATIONS (*Performing Artists*)

The program that sponsors tours abroad of American performing artists and athletes had its origin in 1953, when a group of interested Americans sold Assistant Secretary of State William Benton and President Dwight D. Eisenhower on the idea that it was time to do something to dispel the general ignorance abroad of American cultural achievements, especially in the performing arts.

Government assistance would be needed to make foreign tours possible, especially tours outside of Europe. Such a program would demonstrate to wide varieties of audiences the quality, diversity, and vitality of the American performing artists and athletes and bring about rapport with foreign leaders, performers, and youth. In short, it was in line with the objectives of the educational and cultural exchange program.

In 1954, the program was started as part of the President's Special International Program. Later it became the Cultural Presentations Program of the State Department, which has always administered it.

After twenty years, this program still gives many foreign audiences their first glimpse of American performing artists; it generates much good will, not only through the performances but also offstage, through the contacts that are made between American and foreign professionals in the same arts or sports.*

Workshops and lecture presentations are now frequently arranged as part of the responsibilities of the performing artists. For example, Gary Burton, a top performer and original artist (on the unusual vibraharp) performed professionally in Manila in 1972, but it was in his workshops and lectures that he made the deepest impression on music students, teachers, and serious musicians.

The program tries to reach countries not ordinarily covered by commercial tours or where official relations are strained, where there has been a strong American military presence, or where harsh opinions about Americans and American life prevail. In particular,

---

* Both authors of this book have had heartening experiences as hosts to American performers abroad. We can testify to the extraordinary influence one young American basketball or track coach and his family can have on an entire community over a six- or eight-month period and to the stunning effect of a first-rate American theatrical or musical performance on a foreign audience. During the European tour of *Porgy and Bess* in 1954, the troupe took the city of Munich by storm, and individual members of the cast as well as the performance itself made a tremendous impression on sophisticated Munich music lovers, who were swept off their feet by Leontyne Price, then almost unknown, and astonished at the musicianship and impressive academic backgrounds of most of the cast, whom they met socially on several occasions.

tours to the Soviet Union and to Eastern Europe receive great emphasis. When drastic cuts in the State Department budget were made in 1970, it was decided that they should not affect the sending of performing artists to these areas. The result was that 70 to 75 per cent of all funds available for the performing arts program in 1971 and 1972 were spent for performances in the Soviet Union and Eastern Europe. Regular programs for all countries were supplemented by "picking up" commercial tours already on the road and selecting groups in the United States able to finance a good part of their own tours and/or persuading "name" artists to go out at reduced rates. Thus, the well-heeled Utah Symphony was selected for a Latin American tour in 1971 not simply because it was a fine orchestra but also because it could pay most of its own way. The Newport Jazz Artists were picked up in Western Europe and sent to the "American Jazz Week in Eastern Europe" in 1971; it is now an annual event. The late Mahalia Jackson was on a commercial tour in Japan when Cultural Presentations picked her up to come to India at a greatly reduced rate.

This pick-up technique is also being introduced into the area of sports, and college glee clubs and drama clubs that have arranged their own financing often want U.S. Government or embassy sponsorship, which Cultural Presentations is glad to arrange as long as the artistic quality of the performers meets the standards set by the panel that advises CU on such matters.

After the Duquesne University Folk Ensemble toured the Soviet Union and Eastern Europe in 1969, fully financed by the U.S. Government, the State Department turned down the group's bid for a second tour, but readily gave it a letter of endorsement. Shortly afterwards the Mellon Foundation put up $80,000 for the tour the group made in the summer of 1972.

The cultural agreement with the Soviet Union for 1972–73 called for six attractions in the two-year period. The New York Ballet had a successful tour in the fall of 1972; the San Francisco Symphony, which was picked up in Rome to reduce costs, toured the Soviet Union in June, 1973; and the Arena Stage company of Washington, D.C., presented two American plays, *Our Town* and

Inherit the Wind, to enthusiastic audiences in the fall of 1973. The three-year agreement with the Soviet Union for 1974–76 calls for the exchange of ten attractions.

The Cultural Presentations Program had difficulties obtaining funds even in the days when it was known as the President's Program. The powerful House Subcommittee for (State Department) Appropriations has been especially unsympathetic to its purposes and operations.* Greater reliance on private sources is a welcome development, but adequate government assistance is needed to maintain the quality and to cover the areas that should be covered.

EXCHANGES WITH THE USSR AND CHINA

Cultural exchanges with the Soviet Union were started in 1958, when the first government-to-government agreement was negotiated. New agreements have been negotiated every two years. The current one does not differ markedly from earlier agreements, although as a result of the 1972 Moscow summit meeting, several supplementary agreements have been signed, establishing a Science and Technology Commission to further cooperative efforts in specified fields and establishing joint projects in cancer, heart, and en-

---

* When one of the authors defended the program before Chairman John Rooney and his committee in the late 1950's, the annual appropriation averaged a little over $2 million. This went as high as $2.8 million in fiscal year 1966, but by FY 1971 it had reached an all-time low of only half a million dollars. By FY 1973 it was around $700,000. This continuing cutback has come at a time when the funds for the entire educational and cultural program have been reduced, but to nowhere near the extent of the cut in Cultural Presentations. CU faced a general policy of retrenchment and had to reassess priorities; Cultural Presentations was vulnerable. Its effectiveness was not at issue, but the President's Office of Management and Budget (OMB) and the Rooney Committee had been critical of the management of several tours; CU leadership had been more interested in academic programs; and Cultural Presentations was considered trouble-prone because of its annual difficulties with Representative Rooney. In fact, the immediate cause of the big cut in 1970 appears to have been the Rooney Committee's displeasure over the tour of a Kansas State University theater group and its presentation of a play containing some "dirty words." It made no difference to the committee that this particular tour had not been approved or financed by the Cultural Presentations staff.

vironmental research. The basic agreement provides for an annual exchange of about forty graduate students, several scholars, and twenty-five language teachers annually. The U.S. National Academy of Science handles the exchange of twenty to thirty scientists. Delegations of specialists in scientific and technological fields, agriculture, and public health are also to be exchanged. During a two-year period, six performing arts groups will be exchanged. Since this program was started, close to 1,000 Americans have studied under it, and today it is hard to find teachers of Slavic languages or Russian studies in American colleges who have not participated in it.

The United States would like to increase contacts between Russians and Americans. Both sides stand to benefit. There have been many more official delegations exchanged since the Moscow summit meeting, and the attitude of the Soviet participants has been noticeably more friendly and cooperative. The Soviet Government, however, continues to be distrustful of outside influences; it keeps tab on the contacts American exchangees have with Soviet citizens in Russia and occasionally steps in to restrict them. The Soviet system would have to change radically before its government would permit an appreciably larger exchange program.

The communiqué issued in Shanghai at the time of the first American Presidential visit to Communist China early in 1972 led to speculation that cultural exchanges with the Chinese People's Republic could be developed prior to the settlement of political problems. This has happened. First there was a series of Chinese invitations to individual Americans to visit China. Along with this there has been a certain liberalization in the granting of entry visas. However, the number of visas granted has been very small in relation to the avalanche of applications. Lack of interpreters and of adequate hotel and other accommodations would limit the possibility for tourist travel, even if the Chinese Government were ready to open its doors. Nevertheless, an ever increasing number of exchanges of athletes, entertainers, scientists, physicians, and representatives of other professions has been arranged since Dr. Kissinger's Peking visit in February, 1973, accelerated progress.

THE ROLES OF USIA AND OTHERS

The Smith-Mundt Act of 1948 placed the administration of all information and cultural programs under the State Department's assistant secretary for Public Affairs (P). In 1953, the information programs were removed from State's jurisdiction and given to the new United States Information Agency (USIA). The rationale given at the time was that Secretary of State John Foster Dulles wanted his department to stick to policy and not get involved in operations. He did agree to let the State Department continue to direct the educational exchange and cultural programs (which were not contaminated with the stigma of "propaganda"), but USIA had to provide the Cultural Affairs officers to run the programs at U.S. embassies abroad. This remains the basis for the operation today.

The division of responsibilities between State and USIA in the cultural field has always been an administrative headache. That it works as well as it does is a tribute to the people in the two agencies who make it function. One needs no special experience to picture some of the personnel problems, involving assignments, career advancement, and morale, that result from operating a program abroad that is staffed by personnel provided by and responsible to another agency. There is some interchange of personnel between the agencies, which permits USIA cultural officers to serve in CU after field assignments and Foreign Service officers occasionally to be assigned to cultural affairs abroad. It would be an improvement if there were a much more systematic interchange of this kind, but even this could never solve the problem. Many people in and outside of government, including the authors, who have had long associations with this program, are convinced that the only solution is to put all government-sponsored educational and cultural activities under one agency. This could be USIA, which would then handle both information and cultural activities, or it could be the State Department, which might also take over information activities as well. In that case, the information and cultural activities presumably would be part of a semi-autonomous unit functioning under the Secretary of State.*

* See Chapter VI for discussion of State-USIA relationships, a subject

In 1959, an internal change in the State Department separated the educational and cultural activities from the P Bureau and consolidated them in a new Bureau of Educational and Cultural Affairs (CU). (Exchanges with the Soviet Union and Eastern Europe remained under the administration of the Bureau of European Affairs.) In 1961, the Fulbright-Hays Act became the authority for an expanded exchanges program. CU's budget increased from $33.6 million in fiscal year 1960 to over $50 million in the years FY 1963–67. The program dropped drastically to the $36 million level in FY 1969 and 1970 but was up to $40 million in FY 1971 and 1972 and over $45 million in FY 1973.

The CU staff work closely with the personnel in American embassies abroad who carry out the program in the field. They plan the whole program, working out the complicated arrangements with the other government agencies and private organizations and educational institutions that are involved. Binational commissions, set up in the forty-five countries that have active exchange agreements with the United States, are responsible for the administration of the academic exchange program in each country. Their membership is made up of an equal number of distinguished foreign nationals and resident Americans. (In instances where there is no commission, the U.S. Embassy or Consulate performs this task.)

Several especially appointed boards and advisory commissions give their cooperation and counsel to the State Department. The *Board of Foreign Scholarships* supervises the academic exchange program and selects all academic grantees. The *U.S. Advisory Commission on International Educational and Cultural Affairs* recommends to the President broad policies on the conduct of educational and cultural programs. The *Government Advisory Committee on International Book and Library Programs* helps the Department in a continuing review of U.S. Government book and library activities abroad. The *Advisory Panel on International Athletics* helps in the planning and selection of exchanges involving athletes and coaches. The *National Review Board for the Center*

---

that has become highly topical as a result of studies made in 1974–75 by the Stanton Panel and the Murphy Commission.

for Cultural and Technical Interchange between East and West (East-West Center) reviews the programs and operations of the Center and advises the Secretary of State on these matters. CU staff keep in close touch with the work of these boards and commissions; actually, CU furnishes the executive secretaries or staff directors for the four principal advisory bodies that assist the program. State's International Organizations Bureau (see also Chapter IX) provides the secretariat for the *U.S. National Commission for UNESCO,* which acts as an advisory body to the U.S. Government regarding the programs and policies of the United Nations Educational, Scientific, and Cultural Organization and serves as the informational and community link between UNESCO and the American people.

The U.S. Office of Education is active in the selection of American teachers for exchange grants, and it also assists in their placement abroad and arranges for the placement of exchange teachers in American schools and for their supervision. Exchange of students is handled for the State Department by the Institute of International Education (IIE), a private organization with long experience in international exchanges. Under a contract with State, IIE handles the preliminary screening of American students applying for exchange grants and also provides the placement and supervision in U.S. institutions for most of the U.S.-sponsored foreign students. The Conference Board of Associated Research Councils, a private body representing leading U.S. professional and scholarly organizations, works through its Committee on International Exchange of Persons to recruit and screen American lecturers and research scholars and also handles the placement and program arrangements for their opposite numbers visiting the United States.

Altogether some fifty private agencies work under contract with the State Department in the exchange program. The Governmental Affairs Institute arranges itineraries for international visitors. The Asia Foundation, the American Friends of the Middle East, the African-American Institute, and Operations Crossroads Africa all help program international visitors and place and supervise students from their particular areas. The National Association for Foreign Student Affairs assists in counseling and enriching the experience of many nonsponsored, or at least non-U.S.–sponsored, foreign students in the United States. Approximately twenty-five American universities provide orientation, language training, special study programs, and professional training for selected foreign visitors as well as foreign students.

The rich and varied exchange-of-persons programs in which Americans have been involved for at least twenty-five years attest to the extraordinary cooperation and team work that has developed over the years between the government and the private sector in the exchanges field. All cultural relations activities depend heavily on the support of some 2,300 private institutions, organizations, foundations, and business and professional groups. The scholarships granted by educational institutions and foundations amount to over $9 million annually, or roughly one quarter of the State Department's entire budget for all exchanges. Every State Department exchange program relies on private cooperation, and many foreign visitors complete their stay in the United States without having any direct contact with the government. Community organizations along the way assist the visitors at each stop, arranging appointments and visits to factories, and providing transportation and hospitality. It is estimated that about 100,000 private U.S. citizens actively and generously assist in some aspect of the exchange program in the United States.

VI

Interagency Relationships

The Department of State must maintain relationships—established by law, by formal or informal agreements, by common-sense procedures worked out by individual officials, or by the requirements of a specific foreign affairs problem—with all departments and agencies directly or indirectly responsible for activities that affect or are affected by U.S. foreign policy.

The growth and proliferation of foreign affairs interests in the post–World War II era stems from both political and economic considerations. The wave of nationalism brought independence to a number of former colonies that became sovereign states, most of which established diplomatic relations with the United States and to which the United States gave some form of economic assistance. As a means of protection and security, the United States negotiated a series of mutual defense pacts, notably NATO (North Atlantic Treaty Organization). The United States participated in the formulation of a new international economic system after World War II which established new foundations for economic and fiscal cooperation among the free nations of the world: GATT (General Agreement on Tariffs and Trade), the IMF (International Monetary Fund), and the World Bank.

Through the 1950's the Department of State was able to maintain leadership in the coordination of foreign affairs matters among the several agencies which at that time had overseas interests. One reason, certainly, was the predominance of Secretary John Foster Dulles, who had the complete support and confidence of President Eisenhower. The heads of other departments and agencies knew that in a showdown involving jurisdiction in foreign affairs, the decision would go to the Secretary of State. On the other hand, potential conflicts were greatly reduced by the Secretary's decision not to become involved in overseas operating programs—such as the economic assistance and information programs.

In addition to formal mechanisms, there are, of course, many less formal arrangements for maintaining effective interagency relationships, from person-to-person contacts among working-level officials to ad hoc meetings. The magnitude of the coordination problem becomes evident when it is realized that State not only must maintain relations with more than fifteen departments and agencies but is also represented on about forty committees, commissions, and advisory groups. The following discussions of the Department's relationships with the White House and a few of the principal executive departments and agencies cannot go into detail. It can only indicate the wide variety of overseas activities that State attempts to coordinate.

THE EXECUTIVE OFFICE OF THE PRESIDENT

The degree or kind of coordination between the President and the Secretary of State depends primarily on what role the President wishes the Secretary to perform. When Presidents choose to give great powers to special assistants, the role of the Secretary is greatly reduced. With little influence there is not too much left to coordinate. As pointed out before, the President alone decides the kind of people and system he will use to aid him in the conduct of foreign policy for which he alone has ultimate responsibility in the executive branch, and which he shares only to a limited degree with Congress. A Secretary of State who does not like the role chosen for him by the President can resign, as Thomas Jefferson and William Jennings Bryan did rather than carry out Presidential policies. Some secretaries—such as Acheson, Dulles, and Kissinger in recent times—have been delegated very great powers by the President. Secretary William P. Rogers enjoyed the President's confidence and friendship but was not given responsibility in matters of high policy, which were given instead to the National Security Adviser.

The system used by a President or a strong Secretary of State to manage foreign affairs is especially important in interagency relationships, since who coordinates with whom usually indicates the real power centers among the departments and agencies. Also as discussed earlier (Chapters II, III, and IV) the statutory system for the conduct of interagency matters involving national security resides in the National Security Council (NSC), established in 1947 to advise the President on the integration of domestic, foreign, and military policies, which every President from Truman on has shaped, used, or ignored to meet his own particular method of conducting foreign affairs. When President Nixon made the NSC his "principal forum" for the consideration of national security policies in 1969 under his National Security Adviser, he undermined to a large extent the authority of Secretary Rogers, who, however, was permitted to handle day-to-day departmental business and to continue to be responsible, at least on paper, for the direction of U.S. Government operations overseas. This situation produced a unique relationship between the Secretary of State, the President, and the National Security Adviser during the years 1969–73.

The Secretary of State and the National Security Adviser

With the President relying primarily on his National Security Adviser rather than his Secretary of State to advise, assist, negotiate, and otherwise take over the direction of some of the most important and delicate problems facing the United States in the world arena, there was bound to grow up a strained relationship between the two appointed officials and their staffs. Although the great majority of Department personnel were engaged in work that was unaffected by the leadership at the top, and although the White House was not interested in or capable of taking on the bulk of the State Department's activities, no one in the State Department was happy with a situation which in effect excluded its leadership from the big decisions and operations. Even U.S. ambassadors in foreign posts found themselves ignored by the new model Presidential emissary whose visits to foreign chiefs of state were more than once undertaken without prior information being given to the ambassador on the scene. Foreign governments and their ambassadors tended to prefer to deal with the White House direct if they could arrange appointments. Even heads of U.S. Government agencies participating in interdepartmental committees began to bypass the Secretary of State. This state of affairs, while it lasted, undermined the prestige, power, and usefulness of the State Department, the Secretary of State, and Foreign Service officials on duty in the Department or abroad.

Despite admiration for Dr. Kissinger's performance, many State Department officials did not understand why the President felt that he or his National Security Adviser must be directly involved in operations and in the kind of diplomatic negotiations that have traditionally been handled by the Secretary of State or ambassadors. They did not believe that tight White House control over the NSC committee structure was the only way to operate that system. They believed that the State Department should be allowed to reassert its primacy in foreign affairs but that this could be done only when the President decided to give it strong leadership. The heart of the problem appeared to be not so much structural, or organizational, as one of personalities. During the whole period the processes of interdepartmental coordination were of course used extensively, since that was one of the main purposes of the rejuvenation of the NSC system. But it also served to reduce the role of the Department because the real power rested with the dynamic White House adviser. The situation was, of course, completely altered at the end of August, 1973, when President Nixon announced his intention to nominate Dr. Kissinger to be concurrently his National Security Adviser and his Secretary of State. Kissinger's authority in foreign policy decision making reached a high point when he came to the Department; he was all the more indispensable to the President, who gave him even more authority than before; the Department basked in reflected glory; and, as the new Secretary of State remarked at a news conference shortly after he assumed his Cabinet post, the National Security Adviser and the Secretary of State were extremely close and cordial.

Office of Management and Budget

The Department of State's administrative relations with the Office of Management and Budget (OMB) are closely linked to its substantive, national security-oriented relations with the White House Office and the NSC. Proposed policies or programs without financial resources remain plans; they become realities only when funds are requested, justified, and approved, and it is the OMB that presides over the budgetary process within the executive branch.

No request for funds or legislation goes to Congress without the concurrence of OMB, which is authorized to "bring about more efficient and economical conduct of Government service" and "assist in developing efficient coordinating mechanisms to implement Government activities and to expand interagency cooperation." In brief, OMB, serving essentially as a coordinator and clearing house orchestrating the multitude of programs and activities of the executive branch, can do just about anything on budgetary matters that it decides will help the President meet his heavy responsibilities.

The Department's relations with OMB are unlike those it has with other agencies because of OMB's overriding authority in its field. The Department basically must persuade OMB to approve its proposals before going with them to Congress. The experts OMB assigns to work on the Department's annual budget are— like most of OMB's staff—highly competent, and they soon become as knowledgeable of the details and justifications of the complicated State Department budget as its framers are. The process of State–OMB collaboration on State's budget each year takes place at several levels as the OMB people examine the requirements of each bureau and program of the Department. Against their standing instructions to pare down costs, they have to weigh the hard-to-quantify value to the United States of the Department's varied activities. Resolution of differences on such matters is not easy for the Department because the burden of proof is always on it to justify its case. When important programs are involved, it is especially helpful if the Department has a strong Secretary at the helm.

THE DEPARTMENT OF DEFENSE

The importance of the relationship between the Department of Defense and the Department of State is second only to that State has with the White House. It is obvious that in major crises, such as Berlin in 1961 and Cuba in 1962, diplomacy alone could not have resolved the issues; the strength of the armed forces was an essential ingredient. Conversely, military strength alone, without the skillful and determined diplomacy manifest in those two crises, could have resulted in a bloody war. Not surprisingly, strong differences of opinion have always existed between diplomatic and military personnel, but because of the habit of working together on foreign policy problems in and out of the NSC system since the end of World War II, relations have improved.

One of the first steps toward better cooperation was the establishment of political advisers in several military headquarters overseas just after World War II. This cooperation was continued informally, in fact almost clandestinely, by lower-echelon officers of both departments who realized the necessity of coordinating their efforts. Their efforts were reinforced in 1958 by a Defense Department reorganization that enhanced the role of the Joint Chiefs of Staff and provided a focal point for State-Defense relations.

Two years later, in 1960, a study prepared by the Brookings Institution at the request of the Committee on Foreign Relations recommended:

There should be increased exchange of personnel among military and civilian agencies. Foreign Service officers should be assigned for regular tours of duty in the Department of Defense. Military officers and certain career civilians in the Military Establishment should be assigned for tours of duty in the new Department of Foreign Affairs as well as other relevant agencies. There should be increased civilian participation in the several war colleges and strengthened in-service training programs within the Department of Foreign Affairs.

Most of those recommendations were adopted. About fifteen military officers are currently assigned 2-year tours of duty in the State Department in exchange for an equal number of positions for Foreign Service and civil service officers in the Pentagon—in the Office of the Secretary of Defense, in the Joint Chiefs of Staff, or in any one of the three military departments. Civilian exchange officers also occupy vital positions twenty-four hours a day in the National Military Command Center, the focal point in the Washington area of a worldwide warning and communications network; military exchange officers hold comparable jobs in the State Department's Operations Center, which is patterned after and linked with the National Military Command Center. (The White House Situation Room is part of this network as are other key crisis centers in Washington.) A warning of an impending crisis from military commands or embassies is immediately monitored and evaluated by these combined teams of military-civilian experts, and officials responsible for taking action can be notified literally within minutes.

Fifteen or sixteen State Department officers spend an academic year as students at the National War College, and two or three more are assigned to each of the military service colleges and other military training centers. Foreign Service personnel serve on the faculties of the three military academies, as well as the National War College, where a senior Foreign Service officer is one of the deputy commandants. FSOs also are assigned as top advisers to the heads of the military service colleges and training centers and as political advisers in the major military commands at home and abroad.

Military officers spend an academic year at the Foreign Service Institute as students in the senior seminar on foreign policy, the highest level of training sponsored by the Department of State, and flag and general officers hold key positions in the Arms Control and Disarmament Agency (see Chapter IV). Military attachés have been assigned to U.S. embassies for many years. After World War II, the establishment of Military Assistance Advisory Groups in various countries abroad under the over-all supervision of ambassadors served to help civilian and military personnel understand each other and work together as a team. The military assistance programs are now coordinated in Washington by the under secretary of State for Security Assistance, and his office works closely with the Bureau of Politico-Military Affairs (PM) and the Pentagon's office of International Security Affairs.

The NSC system also provides a formal means of achieving better coordination between the two departments. In particular, it gives State an opportunity to review, primarily through its PM Bureau, proposed Defense policies and overseas programs in the light of national foreign policy. Of course, other channels and points of contact also exist between personnel of the two departments, including those developed between the top ranking officials.

Despite the mechanism available to ensure better working relationships between State and Defense, differences still occur—and doubtless always will. The important point is that they are generally resolved. For example, during one heated interagency discussion of a political-military matter, the civilian leader of the Defense team finally refused to continue the meeting. Although it seemed that an appeal to the Under Secretaries' Committee might be necessary, the group eventually reached a mutually satisfactory solution—undoubtedly having benefited from having had the alternatives thrashed out in a frank, if for a while acrimonious, exchange of opinions.

CENTRAL INTELLIGENCE AGENCY

State's relations with the Central Intelligence Agency (CIA) are also sensitive and complex. Like the Department of Defense, CIA was established by the National Security Act of 1947. Basically, the Act consolidated in the new CIA most U.S. intelligence activities. However, the military continued to operate independent specialized intelligence services and the State Department's reporting activities and Bureau of Intelligence and Research (INR) constituted another intelligence-gathering operation. Hence it was highly important for all of these agencies making up the intelligence community to coordinate their activities to the extent possible. This has been done formally and informally at several levels—formally through the NSC system, where CIA participates in all the key committees, including the Committee of Forty.

Much of the coordination is accomplished routinely by exchanging written intelligence reports. In the Department most of the raw material going into intelligence reports compiled by INR is from information contained in the normal flow of foreign service reporting from overseas posts. The same is true of much of CIA's reporting (despite what "now it can be told" books on CIA may claim).

The State Department's interest in CIA's cloak-and-dagger activities is largely confined to making sure that a specific project is consonant with U.S. policy objectives. Various methods have been used to check out such projects with the ambassador abroad and the appropriate State Department officials in Washington, and over the years lapses have occurred. However, the consequences of failing to coordinate these sensitive matters have been so serious that the chances of CIA's going it alone have become progressively smaller.

Designated liaison officers in the Department facilitate the coordination and distribution of intelligence, and they see that top officials receive the most sensitive reports promptly. Informal contacts between CIA and State experts dealing with similar problems have always been useful and take place at many levels, with the most influential discussions occurring when the President brings together the Secretary of State and the CIA director before making an important decision.

COMMERCE DEPARTMENT

Foreign Service officers serve as commercial attachés or commercial officers in overseas posts, reporting on market conditions and trade opportunities for U.S. importers or exporters, and providing assistance and protection to American business interests.

From time to time, American businessmen have been recruited to serve as commercial attachés for limited periods, usually two to four years.

Commercial services to American businessmen abroad were run by the Commerce Department until 1939, when they were consolidated in the United States Foreign Service run by the Department of State. Since that time almost as soon as each new administration has taken office, there have been moves to re-establish a separate commercial service, and that is what happened shortly after the Nixon Administration came to power. This crystalized in the so-called Magnuson bill, which would have transferred the entire foreign economic function from State to Commerce.

One of the important issues at stake for the Department was the basic question of whether a single Foreign Service—or several services, possibly one for each agency—should be responsible and responsive to all civilian agencies. If a single service is to be administered by *one* agency, the State Department is the logical choice, since the Secretary of State is responsible, under Presidential directive, for directing and coordinating all U.S. foreign relations. On the other hand, critics have contended that it is more important to have business-trained specialists, not generalist Foreign Service officers, to assist American business abroad, and therefore they favored restoring control over commercial work and commercial personnel to the Department of Commerce.

In 1972, Secretary of State Rogers and Secretary of Commerce Maurice Stans directed that a survey be made to suggest how commercial operations serving American business could be strengthened. The survey team, headed by Ambassador John C. Pritzlaff, Jr., reported to the two secretaries on June 21, 1972, that since World War II national priorities had centered on political and military interests. If the government was committed to assisting American business abroad, the report argued, major changes would be required in organization, attitudes, and procedures. Eight recommendations were submitted, in effect calling for an upgrading of commercial work, with joint State-Commerce action on resource requirements and congressional support. In this connection, the report stated: "The need for the Department of Commerce to obtain supplemental funds and positions and other resources clearly undermines the concept of the unified Foreign Service." The Department reacted to these and other recommendations—and to the threat of congressional action—by establishing new priorities and procedures to improve the services provided by the Foreign Service to Commerce and to American business. Following an OMB study at the end of 1973, the President reaffirmed the Department's continuing responsibilities in providing these services and during 1973 and 1974 Congress took no action on the Magnuson bill.

In economic and trade policy matters Commerce has always played an influential role. The American side in trade negotiations, such as those undertaken by the GATT, is generally headed by Commerce, assisted by State. In fact State and Commerce complement each other in many areas where they may at first appear to overlap. Both have responsibilities in international trade policy, both serve the American business community, with Commerce being in especially close touch with it in this country and State abroad. Occasionally there is friction and often rivalry but each needs the other and cooperation can be close. Commerce, especially when headed by a strong Secretary, is influential in the important Council on International Economic Policy in the White House. Top-level Department officials handling economic and business affairs have worked hard to cooperate with Commerce and to win the confidence of Commerce leadership. This has helped stimulate better cooperation at the working levels.

TREASURY DEPARTMENT

In the last few years, at least at the most senior levels and with specific reference to international monetary and financial matters, relations between State and Treasury have left something to be desired. Many civil service professionals in both departments, however, have held the same liaison positions for years and they know how to keep the machinery working, regardless of frictions higher up. As has been evident in recent years there is likely to be less cooperation between the departments at times when an aggressive political figure, rather than a banker or economist, heads the Treasury Department. Another situation that temporarily marred relations occurred some years ago when Internal Revenue Service agents of the Department of Treasury were first assigned to a few embassies—ostensibly to assist Americans or branches of American firms in reporting their U.S. taxable income. It was not entirely clear to the ambassadors or to the State Department that such assistance was really necessary and there was also uncertainty as to what the Treasury's agents were actually doing. The situation was improved by the State-Justice Agreement of 1958, and by subsequent Presidential letters clarifying the authority of ambassadors over all American officials serving abroad. In the words of the agreement: "You (ambassadors) have, of course, the right to be informed, to the extent you deem necessary, of all the information or recommendations reported by any element of the Mission."

The establishment of the Council of International Economic Policy in 1971, as well as the new responsibilities of the Treasury Secretary for coordinating both foreign and domestic economic affairs, also probably helped to improve interdepartmental coordination. At least it was quite clear where the main responsibility lay. Later, after Kissinger became Secretary of State and William E. Simon became Secretary of the Treasury, without the coordinating role, the State Department was able to reassert a good deal of its former leadership in the U.S. Government for international economic affairs.

DEPARTMENT OF AGRICULTURE

The Department of Agriculture won the battle for restoration of a separate Foreign Agricultural Service early in the mid-1950's during the Eisenhower Administration. However, although the Department of Agriculture has many professional agricultural attachés and officers stationed abroad, it also relies on Foreign Service personnel stationed at small posts, in countries where there is less opportunity to dispose of surplus foods or where local crops do not compete with American crops in the world markets. Generally speaking, relationships between officials of the two departments are good, and the services cooperate well in the field. Those who advocate separate overseas services with professionally trained personnel that meet the agency's requirements point to the Foreign Agricultural Service as a model.

LABOR DEPARTMENT

The proponents of a single Foreign Service, obversely, point with pride to the successful arrangements between the State and Labor departments. There are relatively few labor attaché positions, and much of the normal reporting of interest to the Labor Department and organized labor is done by Foreign Service officers. These specialists in labor matters have been fully supported and generally promoted along with their peers in the rest of the Service. Union-sponsored labor attachés have been given temporary or long-term assignments abroad, and some have been integrated into the "regular" Foreign Service, where they have risen to the highest ranks. The Labor Department always makes certain that officers working on labor matters are given proper recognition. When the annual selection (promotion) boards meet, a Labor Department representative sits on every board (as does a Commerce representative), and votes on *all* candidates for promotion, not just those in which his department has a special interest. His presence also helps to ensure that no unintentional favoritism is shown toward Foreign Service personnel in other areas of activity.

DEPARTMENT OF JUSTICE

Because visas for entrance into the United States are issued by State Department officers, most people think the Department of State decides who shall enter the country and who may stay. Not so. It is the Immigration and Naturalization Service of the Department of Justice that determines those matters, subject only to rulings of the courts. For example, an immigration officer who examines the credentials of a foreign national and decides he is not eligible may refuse him admittance, even though a consular officer, thinking the latter met the legal requirements, had issued an appropriate visa. To avoid these somewhat rare situations—and to facilitate tourist travel to this country—immigration officers have been stationed at departure points in several countries, including some Caribbean islands, and, most recently, West Germany. Foreign visitors are practically guaranteed entry to the United States when they receive a visa from a U.S. consul in one office and have it approved by an immigration officer up the hall.

Relationships between State and Justice, and its Immigration and Naturalization Service, become involved because visa problems entail highly technical points of law, administrative procedures, and sometimes difficult interpretations. On the whole, these matters are left to the professionals in the agencies.

GENERAL SERVICES ADMINISTRATION

The General Services Administration (GSA) is the landlord/ housekeeper/contractor of the U.S. Government, building or renting the buildings occupied by State within the United States (the Department's Foreign Buildings Office handles its overseas real estate) and setting the rules regarding the use of all space to which the public has access. GSA guards the buildings, cleans them, and keeps them in repair—all on a reimbursable basis—and only GSA can make alterations to owned or leased property. It is also the supplier of all office equipment, supplies, and furnishings, which it purchases in massive quantities and then "sells" to government agencies. All of the vehicles and trucks used by the Department are also, as a rule, acquired through GSA, with which State personnel have had an excellent working relationship.

GENERAL ACCOUNTING OFFICE

The General Accounting Office (GAO), an arm of Congress, no longer confines itself to auditing accounts and verifying the legality of expenditures of public funds; in accordance with provisions of the Legislative Reorganization Act of 1970, it is now involved in the substance of foreign policy as well. GAO professionals occupy offices in State, and others travel abroad conducting in-depth studies—as many as forty at a time—of specific U.S. policies in individual countries, the operating efficiency of various programs, and the degree to which they achieve policy objectives. In spite of a natural tendency to highlight what is wrong, the reports have generally presented a balanced picture, and relations between the Department and the GAO have been good.

The 1973 GAO report on United States development assistance to Ecuador, for example, criticized the United States for sponsoring ineffective and politically motivated aid programs but also found fault with the Ecuadorean Government for its failure to mobilize its own resources for economic development. The report pointed out the irony in the way the Ecuadorean Navy uses patrol boats provided under U.S. military assistance programs to seize American fishing boats 200 miles off the coast in Ecuador-claimed waters.

Given the investigative mission of the GAO personnel on behalf of Congress, it is not surprising that problems arise from time to time over GAO's access to documents affecting U.S. relations with some other country. For example, the Department is concerned lest a GAO-published report reveal information taken from documents pertaining to pending negotiations, which might be embarrassing or damaging to the United States. The problem is the timing of the publication of the material. This kind of problem can be touchy because it may involve a form of executive privilege—a delicate subject these days. In general, however, these problems get resolved, if necessary by reference to higher authority. One helpful method of avoiding confrontations has been GAO's willingness quite often to submit its reports in draft form for informal review and comment by the people whose operations are being evaluated.

USIA: Its Special Role

What is now the U.S. Information Agency (USIA) was once part of the State Department. It was established as an independent agency under Reorganization Plan No. 8 of June 1, 1953. Secretary of State John Foster Dulles, like many Department and Foreign Service personnel, was not persuaded that the organization's diverse international and cultural functions were properly part of the Department. However, he and subsequent secretaries of State retained certain responsibilities under the U.S. Information and Educational Exchange Act of 1948, including the provision that "the Secretary shall direct the policy and control the content of a program for use abroad," and that he shall "provide to the Director (of USIA) on a current basis full guidance concerning foreign policy."

Mandates such as these cannot be carried out by the Secretary and the director of the Information Agency in chats over the telephone; common-sense guidelines that both organizations can follow are needed. The situation is further complicated by the requirements of other acts for joint educational and cultural exchange activities, for which the agency has primary responsibility abroad (see Chapter V).

John W. Henderson, in a detailed account of the procedures for foreign policy guidance provided USIA by the Department of State, alludes to the involvement of other agencies in activities abroad and the lack of centralization and control, except to some extent— on a long-range basis—in the NSC and the Cabinet itself.* He sums up the special relationship between State and USIA clearly and factually:

> There are also many unofficial exchanges daily between various areas of USIA and corresponding elements of the State Department. Such exchanges have no official standing as policy guidance, but both the Department and the Agency consider them to be, on the whole, helpful. They assure complete understanding among all concerned. Most of the policy and area specialists in USIA have served side by side overseas with their counterparts in State. Their common interests and many mutual associations help to lubricate the policy apparatus. This is one of the reasons why coordination between State and USIA has improved over the years to the increasing satisfaction of both. Some experienced officers believe that policy

* See John W. Henderson, *The United States Information Agency* (Praeger Library of U.S. Government Departments and Agencies, No. 14), 1969.

coordination is closer and more effective now than it was when the overseas information program was administered as part of the State Department. Officials agree that in general the existing machinery is adequate for its purpose so long as there is mutual confidence between State and USIA personnel. Although such mutual confidence ordinarily prevails, at least in the area of policy guidance, periodic replacement of Foreign Service personnel on both sides requires continual reconditioning of bureaucratic fences.

Present-generation officials and the American Foreign Service Association tend to favor reinstatement of USIA in the Department of State. There has been some indication that such a change is in sight, but similar indications have surfaced and vanished before. Meanwhile, problems of coordination remain, and their solution continues to depend largely on the mutual confidence and common interests of those who must work together on these complex issues.

THE PEACE CORPS: ITS PLACE IN THE FOREIGN AFFAIRS FAMILY

The Peace Corps, established in 1961 by the Peace Corps Act, was designed to supplement the U.S. Government's economic assistance programs by making available to interested developing countries American volunteers who would go abroad and provide their skills to help the people in those countries. Since 1961, over 50,000 American volunteers have served in seventy-three countries throughout the developing world. The Peace Corps accent from the beginning has been on the grass-roots approach to help people in poor countries with problems that directly affect the greatest number, like employment, improved health and nutrition, education and broad-based resource exploitation, instead of through conventional efforts to build up a country's infrastructure and basic economic capabilities. This approach is now increasingly being accepted by AID, the World Bank, and other development agencies.

Part of the Peace Corps philosophy, which is important to its success, has been for its volunteers overseas to have as little as possible to do with U.S. Government officials—in the U.S. Embassy, for example. The State Department respects this requirement. Nevertheless, the ambassador in a country in which the Peace Corps is active—and there were sixty-nine such countries in 1974—must keep track of Peace Corps programs and activities, on behalf of the Secretary of State, who has statutory responsibility under the Peace Corps Act to guide the programs to the end that they "are effectively integrated both at home and abroad and the foreign policy of the United States is best served thereby." A Peace Corps director generally keeps in touch with the ambassador or his deputy on an informal basis and he may attend an embassy staff meeting from time to time. In short, coordination does not need to be close and continuous as long as the programs themselves are consonant with U.S. policy in the country concerned. Embassies have often been helpful to Peace Corps volunteers in times of illness or emergency.*

The Peace Corps became part of ACTION in 1971 when several volunteer programs operating at home and abroad were brought together under this new organization to assure better coordination. Nevertheless, the Peace Corps needs to and does maintain its own separate identity.

OTHER INTERAGENCY RELATIONSHIPS

It would be difficult to find a government agency without some interest or involvement overseas. Foreign Service personnel service most of these agencies, meeting their requests for information through procedures established by the Department. A few departments, however, prefer to have their own representatives overseas responding directly to their individual reporting or action requirements. The assignment of representatives for these agencies is provided for either by law (as for agricultural attachés) or by formal or informal agreements (see below). The Department extends its overseas facilities and services to these agencies—on a reimbursable basis—and offers its cooperation in many other ways, always assuming that the agencies' activities are in consonance with U.S. foreign policy objectives in the area.

* See Robert G. Carey, *The Peace Corps* (Praeger Library of U.S. Government Departments and Agencies, No. 22), 1970.

The following list of selected agreements, published in the *Organizational Manual of the Department of State,* indicates the wide variety of interests other departments have in foreign countries and the role of their representatives:

State-Commerce Agreement Regarding Assignment of Civil Aeronautics Administration Technicians, April 3, 1945

State-VA Exchange of Letters on Administration of Certain Functions Abroad, November 4 and 18, 1946

Memorandum Agreement Between State and Department of Defense–Marine Corps Personnel in the Foreign Service, December 18, 1948

State-Agriculture Agreement on Foreign Agricultural Activities, April 1, 1955

Basic Agreement Between State-USIA for Overseas International Educational Exchange Program, June 24, 1955

Agreement Between State and Commerce (Maritime Administration) on Foreign Maritime Activities, December 8, 1955

Arrangements Between State-AEC for Stationing AEC Representatives Abroad, September 22, 1956

State-Justice Agreement Governing Immigration and Naturalization Service Activities Abroad, May 1, 1958

Memorandum of Understanding Between State-AEC Regarding Appointment of AEC Officers to USEC, January 20, 1959

Memorandum of Understanding Between State-Interior with Respect to Minerals and Fisheries Officer Program, May 5, 1959

Memorandum of Agreement Between State-Commerce on International Commercial Activities, November 15, 1961. [All portions of this agreement except paragraph XVI, cost-sharing arrangements, were canceled by Secretaries Rusk and Connor in their January, 1967, exchange of correspondence approving the concept of economic/commercial integration.]

Memorandum of Agreement Concerning Joint Compensation Plans for Local Employees of State, AID, USIA, Certain Designated Units of DOD, FAS, and Other Designated Units of Department of Agriculture, October 5, 1962

State-CAB-FAA Interagency Arrangement on International Civil Aviation, January 15, 1963.

The Department sits on seven or eight interagency committees involved in trade, fiscal, and agricultural matters, and on over thirty-five advisory committees in which public organizations participate. The latter deal with shipping, fishing, international law, architecture of U.S. buildings abroad, cultural and technical interchange, travel, public opinion, and international monetary and financial policies—to name only a few. Like the strictly intergovernmental relationships, which the Department of State must strive to maintain in good order, all are carrying out the President's and his Secretary of State's mandate in the conduct of foreign affairs.

VII

Foreign Affairs and the U.S. Congress

The framers of the Constitution in 1787 were not about to hand over to an executive power of which they were still highly suspicious their control over foreign affairs—however little they had exercised it in those beginning years. When the drafters made certain that Congress alone had the power to grant funds for the executive (and judiciary) branches, ensuring their dependence on the legislative arm of government, it is clear that a major concern was the conduct of affairs with other governments. The organizational relationships between the Department of State's predecessor Department of Foreign Affairs and Congress are still relevant today.

The procedures that have since been established to appropriate funds—first through the authorization and then the money bills—are in themselves an important part of the conduct of foreign relations. There is little question about the sole authority of the legislative branch to grant or withhold the money necessary for the implementation of programs and day-to-day operations of the Department.

Twenty-five years ago, in *Congress—Its Contemporary Role,* Ernest S. Griffith observed:

It is apparent that Congress of late is far from being passive or obstructive in international affairs. More and more it is searching for and finding ways of making itself felt in a most constructive and affirmative position.

In recent years, especially following the Vietnam War, Congress has progressively participated ever more directly in matters of foreign policy, restricting the President's war powers and utilizing the Appropriations authorization procedure as a vehicle for influencing (or making) important foreign policies.

THE SECRETARY OF STATE AND CONGRESS

Except at times when the President is under fire, the Secretary of State is the focal point of legislative interest in foreign policy, economic and military assistance abroad, and the funds requested to operate the programs authorized by Congress. When the Administration is in the hands of one political party and Congress another —particularly when the President's foreign policies are unpopular —the Secretary of State may find himself before congressional committees more often than is normally the case. Because the President and his White House staff can fall back on executive privilege to avoid testifying before congressional committees, the Secretary may then become the target of questions and criticisms actually intended for the President or his White House advisers.

Ordinarily, the Secretary's presence before congressional committees is required several times a year on major legislation and he may be called to explain and justify policies and actions that are likely to be controversial. Like most of his recent predecessors, Secretary Kissinger has met frequently with members of Congress on an informal basis as well, hosting breakfasts at the State Department for the House and the Senate leadership and inviting groups of legislators to accompany him on some of his many trips abroad (for example, to his meeting in Mexico in April 1974 with the Latin American foreign ministers).

Executive Privilege

A further word should be said here about the matter of executive privilege, which Secretary of State Rogers defined on August

4, 1972, in a formal statement submitted to the Senate Subcommittee on Separation of Powers, as "the power of the President to preserve the integrity of his constitutionally assigned functions by withholding information the disclosure of which would impair the process by which the Executive Branch carries out those functions or would be contrary to public interest." This sensitive issue is not just a recent aspect of executive-legislative differences; it began with President Washington and is certain to continue. Occasions will from time to time arise when Presidents will declare that it is not in the public interest to disclose certain information.

Of course, it had never been assumed that executive privilege would be used to protect individuals from criminal charges or to withhold information needed to conduct an impeachment investigation. These are situations that do not involve the State Department, which has found that the executive privilege problems it has faced have been manageable.

Historically, the State Department has generally been able to honor almost all congressional requests for information. In the rare cases in which executive privilege has been invoked, a way has usually been found to pass on to Congress the essential information without giving out the text of sensitive details. The text of telegrams relating to a critical situation abroad, for example, might be withheld from the Foreign Relations Committee, but the basic information in the cables would be made available. In other words, the problem has been worked out informally with the Committee to the satisfaction of both parties. In any case, in the light of the sensitivity of the issue in 1974, the Secretary of State had less reason than ever to attempt to invoke executive privilege in his dealings with Congress.

OFFICE OF CONGRESSIONAL RELATIONS

The main responsibility within the Department of State for liaison with Congress devolves upon the assistant secretary for Congressional Relations. The deputy under secretary for Management serves in a congressional liaison capacity for organizational matters and he shares responsibility for budget and fiscal liaison with the assistant secretary for Administration and deputy assistant secretary for Budget and Finance. In 1973 senior officers of the Department made 181 appearances before congressional committees. The Passport and Visa offices aid members of Congress in behalf of constituents who travel abroad or who assist foreigners to come to the United States. But although these direct and other indirect contacts between officials of the Department and senators, representatives, and their staffs do exist, within the Department of State itself all foreign affairs legislation is coordinated and most inquiries from and service for members of Congress are processed through the Office of Congressional Relations. Experienced personnel of that office maintain close contact with individual members of Congress (and, of equal importance, with congressional staff members), organizing briefings (including regular Wednesday morning meetings whenever Congress is in session) for congressional committees, informal groups, individual members, and staff members. In short, the Office arranges in a variety of ways to bring together the Department's best-informed personnel with congressmen and staff for informal discussions. It also arranges hospitality and meetings to introduce foreign visitors to members of Congress. Subcommittees of the House Committee on Foreign Affairs, moreover, are provided with special services and briefings on particular subjects.

The Office of Congressional Relations sees to it that congressional correspondence receives prompt handling and is answered as quickly and completely as possible. It also tries to ensure that questions on the same subject are answered consistently, even though replies to similar questions are sometimes prepared in different areas of the Department and may tend to reflect the views of a particular unit rather than those of the Department as a whole. In 1973, nearly 19,000 congressional letters were received and answered by the Department, in addition to the more than two hundred telephone inquiries received each day in the Office of Congressional Relations alone.

Another exacting responsibility of this office is arranging for the overseas travel of members of Congress—except for those on the Appropriations committees. Special messages called "CODEL" (for congressional delegation) are sent to all the embassies and consular offices that the travelers will visit to ensure that proper administrative arrangements are made and to provide other guidance for the officers at each post who will be responsible for briefing and escorting the delegation. Considerable criticism has been voiced in the press and elsewhere about congressional visits abroad, often called junkets. In some instances, there undoubtedly is justification for this criticism, but the feeling in the Department and the Foreign Service has generally been that the more members of Congress travel to foreign countries and observe conditions for themselves, the better they—and their constituents—will understand foreign policies and programs.

THE SENATE'S ROLE

The constitutional powers of the Senate in foreign affairs are considerable when that body chooses to exercise its authority. This derives from the fact that the President has the power to make treaties but only "by and with the advice and consent of the Senate" (provided two-thirds of the Senators present agree). Similarly, the President may nominate an ambassador, but he cannot appoint him to serve abroad, except "by and with the advice and consent of the Senate." And only Congress can declare war.

However, a President has the power to circumvent congressional participation or Senate approval. For example, in lieu of treaties, Presidents can make executive agreements or sponsor concurrent resolutions that are not subject to a two-thirds vote of approval by the Senate. Congressional approval of the two agreements with the Soviet Union following the first SALT talks in 1972 were concurrent resolutions. Moreover, as commanders-in-chief of the armed forces, Presidents have demonstrated that they can deploy forces abroad without a declaration of war. President Johnson, for example, sent troops to Vietnam. The 1973 War Powers Act may inhibit such actions in the future, and in any case Congress always has the power to control the size and use of U.S. armed forces by granting or withholding the funds that alone make possible the operation of any military program or action overseas. Its threat to do so at various times during the Vietnam War never materialized, but military appropriations for Southeast Asia in the postwar period have been carefully scrutinized and may be subject to sizable reductions by congressional action.

Foreign Relations Committee

A major role in initiating and guiding senatorial action on foreign affairs legislation has always been played by the Foreign Relations Committee. It drafts authorization bills for important legislation in foreign relations and approves (or disapproves) the appointment of ambassadors and even the class-to-class promotion of every Foreign Service officer. The committee is also the principal organ of the Senate to receive explanations and justifications of foreign policy from the Department's officers, an activity that has increased because of the new system of annual authorization for the Department's budget. Hence, the State Department is especially active in keeping this committee fully informed—as far in advance as possible—on proposed legislation.

The Committee is composed of several regional and functional subcommittees, which are mainly consultative bodies. Under Chairman J. William Fulbright, who preferred to operate in the full committee, they have not been very active. However, the Department of State, mainly through the Office of Congressional Relations, keeps in close touch with the subcommittee members and their staffs. It is a two-way exchange from which both sides benefit. Following through on important pending and controversial legislation, such as foreign aid bills and treaties, can take up a large share of the time of officers assigned to the Congressional Relations Office.

In recent years, the Senate Foreign Relations Committee has sparked much of the legislative effort to reduce the power of the executive branch and has asserted its independent views on many foreign policy issues. During most of the history of the United States, the country has generally been united behind the President in times of war and important diplomatic as well as military decisions have had bipartisan support. Neither public opinion nor increasing numbers of congressional members so supported the Vietnam involvement as it burgeoned. Participation in the Vietnam War became a seeringly controversial issue, and many legislators came to feel that Congress should play a more active role in foreign affairs.

As far back as June, 1969, the Senate passed Resolution No. 85, proposed by its Foreign Relations Committee, which expressed the "sense of the Senate" that commitments to foreign powers can be made only by treaties or other means requiring legislative approval. Although not a law, the resolution indicated which way the wind was blowing.

An amendment to the Foreign Assistance Act of 1971 required State to obtain an annual authorization bill—complete with ceilings for expenditures—as the basis for the Department's annual budget, although for many years, a standard authorization act had been considered sufficient for legislative action. As a result of the new requirement, the Senate Committee on Foreign Relations and the House Committee on Foreign Affairs held extensive hearings in 1972, delving into the details of the State Department's policies, operations, and programs. From this work emerged the Authorization Act of 1972. This kind of annual investigation provides both the Senate and the House with the opportunity to project Congress into foreign policies and operations that would not have been dreamed of only a few years ago.

In February 1972 the Senate Foreign Relations Committee made an effort to limit the President's war powers by severely restricting his freedom to deploy American forces abroad in emergency situations. The House Foreign Affairs Committee would not go that far, however, and after much debate, Congress took no action. Not until the revelations regarding the bombing of Cambodia in the summer of 1973 and the Watergate hearings jarred the nation did both houses of Congress finally agree on a warpowers bill, limiting the President's ability to commit troops by executive action. The bill was passed over a Presidential veto early in November 1973.

Nevertheless, this congressional "victory" does not really alter the validity of Thomas Jefferson's observation that "the transaction of business with foreign nations is executive altogether." Presidential ascendancy over Congress in the conduct of foreign policy has grown over the years because modern foreign policy requires almost continuous actions of the kind that no legislative body is capable of undertaking. Nor can Congress collectively undertake responsibility for foreign policy decisions in the way the President must. Hence, Presidents and Secretaries of State invariably oppose any moves to bring Congress into foreign operations that would deny them the necessary flexibility. In times of disagreement with the Congress it is all the more important for the executive branch to maintain a dialogue with the Congress. Secretary Kissinger's efforts in this regard have been acclaimed but the problem became complicated in 1974 as a result of the nation-wide loss of confidence in White House leadership. This has tended to bolster a more independent position on the part of Congress, especially in the once docile House.

Senate Appropriations Committee

Although the Foreign Relations Committee receives more publicity, the Senate Appropriations Committee also wields great power, derived from the Constitutional clause that states "no money shall be drawn from the Treasury but in consequence of appropriations made by law." Other committees may recommend —and the Senate, in conjunction with the House, may authorize— programs and the maximum amount of money needed to pay for them. But such authorizations are meaningless until the Senate Appropriations Committee (in conjunction with the comparable House committee) goes into action to decide on the actual amount to be granted. More often than not, this is less than the maximum authorized by the two branches of Congress, but is generally accepted by the Senate—although sometimes with important revisions. A similar procedure in the House can produce still another result, and then the differing Senate-House versions are reconciled by a special Senate-House conference committee.

The Senate Appropriations Committee delegates most of the

work to its subcommittees, which have a reputation for sober and careful consideration of appropriations bills.

Other Senate Committees

Several other Senate committees handle matters relating directly or indirectly to foreign relations, and the Department must keep itself informed of their activities and be prepared to provide information they need.

The Commerce Committeee, handling many matters involving international trade and commerce, is naturally much interested in the services the government provides to U.S. businessmen abroad. Through its subcommittee on Foreign Commerce and Tourism, it has for several years been considering various proposals for giving greater authority to the Department of Commerce to handle or otherwise control economic and commercial reporting and services to U.S. businessmen at U.S. embassies abroad. Already noted is the bill introduced by Senator Warren G. Magnuson in 1971, which would, if passed, have re-established a separate commercial foreign service under the Department of Commerce, taking away from State responsibilities it has had since it absorbed the old Commerce service in 1939. The Department responded by taking action to try to restore the confidence of the business community and of the Department of Commerce in the competence of the Foreign Service to handle economic and commercial work. New priorities were assigned and appropriate programs emphasizing trade promotion were inaugurated. The name of the Economic Bureau was changed to Economic and Business Bureau and trade promotion was upgraded within the Bureau. These efforts appeared to be quite successful. The President, at any rate, informed the secretaries of State and Commerce in May 1973 that he looked to the Secretary of State to continue to oversee the activities of personnel engaged in commercial and economic work at our posts abroad. The Watergate hearings in the summer of 1973 also had the effect of sidetracking consideration of the Magnuson Bill.

Subsequently, a new version of the bill was introduced that was equally an anathema to the Department. Although it no longer provided for a separate Department of Commerce foreign service, it called for Commerce Department inspectors, separate from State's Inspection Corps, to watch over the commercial and economic work at overseas posts. The Department has discouraged passage of this bill—successfully, to date.

The Senate Armed Services Committee, with its influence over defense spending limits and problems dealing with bases and troops abroad, is important in many matters affecting foreign relations. The Committee (like its House counterpart) may call State Department officers as witnesses, for example, at hearings on funding military operations or military procurement for assistance to Israel or construction facilities for a home port for the navy abroad. An illustration of how the Committee can make foreign policy is the so-called Byrd Amendment, exempting chrome and other strategic materials from the U.N. Security Council's list of forbidden imports from Rhodesia. Although this issue had no connection with the Defense budget, it was nevertheless tacked on to one of the Armed Service Committee's authorization acts. As of mid-1974, State Department representations to rescind this amendment have been fruitless.

Several other Senate committees with which the Department is in touch are the Post Office and Civil Service Committee, important not because of its postal service oversight but because two-thirds of the Department's employees are in the civil service; Government Operations, which keeps a watchful eye on the way the Department manages itself and its programs; Agriculture, which has its own people stationed in the larger countries and is greatly concerned with the sale (or other disposal) abroad of American food surpluses; and Labor, with its increasing role in international labor activities, especially in the developing countries. More recently, the value of the U.S. dollar in relation to other currencies has become a matter of concern and State has therefore become involved with the Finance Committee, although Treasury has major responsibility in this area.

THE HOUSE OF REPRESENTATIVES'S ROLE

Traditionally the House of Representatives, as the lower chamber with more numerous membership, is considered less prestigious than the Senate, but events since mid-1973 have tended to change the picture. People became aware that the Speaker of the House is third in line for the Presidency; that the House has sole power to decide whether to request the Senate to hold an impeachment trial; that the House has the sole right to originate bills for raising revenue, which some consider more than balances the "advice and consent" power of the Senate in foreign affairs.

In foreign affairs the role of the House Foreign Affairs Committee in reviewing policies in connection with the annual authorization act for the State Department's budget has given the House the means to exert its influence in a wider range of policies than hitherto. In fact, recently the House Committee may have been more influential than the Senate Foreign Relations Committee in such important legislative fields as foreign aid (Foreign Relations Act of 1973), executive agreements, and State Department authorization and funding bills.

Although the Department has generally looked to the House to support the President's policies, this new involvement of the House has been accompanied by a more independent attitude, sparked by public opinion and the activities of its Foreign Affairs Committee. There have been frustrations in the Department's relations with the House. Representatives, facing re-election every two years, tend to be less interested in foreign policy than the elder statesmen of the Senate and to be more susceptible to pressure groups such as those claiming that foreign aid programs are "giveaways."

The House operates through its committee system, and especially through the numerous subcommittees and their chairmen, whose power is such that a handful of representatives, in effect, may well determine the course of action the House as a whole will take. This is especially evident in routine organizational and budget matters in which the subcommittee chairman, supported by the ranking minority member, can practically determine how an agency of the government will operate. Nowhere in the Constitution does the phrase "sense of the committee" appear, but these words in the Appropriations Committees report on a budget, followed by an instruction, have the force of law for the affected agency administrator.

Committee on Foreign Affairs*

Even during the years when the House Committee on Foreign Affairs was overshadowed by its much more publicized sister Committee on Foreign Relations in the Senate and by the powerful House Committee on Appropriations, the Department was highly respectful of the leadership of the Committee and of the effective leadership of many of its subcommittees. Taking into account the suggestions, views, and opinions of the subcommittees has helped reduce the number of hearings and expedited foreign policy legislation. The stronger position the Committee has assumed, as a result of participation in the annual authorization bills and several major foreign policy measures, means that State is in closer touch than ever with the Foreign Affairs Committee and its subcommittees.

The influence of the chairmen of congressional committees and subcommittees is particularly great when a chairmanship is held by one person for many years, as is the case with the Foreign Affairs Committee. Chairman Thomas E. Morgan did not join in challenging the President's war powers until public opinion and the events of the latter part of 1973 virtually forced a policy change. His committee for a long time opposed the Senate Foreign Relations Committee's efforts to do so, as well as its position on a good many other issues. Representative Morgan has tried to follow his longtime philosophy to support, in so far as possible, the foreign policy of the incumbent President, as he did during most of the Vietnam War and in opposing the unilateral withdrawal of U.S. troops from Europe and drastic cuts in foreign aid. But if the Committee has become much more independent only of late, it has never been possible to consider it a tool of any Administration.

The House Committee on Foreign Affairs has ten very active subcommittees, including a subcommittee on the State Department and Foreign Operations under the chairmanship of Congressman Wayne Hays, who has been a constructive critic, friend, and foe of the Department for many years. This subcommittee's members are as active in observing the Foreign Service at work overseas as they are in Washington; they keep well informed, and the Department

* Name changed to *Committee on International Relations* in January, 1975.

does its best to assist. Several of the other subcommittees have been noticeably more active since January, 1971, when the 92nd Congress was organized under new rules. Through attrition and the new prohibition on any member's chairing more than one subcommittee, four more aggressive, younger congressmen became chairmen of Foreign Affairs subcommittees. For the first time, moreover, subcommittees were authorized to employ their own staffs, leading to improvements in efficiency and subcommittee initiatives.

Notwithstanding these developments, the Committee on Foreign Affairs did not basically alter its generally conservative outlook until the end of the summer of 1973. Its prestige and influence still rested mainly on the continuity of its leadership and professional staff, although these were not always sufficient to move the House to go along with legislation favored by the committee. Opposition to foreign aid runs high, because of current prejudice against any kind of "handouts" to foreigners. State Department facts and figures in support of committee positions often have little effect in swaying members' views on this highly charged issue. For example, unless a business firm in a congressman's own district is hurt by curtailment of foreign aid funds, he is not likely to be impressed by the fact that over half of the funds appropriated for military and economic aid are spent in the United States (on goods, labor, and salaries), when his main argument has been that the aid programs help only foreigners.

After the return of U.S. troops and prisoners of war from Vietnam many members of the House came to feel that the time had come to reduce the military factor in foreign policy. This led to a shift in the power structure in the Foreign Affairs Committee closer to that of the Senate's Foreign Relations Committee, notably on restricting Presidential war powers.

House Committee on Appropriations

Holbert N. Carroll, an experienced and perceptive observer, has written:

> It is possible to study the Committee on Foreign Affairs and most of the other House committees as units. To write of the Committee on Appropriations as a unit is to employ a fiction; this committee is

but a sum of its parts. The realities of power rest with the dozen or so subcommittees to which are assigned parts of the annual budget.

The Appropriations Committee convenes as a body to consider the findings of its subcommittees, whose proposals are usually accepted with few, if any, changes. This certainly applies to the subcommittee, chaired for many years by the powerful John J. Rooney of New York, that handles the State Department's budget. Discussing the appropriations process in an address at a Foreign Service Association luncheon in the mid 1950's, Rooney said that once "he decided"—and immediately amended his statement amidst the gale of laughter to say that once "the *committee* decided" how much a department should have, he would defy anyone who attempted to reduce that amount by a single penny. Rooney, who epitomizes the seniority process and the appropriations procedure, knows the Department's budget better than most of the witnesses who come before his subcommittee. He has sufficient seniority, power, and paliamentary skill to defend his bills—with remarkable success—on the House floor, but the Senate has been careful not to challenge him in open hearings. In one instance, the personal appeal of a President of the United States was necessary to get him to change his position. His arbitrary use of power is well illustrated by the way he held up the U.S. contribution to the International Labor Organization for two years. His influence in his subcommittee and in the House was strong enough to put this over, by failing to appropriate the funds in fiscal years 1971 and 1972, allegedly at the behest of his old friend President George Meany of the AFL/CIO, who disapproved of ILO appointments of several Soviet officials.

Some observers think that the Department benefits from this extraordinary process: The chairman and members of his committee have built up a detailed knowledge of the Department's operations; they give the witness a fair hearing; and Representative Rooney successfully justifies and defends the resulting bill before the full committee and the House. Many critics, however, believe there is no excuse for any one congressman to wield such power over the funds and programs of State (or any other department or agency). Certain changes that are taking place in the committee system should indeed make it difficult in the future for chairmen to rule with such an iron hand: the inroads in the seniority system, open hearings and the new rules that encourage all committee members to participate in the hearings. This trend may soon affect the chairman's conduct of the hearings on the State Department's budget, especially if Rooney loses his House seat in the 1974 election.*

The State Department also has much to do with the Subcommittee on Foreign Operations, which handles appropriations for military and economic assistance. This subcommittee has long been chaired by strong-minded, elderly, and powerful Otto Passman of Louisiana, who, like Congressman Rooney, has usually been able to exert his will on his subcommittee and Congress. An exception was the 1973 foreign assistance (AID) appropriations bill, which the House Appropriations Committee approved for $5.8 billion. This amount restored nearly all of the $2.2 billion to help Israel replace arms losses that Passman's subcommittee had reduced to $1.7 billion. Immediately afterward, the chairman was quoted in the press as stating that he would go along with restoring most or all of the $2.2 billion because the Administration had (now) made a strong case which "has fortified me." His power, too, should be somewhat circumscribed by the reforms and trends in the committee system referred to above.

The Agency for International Development (AID) takes the lead in supporting the development-humanitarian (economic) assistance budget in the subcommittee hearings, while the State Department together with the Defense Department heads the effort on behalf of security (military) assistance. For the latter the Secretary of State makes the initial request and the under secretary for Security Assistance is in charge of justification efforts and of State's many witnesses from the geographic and functional bureaus. The Office of Congressional Relations, working closely with its counterpart office in AID, spent much time in 1972 and 1973 trying to move this foreign assistance legislation along. After the hearings were completed, however, the 1972–1973 authorization

---

* Because of ill health, Mr. Rooney did not run for re-election. John M. Slack of West Virginia succeeded to the chairmanship of the subcommittee.

bill was defeated in Congress. Finally, in December 1973 the bill for fiscal year 1973–74, passed, as well as the money bill to go with it. Since July 1, 1972, the programs had been operating on the basis of a continuing resolution, which held expenditures at the same level as the previous year. This unfortunate situation was not the fault of the budgetary process but a reflection of the extremely controversial nature of foreign aid programs.

The Appropriations Committee and its subcommittees, ruled by powerful chairmen, have paid little heed to other committees, but the new responsibilities of both the Senate Foreign Relations and House Foreign Affairs committees to authorize annual appropriations levels for the Department should stimulate better coordination among the committees. The fact now is that the autocrats of the appropriations subcommittees no longer are the only powers to be reckoned with.

Other House Committees

As in the Senate, so in the House State is involved with several other committees from time to time. The House counterparts of the Senate Commerce, Armed Services, and Agriculture committees are important, and the Department must also be attentive to the Committee on Government Operations, whose staff investigates the Department's operations with a view to suggesting improvements in efficiency and economy.

The actions of the House Committee on Agriculture (as well as the Senate committee) impinge strongly on foreign policy. Decisions having to do with the disposal of food surpluses abroad, competition for world markets, and sugar quotas involve large sums of money and affect the political well-being of many members of Congress. Problems with State occur when domestic considerations conflict with foreign policy considerations. From time to time there is a potential conflict between agricultural interests favoring ever increasing exports and a longer-range view that must take into account the total international-relations picture. This is just one aspect of the enormously complicated foreign trade problems facing the United States.

For some years the main problem seemed to be how to increase exports (and the U.S. trade balance) without antagonizing political friends in Europe and Japan by adopting overly protectionist trade policies. With massive grain exports, dwindling surplus grain stocks and rising prices at home, new problems have arisen requiring some basic re-evaluations. The Office of Management and Budget has instituted studies in depth to help guide future policy decisions. Agricultural interests are only one group affected but, whether in Congress or outside, they too will have to learn to adjust to changing conditions, which may require giving up some of the special treatment to which they have been accustomed. In any case, the alternatives to liberal trade policies (policies with as few restrictions on trade as possible) must be carefully weighed. Mounting inflation and threatened depression in the United States will further complicate an already complicated problem.

The House Ways and Means Committee has had the problem of future trade policy under consideration. The Department of State is only one of several executive agencies concerned with trade and international economic policy—Treasury, Commerce and the White House coordinator of economic policies all being influential. The Department has had somewhat more influence in pressing for a liberal trade policy under the leadership of Secretary of State Kissinger. However, on the crucial issue of extending equal tariff treatment to the Soviet Union, a policy favored by the executive branch, congressional opposition, as expressed in amendments to the long-awaited trade bill, has been very powerful.

In February, 1973, Chairman of the Ways and Means Committee Wilbur Mills, with the support of over 250 House members, introduced legislation to block trade concessions for the Soviet Union unless Moscow dropped its tax on emigrating Jews. Senator Henry M. Jackson's similar amendment to the Senate bill had much support in the Senate. The Department, fearing damage to the none too stable détente in Soviet-American relations, suggested a way out of the impasse, but the Soviets rejected it because they considered the objective of the amendment to be unacceptable interference in their internal affairs. (See page 227.) This difficult problem provides an interesting case study of executive-legislative relationships, as well as an example of the great power of congressional committees and their chairmen, to say nothing of the frustrations and the uncertainties of the current détente.

The House Interstate and Foreign Commerce Committee is involved in international activities—airline routes, oil imports, export controls, and promotion of American business overseas—that are of interest to the State Department. It is also interested in the questions raised in the Senate's two Magnuson bills having to do with the responsibility of the State and Commerce departments for economic and commercial reporting and services to businessmen abroad.

Immigration and naturalization, international copyrights, patents and trademarks, and the oftentimes nebulous problems of international law, all of which are of interest to the Department, fall under the jurisdiction of the House Judiciary Committee.

Congressional Staff

An account of relations between the Department of State and Congress would not be complete without a word about the professional staffs of the major committees. These are the legislative experts who provide analyses and information, suggest ways and means, predict the outcome of certain courses of action, and write up reports of conversations and discussions. Their highly skilled work saves committee members time and offers them valuable ideas, speech material, suggestions, and information.

Contact, particularly continuous and personal relationships, between staff members and agency officials who do somewhat similar staff work facilitates the tasks of both groups. Each side recognizes the different approaches that separate their endeavors, but the confidence and respect that seems to develop between pros are mutually beneficial. Of course, even more important in influencing congressional actions affecting the State Department are the calibre of the State Department's top leaders, the authority with which they speak, and the extent of their backing by the President.

The full effect on congressional-State relations of the Watergate investigation and what that whole affair has done to undermine the power and prestige of the Presidency are not discussed in this book, but it is, of course, part of the broader problem of congressional-executive relations. It is clear, however, that Congress is already playing and will continue to play an increasingly active part in the conduct of foreign affairs. This is a development that can be in the public interest, if not carried too far, but that complicates the problems for the President and his Secretary of State, who have the responsibility of running American foreign relations.

VIII

The State Department and
the Public

In a democracy, no foreign policy can long be valid without the support of the public. And during most of U.S. history, with the few notable exceptions of the War of 1812 and the Spanish-American War, getting that backing has presented no problem—a happy circumstance for policy-makers that was, to a great extent, the result of the American public's lack of interest in foreign affairs and not a consequence of government efforts to explain policies. Presidents and secretaries of State tended to direct foreign affairs themselves, and they generally had no reason to worry about public acceptance. In recent years, of course, this has no longer been the case, but the change was not abrupt, and the Department of State, for many years, has carried on programs designed "to provide American citizens with information that will help them to understand U.S. foreign policy and America's role in the world." In this connection, the Bureau of Public Affairs (P) has answered a vast amount of public correspondence, issued countless publications, held briefings and press conferences, sent out speakers, and sponsored conferences.

The P Bureau has had other responsibilities not directly aimed at reaching the American public. When one of the authors served in the bureau in the late 1950's, the foreign propaganda side of information activities was greatly emphasized. The policy direction for the government-sponsored radio programs beamed to Eastern Europe, for example, was coordinated in an *ad hoc* committee chaired by the deputy assistant secretary of State for Public Affairs. The assistant secretary for Public Affairs supervised all Department press relations and, indeed, devoted about 75 per cent of his time to what the Secretary of State's special assistant for Press Relations does today. The P Bureau also handled the cultural and educational exchange programs of the Department, activities that have long since been grouped into a separate bureau (see Chapter V). It could do all this in large part because, as recently as fifteen years ago, the Department of State was organized, with only a limited budget, to do what was basically a routine job of informing the public about foreign policy. As long as there was broad support for government actions, this was an adequate arrangement. No serious criticism handicapped Department action, although Congress always kept a tight rein on funds.

Crisis in Confidence

Instant global communications, nuclear weapons, the influence of television, and the changes that have occurred in American economic and military strength since World War II have meant that the United States becomes involuntarily concerned, one way or another, with just about everything that is happening anywhere in the world. Other countries—millions of human beings—can be critically affected by U.S. decisions. Whereas in the past foreign relations could be adequately handled by the President and his Secretary of State, today some forty government agencies are concerned with foreign affairs. And there is growing public and congressional interest in playing a more significant role in determination of foreign policy.

The broad-based support for U.S. policies of the cold war era, which were formulated by a small, elite foreign policy establishment, has disappeared; the post-Vietnam policies emphasizing greater self-restraint have not achieved the same kind of nonpartisan consensus. Instead, a situation exists in which there are many different opinions, and much perplexity, as to what course the United States should follow—as well as a great deal of public distrust of the Establishment. In fact, many observers fear that this public uncertainty and confusion will result in disillusionment with foreigners and foreign countries generally and in U.S. withdrawal from international affairs—in short, in isolationism. Then, too, the unpopularity of U.S. involvement in Vietnam has caused the loss of public support for foreign policies in other areas, such as aid to undeveloped nations and expansion of world trade through liberal trade policies. The crisis in public confidence became dramatically evident when President Lyndon Johnson announced, in March, 1968, that he would not run for re-election. Richard Nixon's Watergate scandal hardly restored confidence in the top leadership.

MEETING THE CHALLENGE IN THE P BUREAU

The job of meeting effectively the ever more complex problem of communicating with the public is of continuing concern to the State Department and especially its Bureau of Public Affairs. Today the P Bureau receives and answers a quarter of a million letters from the general public, including some 7,000 letters from Congress requesting information to be passed on to constituents. Together with the Press Relations Office, a part of the office of the Secretary (see Chapter II), the P Bureau is now the focal point of State Department efforts to provide the public with foreign affairs information. In addition to assisting the news media, the Department is engaged in many activities aimed at explaining policy to students and scholars, community leaders, congressmen, and the general public. It is also attempting to educate its own officers on the importance of establishing better communications with the public.

The accent on reaching youth and on "openness," a position strongly supported by top officials of State, was articulated in the fall of 1969, when Secretary of State William P. Rogers urged people to understand U.S. policy and communicate their views to the Department so that they could feel they were participants in foreign policy making. He said he expected Foreign Service officers in particular to become involved in a continuing dialogue and noted that they tended in the past to be too insulated from the public. Some of the difficulties in this policy were pointed out by the counselor of the Department, Richard Peterson, late in 1970, when he warned that personnel must be ready to be challenged on fundamental values and assumptions, as well as on specific policies. Young people also, he underscored, must be ready to listen, deal with the facts, and consider the complexities of problems as they actually happened.

Campus Speakers

In April, 1972, four Foreign Service officers, then on assignment to the Department of State, undertook a 5-day speaking tour to North Carolina. They were among the two hundred younger Foreign Service officers who visit more than six hundred campuses and communities each year. Their tour offered a good illustration of what goes on during such campus visits and of the effort to better communicate with the public.

George Mitchell, chief of the Speakers Division, led the group and coordinated the planning that enabled the four officers, singly and as a group, to make 106 different appearances at 15 colleges and universities, 5 high schools, 3 community organizations, 3 television and radio stations, and 2 newspapers.

Yale Richmond, of the Office of Soviet and Eastern European Exchanges, covered the field of changing relations with the Soviet Union and Eastern Europe, and he recalls that "the person-to-person dialogues with inquisitive students and probing professors sharpened my own thinking on foreign policy."

Dr. F. A. Logan, of the African Bureau, a history professor before he joined the Foreign Service, on this trip had an especially heavy schedule. In one day, he undertook as many as eight speaking engagements. A high school history teacher remarked, after one of these sessions, that hearing about Dr. Logan's personal experience in South Africa stimulated her to initiate a class project on that country. Students everywhere showed a deep interest in Africa, and they deluged him with questions after the classes.

Richard Hines, of the Inter-American Affairs Bureau, felt that he had gained more from the trip than his listeners; the question-and-answer sessions stimulated his thinking and improved his prespective on Latin American problems. Young professors in particular sought him out to discuss such issues as economic nationalism in Latin America and the role of private investment there.

It was John Muehlke's task to talk about Vietnam just as U.S. planes were starting to bomb Haiphong harbor. As a member of the East Asian Bureau, he telephoned his office every day to keep in touch with latest developments. Because of the special timeliness of his subject, Muehlke was asked to address statewide audiences on local television and radio stations, and he was able to speak authoritatively.

All four State Department speakers had a rough time at an evening student forum in Greensboro, North Carolina. The student group, primarily black, was sharply critical of American involvement in Vietnam and of U.S. policy in Africa. The Foreign Service officers spoke frankly, gave the facts as they knew them, described how the policies were being carried out, and admitted shortcomings. In retrospect, they felt that it had been a "hot" but worthwhile session and that they themselves had come away with better understanding of grass-roots public opinion towards American foreign policy.

Similar community meetings on foreign affairs were held in eleven other states during 1972. The nine teams that participated had a total of 856 live and media engagements. The program has continued at approximately the same level in FY 1973 and 1974 and has operated in nearly every state in the union since 1963.

Scholar-Diplomat Seminars

The Scholar-Diplomat Program, which began as an experimental meeting of eleven young academicians with State Department officials for a week-long session on African studies, illustrates another way in which the Department responded to the increase in nationwide disillusionment with foreign policy. Through it young Ph.D.'s are given the opportunity to work side by side and issue by issue with responsible State Department officers on problems related to their own specialty. They receive access to classified material and can observe and participate in the handling of current problems; they see the telegraphic traffic, discuss policy papers, attend staff meetings, make suggestions, and have occasion to observe the realistic limitations on seemingly ideal courses of action. In short, they see diplomacy at first hand.

This program owes much to Dr. Robert Caldwell, formerly with the Public Affairs Bureau, who recognized its importance, and promoted it within the Department. In the four years since its inception in 1969, some 62 seminars have been held in the 5 geographic bureaus and several of the functional bureaus of State, and 733 scholars have participated, most of them teachers of political science, history, international relations, and economics. In FY 1973 alone 21 seminars were held with 228 scholars participating. Many of the scholars have kept in touch with their host officers after the seminars, sending them their scholarly papers and inviting them to their institutions. A few have taken government jobs. They have also written many letters to the Department: "Personal contact is the main strength of the program. . . ." "I can recall few experiences in my life that were so rewarding in so short a period of time. . . ." "Without being 'brainwashed,' I came away with an improved image of the Department and especially of its personnel. . . ." "I was extraordinarily impressed by the openness and frankness with which we were treated—at every level in State and in several other of the agencies visited." "I think the major payoff of the program is the opportunity to observe directly the process of foreign policy problem-management. . . ." "It would be too much to say that all questions were resolved, but it was a Great Leap Forward that hopefully will continue. . . ."

Briefings, Conferences, and Educational Programs

Briefings are held twice weekly for the general public at the State Department, and special briefings are arranged for groups from high schools, colleges, churches, and civic organizations. Professors and students are especially welcome in the Department for colloquies and research projects during the midterm break.

Other national conferences on foreign policy for specialized audiences—the news media, nongovernment organizations, businessmen, and educators—are also held regularly in the Department of State. To elicit as much audience participation as practicable, representatives of the attending organizations make up the questioners' panels that lead the discussions following the speakers' presentations, and optional informal sessions covering a wide range of subjects are available for those who prefer smaller group discussions to the plenary conference.

The State Department also takes part in regional foreign policy conferences for similar audiences of civic and community leaders, dispatching top officials to address these meetings and discuss the issues. State representatives to such conferences increasingly attend student conferences at the same time.

Diplomats in Residence

Under another program, six to eight experienced Foreign Service officers are assigned annually to a college or university for a year in residence, giving lectures and talking with students and faculty in classes, meetings, seminars and at community functions. The academic community has an opportunity to see that diplomats do not all have horns or forked tails, nor are they "cookie pushers in striped pants," and students may gain useful insights into the issues and practices of diplomacy from the visiting lecturer-diplomats. For the Foreign Service officers, and their families, moreover, the experience of adjusting to life in an American academic environment after years of service overseas is also valuable. Rubbing elbows with students, faculty, and citizens in a college town many miles from Washington, D.C., provides unforgettable insights into the thinking and attitudes of the American public, an important educational factor for the U.S. Foreign Service.

Senior Seminar

The Foreign Service Institute's Senior Seminar for civilian and military officers from many federal agencies is the most advanced educational program of studies in international relations offered by any government agency. Half of the twenty-five or so talented senior officers who take the 10-month course each year are Foreign Service officers, and the seminar is shaped to their needs. The emphasis is on firsthand observation and study of a wide range of some of our most serious domestic problems. The class travels extensively throughout the United States looking into all possible phases of American life. The similarities between problems in the United States and those in other countries thus become strongly evident, and the total experience of relating and correlating domestic problems with foreign relations is highly useful.

University Studies

Six to eight experienced Foreign Service officers are assigned each year to a college or university. They spend a full academic year to advance their expertise in, for example, area studies, economics, or political science. Equally important is their participation in discussions in the many different forums on campus and their exposure to campus thinking in general.

Summer Interns

Finally, the Department of State, as well as many other federal government departments, welcomes a number of students, summer "interns," who serve as apprentices or junior assistants. The thirty-five or forty students in the program, including at least ten from minority groups, have an opportunity to learn about government and its processes in their daily work.

MEDIA SERVICES AND P BUREAU PRODUCTS

The Office of Press Relations carries on the day-to-day business of dealing with the 120 or more American and foreign correspondents who regularly cover the State Department. Each morning this office prepares for the daily press briefing it conducts at noon by farming out anticipated questions to the various bureaus, whose experts suggest replies. Preparations for a press conference by the Secretary of State are handled in a similar manner.

The Office is always in contact with the press offices in the White House, where there are two press briefings daily, and the Department of Defense, where there is one. This liaison activity is important because foreign policy issues are brought up in all of these briefings, and while the White House spokesman tends to look at foreign policy questions from the point of view of their impact on domestic politics and the Pentagon speaker from the point of view of national security, State must point out the global impact of official statements.

The Press Office may arrange for experts to provide background information on topical subjects at press briefings. For example, on July 21, 1972, after President Nixon congratulated the French Government for seizing three heroin laboratories in France, the subject of American efforts to obtain cooperation from other governments against drug abuse, largely through the work of American embassies abroad, was brought up at the Department's regular press briefing. The Press Office arranged to have an official representing the Department's Narcotics Coordinator on hand to fill in the details of the heroin traffic and what U.S. embassies were doing about it. Besides the briefings, correspondents also have access to individual State Department officers whose special knowledge can help provide background for their stories. Official comments are generally "on the record" and can be attributed to the source, or sometimes to "an official source," without mentioning names.

The custom of having high-level background sessions by the Secretary of State for a few selected correspondents is less in vogue than it was in the time of Dulles and Rusk. The position taken by several correspondents that they are free to expose their sources has certainly put a damper on the tendency of many high officials to "go background" and, in fact, has caused some officials to decline to talk to reporters. Even the President's National Security Adviser and later Secretary of State, Henry Kissinger, began to talk mostly "on the record" after December, 1971, when a correspondent revealed his identity as the source of a sensitive India-Pakistan "backgrounder" during that crisis. Wariness of the backgrounder continues, but both high officials and correspondents have found that they benefit from the additional flow of information that results from frank "off the record" comments. When Kissinger became Secretary of State he developed his own informal way to carry out this special kind of briefing, often taking advantage of long overseas plane flights to give correspondents traveling with him background information. He has, of course, also held large, formal on-the-record press conferences in Washington, as well as similar meetings with the press abroad at the end of official visits.

To supplement and fill out the news provided by the Office of Press Relations in press conferences and briefings, the P Bureau makes available a variety of materials for radio, TV, film, school, and other use.

Radio and Television Features

News features and radio excerpts from the Secretary's press conferences are provided to television and radio stations. Arrangements are also made for officers of the Department to appear on selected television and radio programs around the country. In addition, 5-minute recorded interviews on foreign policy issues, "Reports from the State Department," are used by about 1,000 radio stations in their news programs and by some schools as teaching aids.

A series of half-hour radio programs called "Students and Diplomats" is produced in cooperation with American University in Washington, D.C., for broadcast on campus stations across the country. The program brings together student spokesmen and State Department officers for a frank dialogue on policy issues.

Films and Film Strips

Films are produced mainly for educational use in classrooms or by adult organizations. They are sometimes shown on television when the subject is topical, although the emphasis is generally on basic concepts in order to help Americans understand the complexity of handling foreign policy problems. "From Where I Sit," for example, is a film inquiring into the process of decision-making, illustrating the conflicting elements that are always involved. Other films show the work of an American embassy overseas, and there is a series on the diplomatic history of the United States. One film strip, "The U.S. and the World: An Introduction to Foreign Relations," has been produced for high schools.

Publications

A large segment of the Departmental effort to inform the public about foreign affairs is done through the printed word. Major foreign policy topics are covered in daily press releases, in the weekly *Department of State Bulletin,* and in the documentary series *Foreign Relations of the United States.* Many scholars feel that no foreign office in the world publishes its documentary record in such depth and so soon after the events as does the Department of State.

A pamphlet series, *Issues in United States Foreign Policy,* covers such key subjects as the Middle East, NATO and the defense of Europe, Communist China, commitments of U.S. power abroad, the United Nations, and liberal trade versus protectionism. The series, which seeks to define questions rather than give answers, is designed for classroom use and emphasizes the factors underlying a given problem rather than defense of existing policies. Another series of papers, *International Organizations,* deals with the principal international organizations in which the United States is a member or has an interest—the U.N. and its specialized agencies, regional organizations, international development banks, and the like.

Background Notes on all the nations of the world and numerous special educational pamphlets, such as "How Foreign Policy Is Made" and "The Country Team," as well as the texts of important foreign policy statements are also published by the P Bureau.

The alarming number of Americans under detention abroad on narcotics charges (1013 as of April, 1974)* caused the Department of State to make a major effort to explain some of the pitfalls that can be encountered in foreign travel. A June, 1972, pamphlet, "Youth Travel Abroad—What To Know Before You Go," gives information on, among other things, foreign laws and penalties on illicit sale, use, and possession of drugs; illicit currency transactions; and "educational" programs that actually give no academic credits. The limitations on the power of consular officers abroad to assist American citizens apprehended under the laws of a particular country are explained. These pamphlets, as well as a single-sheet condensation, have been widely distributed at passport offices, travel bureaus, airline offices, and American colleges.

The Credibility Gap

The information and explanations given out to the American public by the State Department derive from policies and actions emanating from the top leadership—often the President's. The Department's task is unenviable when the public distrusts that leadership. Then there is a wide credibility gap. Sometimes the Department's difficulties are compounded by the way the press selects, and plays up or plays down, the news. Criticism is, unfortunately, more newsworthy than stories of positive achievement.

---

* American citizens detained abroad on narcotics charges (not including U.S. military personnel held under U.S. military detention) as of:

April, 1969—153
     1970—522
     1971—711
     1972—919
     1973—1,084
     1974—1,013

A good example of that occurred during the India-Pakistan war in 1971. At the very time the United States was feeding half the Bangladesh refugees and sending immense quantities of food and supplies to India, a national television "special" stated that the United States was doing nothing to alleviate the suffering. The State Department received a barrage of congressional inquiries demanding that something be done for the refugees at a time when the United States was in fact doing more than any other country in the world. This misconception was not the result of the government's withholding information—the State Department had issued a series of situation reports about the relief effort that were distributed to approximately 5,000 newspapers and radio and television stations.

The Press Office is responsible for assuring that the government —all the agencies and departments and the State Department as a whole—speaks with one voice on foreign affairs. The slow-moving committee system helps avoid some problems of conflicting—or apparently conflicting—statements, but more often, coordination is obtained informally by hand-carrying a proposed news release, speech, communiqué, or statement to the interested bureaus for approval.

The Public Affairs Bureau (in the past) and the Press Office (at present) are the State Department's watchdogs to ensure that the right hand of diplomacy knows what the left hand is doing. Occasionally a lapse does occur and the fur flies inside the Department and in a foreign capital where feelings are hurt. For example, at the conclusion of official talks between Secretary John Foster Dulles and the Foreign Minister of Portugal in Washington on December 2, 1955, a joint communiqué was issued. It mentioned *inter alia* that the two foreign ministers had agreed that high-level Russian "allegations concerning the Portuguese provinces in the Far East" did not serve the cause of peace. The release had not been shown to the Far East or Middle East Bureaus or to the Public Affairs Bureau, then responsible for coordination, which would have pointed out the pitfalls in using the word "provinces." The Indian Government was especially annoyed. The status of Portuguese-held Goa within the subcontinent was a hot issue at that time. (Goa was annexed by India in 1961). The United States had therefore carefully avoided taking sides in the dispute and had never referred to Goa as a Portuguese province. Careless handling of a routine release caused an international incident and later clarifying statements did little to mollify the Indian Government.

Several steps have been taken to try to bring about greater top-level attention and more resources to the psychological factors in foreign policy decision-making. Although this has been a perennial objective of those who have worked in the public affairs field, no satisfactory bureaucratic solutions have yet been found. In the final analysis, the top decision-makers themselves must be sensitive to the impact of their decisions domestically and globally. Toward this end, the Secretary of State generally confers daily with his press relations people and also meets frequently with the assistant secretary for Public Affairs to consult "on the public affairs and information aspects of the Department's responsibilities—except for news policy . . . and press relations." The P Bureau has also developed an annual Department-wide public affairs planning procedure to project the requirements of each bureau for information programs and other public affairs activities. This usefully focuses the attention of the leaders of each bureau, as well as the Secretary and his deputies, on public affairs planning.

Another innovation was the formation, early in 1971, of an Interdepartmental Group on Foreign Policy Information, chaired by the assistant secretary for Public Affairs. This group is not part of the National Security Council system, but it performs similar functions by attempting to coordinate the information efforts of all federal departments and agencies that are concerned in any way with foreign policy. Its accomplishments have not been spectacular, but the habit of consulting on mutual problems undoubtedly has its benefits, and some useful coordinating mechanisms have been adopted. For example, a clearinghouse has been established through which agencies notify each other of high-priority topics or information themes that might be worthy of interagency support.

The P Bureau has also expanded and improved its information services on U.S. public opinion as it relates to foreign affairs. Its reports of public opinion polls, on editorial comment from the press and other media, and the periodical *Current Magazine Comment* are widely distributed within the Department and to missions abroad.

Finally, the P Bureau, working closely with the public affairs advisers (PAAs) in each bureau, is responsible for policy guidance to and coordination with the U.S. Information Agency (USIA), whose programs are directed to foreign audiences. The daily press briefing at noon is, of course, the principal channel for representatives of the Voice of America and of the USIA Press Division to get State Department reports on foreign policy developments for use in their radio and news services. USIA policy guidance officers also meet with the PAA's and with representatives of the P Bureau every morning for further background information.

CONGRESSIONAL WARINESS

The expansion of public affairs programs has been limited because of congressional suspicion that the Department's public explanation of controversial policies was influencing the voters to pressure their congressmen. Thus, the Department's role was seen as a partisan one, an intention invariably denied by State, although the timing and content of specific examples, such as advocacy of economic assistance programs, sometimes tended to support the congressional contention.

The Department of State has, however, successfully held that it has the duty to explain and advocate the President's foreign policies, just as other departments with large constituencies, Defense or Agriculture, for example, do, without Congress's objection.

Appropriation bills for the past twenty-five years have prohibited the use of State Department funds for "publicity and propaganda purposes," but neither Congress nor the Administration can readily distinguish information from propaganda. Congressional opponents of controversial Administration policies invariably argue that Department publications and speeches fall into the latter category, while unbiased observers maintain that the Department should reasonably be permitted to explain its policies to the public, whether or not those policies are controversial. Congress has not seriously pressed its strictures against the Department's publicity and has resorted instead to limiting the size of congressional appropriations for information activities aimed at domestic audiences.*

PUBLIC INFLUENCES ON AMERICAN FOREIGN POLICY

This chapter would be incomplete without a word about the efforts of numerous nongovernmental organizations, pressure groups, and individuals to influence the State Department. A relatively new form of such activity has developed out of the mass demonstrations that took place in Washington in recent years, usually in connection with the war in Vietnam. On such occasions, organizations frequently sent delegations to present their views at the State Department. In the spring of 1970, for example, when the President announced the movement of U.S. troops into Cambodia, the P Bureau set up special round-the-clock facilities to arrange for the steady stream of delegations to meet with some of the highest-ranking Department officials. A series of such group visits by concerned, articulate Americans is bound to make an impression on policy-makers, even if their immediate reaction is the standard bureaucratic cliché: "Thank you for coming. We shall certainly take your views into consideration."

Letter-writing campaigns, organized by groups such as ethnic, political, or religious organizations; invitations to Department officers to talk and engage in discussions; hospitality to individual officials by prestigious partisans of specific policies; and requests

---

* A similar congressional sensitivity accounts for legislation barring the dissemination in the United States of USIA productions. Members of Congress, journalists, research students, and scholars may have access to these materials, but this exception required tightening up after Senator James Buckley showed USIA's film about the 1968 invasion of Czechoslovakia on television. Senator William Fulbright and the Foreign Relations Committee objected, and there was a major flap. Amending legislation was finally passed, making it clear that USIA information materials furnished to members of Congress on request are for examination only and not for further dissemination.

for meetings and conferences in the Department by special interest groups, are more normal pressure techniques. Many of these same organizations—labor unions, business concerns, and so on—carry on massive lobbying activities among the members of Congress, supporting or opposing legislation in which they are interested. When the legislation has to do with foreign policy or tariffs, the State Department is also concerned.

Domestic influences on foreign relations have always been a factor in the foreign policy process, but modern communications, increased trade, the Vietnam war, the Arab-Israeli conflict, have meant that special-interest groups now have greater impact than ever. In recognition of this, the State Department maintains contact with domestic interests of all sorts. The various geographic bureaus are concerned with political and ethnic organizations; for example, a Polish anti-Communist group that opposes imports of Polish ham, a Rumanian group protesting an American rubber company's investment in Rumania, or Zionist groups urging the sale of military aircraft to Israel. Domestic race relations also spill over into foreign affairs, because black groups tend to keep their eye on American actions in such countries as South Africa. In 1967, for example, they caused an American aircraft carrier to cancel a fuel stop in Capetown after it became known that the South African Government had stipulated that the crew could go ashore only in segregated groups.

Economic interest groups, including business firms, are among the most active in pressing their case for protection against foreign competition, especially through import duties and quotas favorable to specific commodities. The State Department must try to achieve the right mix of domestic and foreign interests, and the Bureau of Economic and Business Affairs bears much of the brunt of the outside pressures in this area.

Organized labor is a fairly new arrival in the ranks of pressure groups active in foreign affairs. In the Department, these interests have been recognized by the creation of the position of special assistant to the Secretary of State for Labor Affairs. Besides lobbying for legislation, labor can influence diplomatic negotiations when its interests—mainly jobs for American workers—are affected by competition from abroad. Its influence can be seen in many of the terms set in trade agreements.

The activities of pressure groups in behalf of their special interests make complicated, fascinating, and sometimes horrifying stories. They may involve Congress, the White House, the State Department, and many other departments. More often than not, however, the conflicting interests that are presenting their points of view are completely legitimate and State's attention to them is important. It is, of course, the Department's responsibility to see that these special interests are put in perspective against the broader aims and goals of the United States in its relations with other countries—and to see that this perspective is then adequately presented to the press and the American public.

IX

Multilateral Diplomacy

International relations has traditionally been based on one nation's dealings with another, and this bilateral approach is still the most common method of dealing with many issues. Many problems today however are multinational—especially in the economic sphere, where the interdependence of nations often makes it necessary for them to act in concert when dealing with trade, investment, agriculture, monetary policy, and balance of payments.

Another factor that draws the United States into international diplomacy is the emergence of a large number of new problems—created by the technological revolution—that are global in scope: problems of pollution, expanding population, terrorism and hijacking, narcotics, and the uses of the ocean's resources and of the seabed. These issues constitute a whole "new dimension of diplomacy" and occupy an increasingly important part of the State Department's attention. The United States looks primarily to the United Nations (U.N.), which is already organized to cope with global matters, for international action to deal with these problems.

THE ROLE OF THE STATE DEPARTMENT

Within the U.S. Government, the responsibility for working with international institutions rests primarily in the State Department's Bureau of International Organization Affairs (IO), whose respon-

193

sibility it is to see that the nation speaks with one voice—no easy task for the Department itself, not to mention speaking for all the other agencies that may be involved, as described in Chapter VI. The Bureau also coordinates the selection of U.S. delegations to the scores of international conferences that are constantly in session—642 in fiscal year 1973. It must see that U.S. positions are prepared in advance and take care of the housekeeping arrangements for the U.S. delegations. When the United States hosts a meeting, such as the General Conference of the Organization of American States in Atlanta in April 1974, the Office of International Conferences of IO is responsible for running it.

The Bureau oversees the activities of the large U.S. Mission to the United Nations in New York, as well as those in the permanent U.N. secretariats at the headquarters of the big specialized agencies —in Rome for the Food and Agriculture Organization (FAO), in Montreal for the International Civil Aviation Organization (ICAO), in Paris for the U.N. Educational, Scientific, and Cultural Organization (UNESCO), in Vienna for the International Atomic Energy Agency (IAEA) and U.N. Industrial Development Organization (UNIDO), and in Geneva for the World Health Organization (WHO), the World Meteorological Organization (WMO), the International Labor Organization (ILO), and the International Telecommunications Union (ITU). The U.N. secretariats carry on the agencies' business in the intervals between annual or biennial conferences, and the U.S. missions there try to make these sprawling international bureaucracies more effective, hard-hitting, and less bogged down in duplication of effort and red tape.

As part of its obligation to present multilateral thinking to the great majority of State Department officials who are accustomed to thinking bilaterally, IO presides over many meetings to iron out the position U.S. delegates should take at international conferences or U.N. meetings. An IO representative then drafts or reviews drafts of these position papers, which are prepared for every item on the conference agenda. The Bureau has considerable influence on these matters, partially, no doubt, because it controls the funds that are appropriated for U.S. contributions to most international organizations. (The major exceptions are the international financial institutions).

Many other sections of State play active roles in international diplomacy when their functional area becomes involved. The Bureau of Economic and Business Affairs (EB) is the Department's focal point for dealing with the main international economic agencies, banks, and development organs—International Bank for Reconstruction and Development, International Development Association, International Finance Corporation, International Monetary Fund, U.N. Industrial Development Organization, U.N. Conference on Trade and Development, General Agreement on Tariffs and Trade, and others. It develops U.S. policy and represents the nation in international meetings. When a government agency other than State (Commerce, on trade and tariff matters, or Treasury, on monetary and balance-of-payment problems) represents the United States at international meetings or conferences, the Department's bureaus play a strong supporting role, usually furnishing the deputy delegate on the U.S. delegation and technical advisers.

The Bureau of International Scientific and Technological Affairs (SCI), absorbed into the new Bureau of Oceans and International Environmental and Scientific Affairs (OES) in 1974, has played much the same role in international diplomacy that EB does in its field; it represents State in its relations with the extensive official and unofficial scientific community in the United States and with international organizations and U.N. agencies. (These include numerous elements of the U.N. family, its specialized agencies, and several regional organizations, such as the North Atlantic Treaty Organization's (NATO's) Committee on the Challenges of Modern Society, which provides a regional approach to pollution problems.) The Bureau is engaged in many bilateral activities dealing with problems of the environment, outer space, and atomic energy and has taken the lead, along with the Legal Adviser's Office (L), in negotiating treaties with Germany and Japan to stimulate joint research in these areas. The U.S. delegation to the 1972 Stockholm Conference on the Human Environment illustrates well the kind of teamwork that is required: the leader was the head of the President's Council for Environmental Quality, the vice-chairman was from SCI, and other members represented IO and the Secretary of State's Advisory Committee on the Human Environment.

Successful international diplomacy frequently results in an international treaty that becomes part of the framework of international law. The State Department's legal adviser and his office are active in this process, from drafting to negotiating.

The various special assistants to the Secretary—for International Narcotics, Combating Terrorism, Refugees and Migration, and International Labor—are mainly coordinating officers. They do, however, sometimes directly participate in international planning and negotiating at international conferences.

The geographic bureaus, through their regional and functional offices and their special assistants and advisers, tie the bureaus into the United Nations and other multilateral organizations. This type of cooperation is mutually useful. It is important, for example, for the man in charge of U.S. relations with Brazil to be in on plans for expanding a U.N. population control program in that country; and the area man's background in the region is indispensable to the functional man's expertise.

The Agency for International Development (AID) coordinates its bilateral economic assistance programs with the multilateral programs of the U.N. Development Program and other U.N. agencies. It also contributes, through IO, to various U.N. enterprises such as the Population Fund.

The Arms Control and Disarmament Agency, a main channel for international negotiation, besides participating in bilateral talks, also handles a lot of regional work (for example, with NATO on the question of European force withdrawals) and multilateral agreements (for example, with the U.N. Conference of the Committee on Disarmament on chemical and bacteriological weapons, a comprehensive test ban, and nuclear free zones).

The United Nations

The United States fathered the United Nations as World War II was ending, in the hope of preserving world peace through international cooperation. However, because no power, including the United States, has been willing to relinquish enough national sovereignty to allow the world body to make decisions affecting its own national security, the United Nations can take effective action only when all the major nations agree. The United States has supported several successful U.N. actions in the name of collective security—in Korea, the Congo, Cyprus, the Middle East—but it has been reluctant to refer to the international body the kind of disputes that would get bogged down by predictable Security Council vetoes. The United Nations had little, if anything, to do with the Berlin problem, for example, or with problems in Vietnam, Czechoslovakia, or Nigeria. And in 1971, when the Security Council took up the India-Pakistan war, a Soviet veto kept the United Nations powerless to act until *after* the issue had been settled on the battlefield.

Its weaknesses in the peacekeeping area, however, should not blind one to the important work of the United Nations and its associated agencies in other areas of international collaboration. The seating of the People's Republic of China and of the two Germanies, with the prospect of further widening membership, means that the United Nations will at long last represent all the centers of power and influence in the world. And besides helping to prevent serious conflicts in areas where the great powers are not involved, the United Nations is engaged in many highly useful programs: assistance to the economic and social development of the low-income countries (utilizing about 80 per cent of U.N. resources); the sharing of scientific and technological information; the support of international disarmament arrangements; and the extension of international law and protection of human rights. The very existence of the United Nations as an international forum is an asset that can increasingly be used to attack some of the problems that beset the world.

The dramatic increase in U.N. membership—from 51 to 135 nations during its relatively short life span, with most of the new members joining within the last decade—has significantly changed the way the organization functions. The smallest nations each have their vote in the General Assembly, and they tend more and more to vote as blocs, sometimes from a geographic region such as Latin America or Africa, or in larger categories. Some ninety-five countries can be classed as developing nations and these, acting together, constitute over two-thirds of the membership. Another grouping of seventy-five states, overlapping with the developing nations, is known as the nonaligned group, and they have shown that they can organize themselves for concerted action. One result of this trend has been to reduce the ability of the great powers, especially the United States, to dominate the United Nations, which is probably all to the good. On the other hand, there is the unfortunate tendency of the smaller nations to use their majority position irresponsibly by pushing through unenforceable or impractical resolutions in an unrealistic attempt to seek total solutions to complicated problems. As the American representative pointed out during the 1973 General Assembly, "marshalling majorities behind unenforceable resolutions is a meaningless activity" and one that "if it continues, could seriously weaken the United Nations potential as an instrument of international cooperation." It was not particularly encouraging to note that actions of the special session of the General Assembly early in 1974 on problems of the less developed countries were largely limited to resolutions of this very kind.

Focus on Development

The increased ratio of developing countries to total membership has had one very important and salutary effect on U.N economic activities. Whereas the group formerly focused on such matters as the negotiation of international conventions on radio frequencies, air routes, and inoculation cards, it now centers its attention on economic development and on closing the gap between the rich and the poor nations of the globe—particularly on multinational economic assistance, especially technical assistance; preinvestment surveys; and capital development loans through the World Bank and regional banks. The U.N. Development Program, with a total 1974 budget, excluding the international banks, of $800 million, now operates the largest technical assistance program in the world.

The United States took the lead in getting the General Assembly to launch the first U.N. Development Decade on January 1, 1961. Although little progress had been made by the mid-1960's toward stimulating the rate of growth of the developing countries, a concerted effort was launched to meet the growth rate target and to develop a strategy for the second Development Decade of the 1970's. By the end of 1970, a comprehensive program of co-operative measures, embracing economic and social factors, had been agreed upon. This was built around the goal of increasing by at least 6 per cent the annual growth of the gross national product (GNP) of the developing countries as a whole. The U.S. delegation endorsed the strategy—despite never being able to commit the U.S. Government to the target to contribute 1 per cent of its GNP annually to assist developing nations—including the provisions calling for periodic appraisal of progress in order to identify and correct weaknesses. Nevertheless, there are no very optimistic indications that this or any other program has found out how to keep the poor from getting poorer or the rich from getting richer. In its 1971–72 *Commodity Review and Outlook* FAO estimates that the poor countries will have a difficult time reaching halfway to their 1980 goals in agricultural exports (their chief money earner).

American development assistance to individual countries and to U.N. institutions that help them, such as the World Bank Group, is carried out, as far as possible, within a framework set up by the international institutions. This policy has recently met serious opposition in Congress, which has drastically cut U.S. bilateral aid and delayed for long periods the appropriation of U.S. funds for international institutions. Since the United States has been furnishing over 30 per cent of the United Nations' regular budget and around 40 per cent of the voluntary development funds, the uncertainty and delays in obtaining U.S. contributions have seriously impaired important programs affecting many countries—ironically, many of the activities this nation has taken the lead in supporting—peacekeeping, disarmament, problems of the environment, overpopulation, unemployment, use of the seabed, and so on. Far from furnishing 1 per cent of its GNP to help developing countries, the

United States in recent years has contributed less than half of 1 per cent.

Political and Organizational Matters

In recent years, the United States has tried to work for improvements in the efficiency of the U.N. system. In 1971, it participated actively in the work of a Special Committee on Rationalization of the Procedures and Organization of the General Assembly, proposing important reforms to streamline and shorten sessions and improve procedures. Some recommendations were adopted, but these stopped far short of the kind of reforms U.S. spokesmen believe are urgently required. Similarly, no real progress has been made toward liquidating the United Nations' financial deficit of $172 million created by the refusal of several countries to pay their assessed contributions to the U.N. peacekeeping operations in the Congo and Middle East. No more than $35 million in voluntary contributions had been pledged as of the end of 1973.

This situation has long pointed up the need for agreed rules for conducting and financing peacekeeping missions. The lack of such rules has meant that the United Nations has had to improvise at the last minute when faced with emergencies. Essentially the difficulty is that the Russians have been unwilling to give the Secretary General any semblance of operational authority, insisting that the permanent members of the Security Council can intervene in detailed operations through their veto power. The United States has not agreed. Hopes were raised that the impasse might be broken after October 1973 when the United States and the Soviet Union agreed on a new U.N. peacekeeping force in the Middle East. But this turned out to be just another *ad hoc* arrangement, and subsequent concessions offered by the United States at the 1973 U.N. General Assembly failed to produce any progress.

In line with a recommendation of the President's Commission for the Observance of the Twenty-fifth Anniversary of the United Nations (the Lodge Commission), as well as congressional attitudes, the United States Mission to the United Nations in New York has pressed for some time for gradual reduction of its annual assessment from over 30 per cent to 25 per cent of the total U.N. budget. The difference in funds would be made up from the contributions of new or expected members like West and East Germany. The 1972 General Assembly approved the U.S. draft resolution that, in effect, established as a guideline for the Committee on Contributions the principle that no member should pay over 25 per cent of the budget, and the Committee's 1974–76 assessments, reflecting this principle, were approved by the 1973 General Assembly. Although there is no *quid pro quo,* it is generally expected that the United States will continue to furnish up to 40 per cent or more of the voluntary contributions on which the United Nations' specialized agencies are heavily dependent.

U.S. efforts since 1969 towards creation of a new associate membership status for microstates that lack the resources to carry out the normal obligations of regular membership have gotten nowhere. Despite the logic of the U.S. proposal, it has not received much support because no sovereign nation wishes publicly to admit that it cannot afford to maintain the privileges of full membership.

The State Department, specifically IO and the U.S. Mission to the United Nations, spends a great deal of time and effort working on so-called damage-limiting questions—problems that cannot be solved and where the best position is the one that damages the United States least. These have increased in number since 1960, when African problems began to loom large. On fundamental principles the United States generally is sympathetic with the goals of the black Africans who have sought self-determination in Rhodesia and in South Africa, and independence for the Portuguese colonies. Yet the United States cannot vote for highly charged U.N. resolutions that condemn one party in a dispute before all the facts have come to light. On Portuguese colonial issues, for example, the U.S. position has been strongly influenced by security considerations connected with Portugal's membership in NATO and the agreement with that nation for the use of military bases in the Azores.

One of the most difficult American actions to defend is the passage of the Byrd Amendment, which exempts chrome and other strategic materials from the United Nations' list of forbidden imports from Rhodesia. This action resulted, on November 16, 1971, in a General Assembly resolution calling on the United States to comply with the Security Council's sanctions against such imports. State Department attempts to get the Byrd Amendment repealed have failed.

In the Trusteeship Council, the United States must defend its policies governing its administration of trust territories and U.S. territories, such as the Virgin Islands, Guam, and Samoa. Strong criticism from those U.N. nations advocating immediate independence for everyone has been a factor in our negotiations with the representatives of Micronesia over the future political status of that trust territory, which the United States has administered since 1945. The General Assembly's Committee on Colonialism, though not responsible for these Pacific islands, which have been declared a strategic area by the U.N. Security Council, has nevertheless been very critical of the United States for not yet terminating the trusteeship agreement. Negotiations with the islands under a Presidentially appointed delegation, coordinated by IO, with representatives of the departments of Interior and Defense also participating, have been taking place off and on since 1971, but progress to 1974 has been slow.*

GLOBAL PROBLEMS—NEW DIMENSIONS

As the Secretary of State foresaw in his 1969–1970 foreign policy report: "Just as the priority of the United Nations was directed in the 1950's to peacekeeping and in the 1960's to the drive for economic development, we believe that in the 1970's a third basic U.N. priority should be added—the enhancement of the quality of human life." This wide field embraces complex technological and social problems, like the protection of the environment, that are too broad to be handled by one nation or by any one specialized agency of the United Nations and call instead for coordi-

* At least partial success was achieved in 1975 when agreement was reached on a new commonwealth status for part of the Trust Territory, the Mariana Islands.

nated efforts of several countries and several agencies or the creation of entirely new international entities.

Environment

Recognizing the seriousness and global extent of the problem of pollution, the United States and the State Department have been pressing for improved international cooperation and organization to deal with the issue. The Office of Environmental Affairs was established in SCI (later OES) to advance the international program, and a great deal of bilateral cooperation with individual countries has been started, both to deal with common problems, like the U.S.–Canadian negotiations to combat pollution on the Great Lakes, and to share common experiences and expertise. Many national agencies are involved, including the Environmental Protection Agency, Department of Agriculture, Smithsonian Institution, and AID. On a U.S. recommendation, the North Atlantic Treaty Organization (NATO) established in 1969 a Committee on the Challenges of Modern Society, which in less than four years has taken on thirteen projects to protect the environment. A resolution adopted in 1970 initiated action that may lead to outlawing international discharges of oil into the oceans by 1975. An international conference on marine pollution that met in London in the fall of 1973 had this matter high on its agenda. Joint studies on air pollution produced NATO agreements that will serve as a basis for national laws. Solar and geothermal energy studies, proposed by the United States in October 1973, will be coordinated among several NATO countries.

The international programs as a result of the Stockholm conference of 1972 are handled through the U.N. Environment Program with its own Governing Council and Secretariat. This is a recent and important development and one in which U.S. initiatives played a leading part. Therefore some background on how it came about may be of interest.

In general, the industrialized countries are understandably the first to be concerned about environmental problems. Although some developing countries have shown an interest in protecting their environment, others tend to fear that such action may be at the expense of their economic gains. In any case, the need for a full-scale international conference to discuss these problems and to approve plans and future actions in the environmental field became evident several years ago. In 1969, the General Assembly accepted Sweden's invitation to hold a U.N. Conference on the Human Environment in Stockholm in June, 1972. The United States pledged its support—the burden of the preparations and of the later negotiations was borne by IO and SCI in the State Department, with fourteen other agencies participating—and preparatory work began early in 1970.

The timetable of development of one of the most significant decisions of the conference illustrates beautifully multilateral diplomacy at a major international meeting as engineered by State Department representatives:

Autumn, 1969. The General Assembly accepts Sweden's invitation to hold the Conference in Stockholm in June 1972 and establishes a 27-nation preparatory committee.

Early 1970. The United States creates a task force representing fifteen U.S. agencies, chaired by Christian A. Herter, Jr., director of the Department's Office of Environmental Affairs within the SCI Bureau, to prepare the American positions for the conference. For the next two years, this group meets every two weeks.

Spring, 1970. The U.N. Preparatory Committee agrees on the main subjects to be discussed at the conference, the rules, the type of conference (action-oriented), and other guidelines. The United States is represented on the committee by a 2-man delegation led by Herter.

July, 1970. The Economic and Social Council (ECOSOC) approves the committee's recommendations.

November, 1970. Maurice Strong of Canada is appointed Secretary General of the Conference and meets with the preparatory committee.

November 27, 1970. The General Assembly's so-called Second Committee adopts a resolution recommending that the preparatory committee consider special financing to ensure that development programs in developing countries will not be adversely affected by environmental measures.

February–September, 1971. Under the auspices of the preparatory committee, action papers on the major subject areas are prepared by the Conference secretariat and by special intergovernmental working groups.

November–December, 1971. The Second Committee adopts a resolution specifying that action plans to protect the environment must not impede development and indicating that the developed countries are responsible for financing corrective measures.

1970–71. The U.S. task force agrees that a newly created structure will be needed to coordinate the numerous U.N. agencies that will have to carry out the programs decided on at the conference. The IO representative, and vice chairman of the task force, John W. McDonald, Jr., argues that the coordinating agency should not be financed through the U.N. Development Program (UNDP), which focuses on technical assistance for the developing countries, because that agency is not really interested in environmental problems that mainly affect the industrialized nations. He urges the United States to strongly advocate global handling of these problems, with consideration for the interest of both underdeveloped and developed nations.

March, 1971. It is proposed in the task force that the United States delegation at Stockholm advocate the creation of a 5-year fund of $100 million—with specific suggestions as to how the fund should spend its money—operating on the principle that the major polluters shall be the major contributors. The whole package is then presented to the President's Office of Management and Budget, which agrees to recommend it to the President.

February 8, 1972. The President sends a message on the environment to Congress in which he proposes this 100 million-dollar U.N. Fund with the United States putting up $40 million over a 5-year period on a matching basis.

March, 1972. In the preparatory committee Herter presents a draft resolution to be made formally at Stockholm to create: (a) the Fund; (b) a semi-autonomous secretariat to manage the Fund and carry out policies, whose projects would be executed by the specialized agencies, universities, and corporations; (c) an intergovernmental body to define policy; and (d) an environmental coordinating board from the U.N. specialized agencies, chaired by the head of the Fund, to see that the whole action is coordinated. This is the beginning of a battle that lasts throughout the Conference itself three months later, with the developing countries arguing for new programs dealing with the environment to be national projects funded by the UNDP.

June, 1972. The conference begins with four resolutions, proposed by the United States, Brazil, Sweden, and Kenya, on how to implement programs agreed on at the Conference. Representatives of these meet and finally accept the U.S. approach, producing a single text with many disagreed sections in brackets.

During the next five days, meetings are held with representatives of the twenty-six nations most interested in the subject to explain the draft and get their points of view. A 7-nation drafting group produces a new version, taking into account all the comments, and the revised resolution is formally submitted to the Conference for 114 delegates to consider. Delegates having proposals to make are invited to join a working group, which adds fifty amendments to the draft. For two days, the Conference Committee of the Whole discusses the proposed amendments and votes on them, paragraph by paragraph. An agreed text of the resolution is ready at last.

The plenary session takes up the resolution the day before the Conference ends, with twenty nations urging unanimous adoption of the resolution. Then Algeria proposes a major amendment, raising once more the issue of putting the fund under the UNDP. The Brazilian delegate, in an act of true statesmanship, indicates that his country is in general agreement with Algeria but points out that the resolution before the conference is the result of compromises laboriously worked out over many weeks; he urges Algeria to withdraw the amendment. Confronted with such a conciliatory attitude on the part of one of the proponents of the four original drafts, Algeria withdraws its amendment, and the resolution is adopted by acclamation.

The final resolution adopted by the Stockholm conference has retained all four major points of the U.S. draft. Before the conference breaks up, $65 million of the $100 million needed for the Fund has been pledged—$40 million by the United States—and a dozen other countries state that they will contribute.

The 1972 General Assembly approved the declaration of principles and the action plan recommended by the conference, which contained 109 recommendations for actions to be undertaken by the U.N. Environment Program, including an Earthwatch Program with a global plan to monitor levels of pollution around the world and an Information Referral System. It voted to establish a highly professional environment secretariat with Maurice Strong as Executive Director, created a governing council, and established the 5-year Fund to finance the program.

As of the spring of 1974, participating countries had pledged to the Fund over $105 million, including the $40 million pledged by the United States, and the Governing Council had held two annual meetings in March 1973 at Geneva and in March 1974 at the new headquarters in Nairobi.

Population

The United States continues to strengthen and stimulate its own and international programs to control the world's population explosion, among them the U.N. Fund for Population Activities (UNFPA), which is the central funding and coordinating mechanism for population programs sponsored by U.N. agencies. Through AID, the principal U.S. agency in this field, the United States has contributed over $500 million to population programs from fiscal years 1965–73, including about $60 million to the UNFPA, whose other donors contributed a similar amount. Programs in over eighty developing countries have been assisted. American contributions, which increased from $2 million in 1965 to over $125 million in 1973, are now expected to level off along with most other AID-financed projects.

A World Population Conference was scheduled to take place in Bucharest in August, 1974, as the high point in the 1974 World Population Year, with over 100 nations expected to send delegations and to hold discussions on the problems of development, including the consequences of continued high population growth rates. Focusing attention on these problems will, it is hoped, stimulate individual countries to cooperate in population programs.

Narcotics

Since the illicit drugs that flow into the United States are produced abroad and shipped into the country illegally, the government has been increasing its efforts to reduce production and curb drug traffic. In fact, these efforts have become a major objective of American diplomacy, and the Department of State and U.S. embassies abroad have been reorganized to cope more effectively with these problems. Narcotics control coordinators have been placed in the bureaus, and a senior coordinator acts as adviser to the Secretary of State. Interdepartmental committees at the bureau and Cabinet level (the latter chaired by the Secretary) have also been established, and drug control officers have been designated at most embassies abroad.

A major campaign was launched through the embassies to negotiate bilateral narcotics-control action programs with more than fifty countries, including Canada, Mexico, France, Turkey, Thailand, and Laos, with the short-term goal of controlling illicit drug traffic and the long-term goal of eliminating illicit production. Although progress has been made, the problem seems impossible to solve, even with full cooperation of other governments, as long as the demand for the product continues. The story of the poppy-growing ban in Turkey is a case in point. Because of an oversupply in the world, smugglers have no difficulty obtaining opium from other sources, such as those in Southeast Asia, where effective controls are most difficult to enforce. Bilateral agreements with Thailand and Laos represent only a start in what will be a continuing effort. Cooperation among the United States, France, and Canada and between the United States and Mexico has paid off in important seizures of illegal narcotics shipments and the destruction of heroin conversion laboratories in France. In fact, three times as much heroin was seized at U.S. borders in 1971 as in 1970, although the total amount (1,541 pounds) was a small fraction of the 6 to 10 tons consumed yearly in the United States. In 1972 seizures were twice those of 1971.

The bilateral action programs mentioned above are prepared in advance by a complicated coordinated effort on the American side. For example, country X produces poppies whose opium gets into the U.S. market. The Regional Interagency Narcotics Control Committee for Near Eastern and South Asian Affairs exchanges telegrams with the U.S. embassy in X, and it is decided that a country narcotics control action plan is needed. The embassy country team proposes a strategy, action plan, and allocation of resources, which is then examined by the regional committee. This committee, chaired by the State Department's deputy assistant secretary or regional affairs officer for Near Eastern and South Asian Affairs and with representatives from such agencies as Justice, Treasury, Agriculture, CIA, AID, and Defense, meets every two weeks. At the second meeting on the plan for X, the U.S. Customs Service representative points out that there is no provision for exchange of information between the customs services of the United States and X. This valid criticism leads to correction. Issue by issue, the paper is discussed, and finally the plan is approved. It is then referred back to the embassy in X; the country team refines it still further and informally consults the host government and experts from Washington on matters of law enforcement, agriculture, and intelligence. The regional committee gives its final approval; the government of X agrees after brief negotiations; and the program, which involves unilateral, bilateral, and multilateral action, goes into effect.

The United States has worked through the 30-nation U.N. Commission on Narcotic Drugs for improved multilateral cooperation, and as a result, the 1970 General Assembly adopted a worldwide program designed to reduce the demand for and supply of dangerous drugs. This was to be carried out by the competent U.N. bodies and financed by a new Fund for Drug Abuse Control, which was established in 1971, with a program for drug-abuse control in Thailand one of its first projects. The United States had contributed $10 million of the $12.4 million in the Fund as of May 1974.

A March 1972 U.N. conference at Geneva, attended by ninety-seven nations, adopted amendments to the Single Convention of 1961 on Narcotic Drugs that considerably strengthened the international narcotics control system. The State Department, whose senior adviser on Narcotics Matters, at that time, headed the U.S. delegation, assisted by representatives of five other agencies, had drafted the proposed amendments and then organized a big diplomatic offensive to gain wide support for them before the conference. This was done by enlisting the help of U.S. ambassadors in the field, in various regional organizations like the Organization of American States, and at the United Nations. When the Conference convened, there were thirty cosponsors and no opponents.

The United States also has a responsibility toward American drugs—mainly psychotropic substances such as LSD and other hallucinogens, barbituates, and tranquilizers—that are smuggled out of the country. There was no international instrument for their control until a Convention on Psychotropic Substances was signed in Vienna in February, 1971. When ratified, the new convention will close an important gap in the drug-control convention of 1961.

Although these bilateral and multilateral efforts to control drug traffic and reduce production will not solve the problem of drug addiction, they can help moderate the problem and perhaps reduce it to more manageable proportions.

The Seabed and the Oceans

It has been increasingly apparent that changing technology requires changes in the law of the sea. The ability to exploit valuable resources at great depths under the sea and in the seabed has created new opportunities and new conflicts over claims. Coastal states tend to claim jurisdiction farther and farther from their shores. By 1971, only twenty-six countries still adhered to the 3-mile limit. And nations attempting to protect their environment from marine pollution, as in the case of Canada, or from distant-water fishermen, as in the case of Peru and Ecuador, run into conflict with other states that are concerned with free movement of commercial and naval ships, fishing rights, or marine research. Conferences in 1958 and 1960 on these subjects were unsuccessful, largely because they did not deal with the problems as essentially political issues, although a country's control of its resources is really just that.

The situation has continued to deteriorate; Egypt closed the Straits of Aqaba; more countries have unilaterally extended their territorial waters; and more American fishing boats have been seized on the high seas. The United Nations' special seabed committee wrestled with some of these problems for several years, and the same problems were debated within the U.S. Government, where many different interests presented conflicting views. Finally, in May 1970, the President made a definitive U.S. oceans policy statement in which he warned that, unless the basic issues were resolved, "unilateral action and international conflict were inevitable." He therefore proposed a treaty under which all nations would renounce claim to natural resources in the deep seabed off their coasts; an international body would control exploitation of these resources for international benefit and especially for the developing countries. The President also proposed a new law-of-the-sea treaty "to assure unfettered and harmonious use of the oceans as an avenue of commercial transportation and as a source of food." The 1970 General Assembly called for a Law of the Sea Conference in 1973 and expanded the seabed committee to prepare the draft treaty articles. The United States submitted detailed proposals based on the oceans policy statement (a) regarding the deep seabed, (b) for a 12-mile territorial sea and (because this would automatically close 116 international straits) free transit through and over international straits, and (c) for certain fishing preferences for coastal states.

A U.S. interdepartmental task force led by State but also including representatives from the departments of Interior, Commerce, and Defense, develops U.S. policies and positions for the delegations to the seabed committee and to the Conference. State often plays the role of mediator among conflicting interests in the task force, as it tries to keep the focus on the broad national interest—sometimes a difficult task. Oil and coastal fisheries interests, for example, might favor a 200-mile-wide fixed zone of territorial waters barred to foreign exploitation, whereas the U.S. Navy and distant-water fishing interests would prefer to retain the old 3-mile limit, because of their interest in maximum freedom of movement on the high seas. It is the State Department's job to balance these conflicting interests and mesh them into a national policy that will be negotiable in the discussions with other countries.

Top-level policy decisions on law-of-the-sea matters are handled through the National Security Council's Under Secretaries' Committee, chaired by the deputy secretary of State, assisted by a special interagency office, established September 10, 1973, which to all intents and purposes is the Task Force. A former legal adviser of the Department was the President's special representative for the Law of the Sea Conference, and the Department's former counselor on international law was chairman of the Task Force. The Staff Director is from IO.

The U.N. Seabed Committee's meetings for over three years prior to the Conference helped clarify the issues but left many undecided. Most of the important coastal states, for example, have been unwilling to extend the right of free transit through straits that lie within the 12-mile limit, and the countries that claim

100 or 200 miles of territorial waters still insist on controlling "exclusive economic zones" of similar size.

A preliminary (procedural) session of the Law of the Sea Conference was held in New York in December, 1973, the main conference being scheduled for Caracas in June, 1974. Pessimists could find many reasons to be skeptical of the results of the conference but the consequences of failure this time would be so serious that many of those who were closest to the problem believed the international community must find rational solutions rather than leave 71 per cent of the earth's surface open to unregulated national rivalries and hence to dangerous conflicts.

The Department's responsibilities in guiding U.S. initiatives before and during the crucial conference were considerable, and they also extended to many bilateral problems involving the oceans. Within the Department, the geographic bureaus are likely to carry the ball in developing policies and dealing with individual countries, through appropriate U.S. embassies. For example, in the Bureau of Inter-American Affairs (ARA), the then desk officer in charge of Ecuadorian affairs, Rozanne Ridgway, had spent so much time dealing with periodic seizures of U.S. fishing boats by the Ecuadorian Navy that she became the Department's leading expert on the West Coast fisheries problem. Her expertise was recognized in September, 1972, when she became deputy director of ARA's Office of Policy, Planning, and Coordination, prior to a field assignment.

Terrorism and Hijacking

The international community faces mounting acts of terrorism, hijacking of airplanes, kidnapping and assassination of diplomats, and bomb threats to diplomatic missions. The United States has supported international conventions establishing rules of law for hijacking and similar criminal acts (Tokyo, 1963, the Hague, 1970, and Montreal, 1971) and in 1972 took initiatives to press for stronger enforcement of the rules against air piracy and terrorism. Following the terrorism at the 1972 Olympic Games in Munich, the State Department launched a major diplomatic drive toward more effective international action. The timetable below illustrates how the U.S. Government, under State Department leadership, prods and needles American agencies and international organizations to move ahead on this front.

September 6–7, 1972. The Secretary of State calls fifty foreign ambassadors into the Department to discuss collective action against terrorism.

September 6. He goes before the ICAO subcommittee meeting in Washington to urge prompt drafting of a new treaty to deny air services to countries failing to prosecute or extradite hijackers and saboteurs.

September 7. The Secretary appoints Deputy Secretary of State John Irwin to coordinate antiterrorist actions within the Department. Two committees—for international actions and for protection of foreigners in the United States—are established under high-level officers.

September 9. Via U.S. embassies abroad the Secretary sends a personal letter informing other governments that this nation is beginning consultations on problems of terrorism and will welcome suggestions. He urges support for the three aviation conventions.

September 13. Through the same channel, the Secretary informs foreign governments he will stress terrorism in his annual speech to the U.N. General Assembly.

September 14. He writes the U.N. Secretary General welcoming his initiative in including the subject on the General Assembly agenda.

September 25. In his speech to the United Nations, the Secretary urges early concerted action on treaties (a) to enforce earlier hijacking conventions, (b) to establish sanctions against governments that fail to comply, and (c) to prosecute or extradite kidnappers of diplomats and terrorists blackmailing civilians.

September. U.S. delegations to the Interpol general assembly in Frankfurt and to the Interparliamentary Union in Rome obtain resolutions pledging cooperation against terrorism.

September. The State Department presses Congress for action to implement the hijacking conventions.

October 2. The Secretary chairs the first meeting of a Cabinet committee (created September 25) to develop and coordinate actions against international terrorism.

October 3. The Senate approves the Montreal Sabotage Convention.

Despite actions of this kind, however, results are discouraging. When the General Assembly considered the terrorism issue in the fall of 1972, a tough U.S.-sponsored resolution was sidetracked by the Arab and African delegates, whose innocuous resolution—calling for a committee to consider the comments of states on the problem of terrorism and to report on its findings to the 1973 General Assembly—was adopted after weeks of debate. Its report a year later was deferred for the consideration of the 1974 General Assembly.

The absence of international agreement on how to handle terrorism is evident in many areas and can only encourage extremist groups. The highly emotional Arab-Israeli issue has affected some governments' attitudes toward nationalist saboteurs, and it has even been impossible to obtain international agreement on the difference between political activists and ordinary criminals. There is no consensus over meeting ransom demands or on the treatment of captured terrorists. In general, the United States has taken a hard line in these areas, refusing to yield to blackmail demands and urging severe punishment for terrorists.

U.S. efforts against hijacking also suffered a setback in Montreal in January, 1973, when the 58-nation Legal Committee of the ICAO proposed an antihijacking treaty that failed to include the crucial U.S.-supported sanctions against countries that do not sign the treaty or fail to cooperate in international efforts to prevent or punish hijacking. Late in 1972, however, Cuba made unexpected overtures to the United States to negotiate reciprocal arrangements for the handling of hijacked planes and hijackers, which resulted in an agreement signed on February 15, 1973.

The United States has taken several steps to give better protection to its own diplomats abroad and to foreign diplomats in this country. Congress, under strong State Department urging, has expanded federal jurisdiction over crimes against foreign diplomats in this country, and U.S. initiatives at the 1973 U.N. General Assembly helped push through a resolution adopting an international Convention on the Prevention and Punishment of Crimes Against Internationally Protected Persons, including diplomatic agents. This Convention sets up a mechanism for international cooperation to see that perpetrators of attacks against such persons are brought to justice.

Disaster Relief

The United States continues its own support of multilateral and bilateral refugee programs through the Secretary of State's special assistant for Refugee and Migration Affairs. In addition, it works closely with the refugee and relief activities of the United Nations, which, for example, organized the huge relief operations in Bangladesh after the 1971 war there. By the end of November, 1972, nearly $1.1 billion of relief assistance (one-third food grains) had been sent to Bangladesh from all sources, nearly $319 million from the United States. The United States also strongly supports the U.N. Relief and Works Agency for Palestinian Refugees, having contributed since 1950 over half a billion dollars or 64 per cent of the total.

Largely as a result of the succession of national disasters and instances of civil strife requiring emergency relief assistance in recent years, the United Nations, with the United States taking an active role, created the position of disaster relief coordinator in 1971 to improve the effectiveness of emergency multinational relief operations. In less than a year of operations, as of November 1972, assistance had been provided in eleven disaster situations.

INTELSAT and Outer Space

The United States is committed to international cooperation in space and has worked with eighty other countries in a variety of fields: research, design and launching of satellites, tracking activities, collection of meteorological data, and use of satellites for international communications. The United States, particularly State's legal adviser and its IO and SCI bureaus, participates in the U.N. Committee on the Peaceful Uses of Outer Space and worked hard for years to get the General Assembly to put through a 1971 convention establishing, for the first time, liabilities in connection with claims for damages caused by objects from outer space. One of the most far-reaching American proposals is the post-Apollo program in which Europe and the United States are working together in a revolutionary technological experience. Experiments by scientists from thirty-eight foreign countries and two international organizations are already being carried out on the first U.S. earth resources technology satellite.

State was especially interested in using satellites for communication, and it made all the arrangements for five international conferences on that subject at the Department between 1969 and 1971. The conference in May, 1971, which was handled by IO's Office of International Conferences with State's Bureau of Economic Affairs playing a major role, along with experts from the Federal Communications Commission and the Communications Satellite Corporation, concluded plans for the establishment of the International Telecommunications Satellite Consortium (INTELSAT), a worldwide communications system that had been functioning on an interim basis since 1964. Some eighty member states "share its costs, its services and its benefits on an equitable businesslike basis," making this a new form of international cooperation.

Multinational Enterprise

The spread of U.S.-controlled multinational enterprises over the globe, usually through the formation of national subsidiaries owing double or multiple allegiances, is a phenomenon of the last two decades. As these businesses continue to proliferate, they have a significant impact on the structure of the world economy. One authority on the subject has written, "Within a generation about 400 to 500 international corporations will own two-thirds of the fixed assets of the world."

It is generally accepted that these far-flung enterprises have brought economic benefits to the foreign countries in which they operate as well as to the United States. American labor, however, understandably feels that the competition of foreign-based firms is not good for the domestic job market. The psychological and political tensions aroused by the presence of these foreign subsidiaries powerfully affect their relations with local businessmen and governments, and clashes of interest are inevitable.

Difficulties generally arise when it is too late to correct them, as in the cases of expropriation of American-controlled subsidiaries in Peru and Chile. At that stage the parent corporations, which normally tend to keep the U.S. Government at arm's length, were happy to ask the State Department for assistance in negotiating "fair compensation" on their behalf.

A better solution, of course, would be to deal with these tensions before they get out of hand, but neither foreign governments nor corporations have gone very far in arriving at joint understandings or formal international agreements. The practice of offering subsidies and tax inducements to international corporations, for example, is unregulated, and governments wheel and deal fantastically in these matters. If some international control were recognized, the problems would be subject to international checks and balances.

The oil industry presents special problems. Consumers of oil all over the world are affected by the steadily mounting prices that have resulted mainly from the successful efforts of the producing countries, acting as a cartel, to demand ever-increasing taxes and shares in ownership of the oil industry and from the profit hunger of the huge international companies themselves. The State Department has long advocated a cooperative approach by the consuming countries and late in 1972 the European Common Market and Japan seemed to have a policy that would not only have sought new sources of energy but would have set up an international authority to reduce cutthroat competition in times of oil shortage. Unfortunately, it takes a long time for policies to be transformed into action in international or regional organizations and the industrialized countries have been very timid in their reaction to the near-monopoly of the Arab states. Even the arbitrary oil cutoffs from October, 1973 to March, 1974 failed to jar the consuming countries into taking concerted action despite the initiatives of Secretary Kissinger early in 1974.

REGIONAL ORGANIZATIONAL RELATIONSHIPS

The United Nations is not always the best forum for the conduct of multilateral diplomacy or the handling of international disputes. Sometimes problems that involve several nations have distinctly regional boundaries, or they can be tackled initially at the regional level and on a broader base later. The U.N. Charter urged member nations to make every effort to settle disputes at the local level before referring them to the Security Council. Where homogeneity exists, regional organizations tend to be more effective. In any case, these groups have grown up over the years in all major areas of the world, and, in general, their purpose is to help countries in the region work together for their political, military, economic, and social benefit.

The United States was instrumental in organizing several of these organizations, especially in the security field, after World War II, basing them on mutual defense treaties that the United States initiated because of the ineffectiveness of the U.N. Security Council and the threatening posture of the Soviet Union. The Rio Treaty (1947) and the Bogotá Pact (1948) supported the military side of the Organization of American States (OAS), and beginning in 1949 NATO became the shield for the security of Europe. Events in China, Korea, and Indochina led to the special defense arrangement known as the Australia-New Zealand-United States (ANZUS) Agreement in 1951 and to the formation of the Southeast Asia Treaty Organization (SEATO) in 1954. Similarly, the Baghdad Pact or Central Treaty Organization (CENTO) provided a buffer organization against the Soviet Union in the Middle East.

Regional organizations, like the United Nations itself, are only as effective as their members are willing to make them. In recent years, as the threat of communism has subsided, they have tended to lose their vitality, as in the case of CENTO and SEATO, or to broaden their interests as with OAS and NATO. The origins and purposes of the alliances were essentially political, and the highest executive bodies controlling them are high-level councils of foreign ministers and ambassadors. The American council members are served by permanent staffs of State Department (Foreign Service) personnel.

OAS

Political regional organizations, such as the OAS, the Council of Europe, the Arab League, and the Organization of African

Unity, from time to time are called on to mediate disputes in their areas, but, with the exception of the OAS they do not generally engage in peacekeeping operations, which come under the United Nations. In 1965, the OAS participated in the Dominican Republic operation—on the heels of the U.S. action and in accordance with a U.N. Security Council cease-fire resolution. The organization, moreover, has been periodically called on to aid a member state that has been attacked by a neighbor. The OAS responds promptly by sending a fact-finding mission with conciliatory powers (more psychological than real) to the trouble spot to try to calm things down, prevent bloodshed and, if possible, settle the dispute.

The United States accepted the principle of collective hemispheric defense in the Rio Treaty of 1947, an important landmark in U.S.–Latin American relations, which had long been characterized by unilateral American intervention, often in the name of the Monroe Doctrine. When its security appeared to be threatened, however, as happened in the Dominican Republic and in Cuba in the 1960's, the United States has not hesitated to step in. The OAS obviously cannot prevent this type of action, but current trends make such unilateral actions less likely than in the past.

In the economic and social sphere, the OAS actively assists member countries in their programs for development. Other regional or subregional organizations similarly interested are the Latin American Free Trade Area, the Central American Common Market, and the Inter-American Development Bank (IADB).

The United States, which has long operated bilateral economic assistance programs in Latin America, launched its highly publicized Alliance for Progress at Punta del Este in 1961, but the program was not a success, partially because of fears, suspicion, jealousy, and animosity, growing out of American exploitation of Latin America in the past. Regional development goals were not realized; economic growth that did occur did not necessarily lead to social equity or political stability. On the other hand, a number of countries have had impressive growth rates, and foreign investment, despite setbacks, has expanded. The Alliance has also come very close to reaching some important limited goals, providing adequate potable water for urban communities, for example. In seven years, from 1961–68, over $400 million was spent for sewer and water systems.

The OAS, through its influential Inter-American Committee on the Alliance for Progress, reviews country plans each year, with the help of the principal lending agencies, and has generally stimulated long-term development planning in many countries.

Within the State Department the Bureau of Inter-American Affairs (ARA) was reorganized, actually absorbing the entire Latin American Bureau (LA) of AID, to reflect the needs of the Alliance. The assistant secretary for ARA-LA put on an additional hat as coordinator of the Alliance for Progress, and the AID assistant administrator became his deputy coordinator. The result has been a unique, fully coordinated State-AID operation, both in Washington and in the field.

As disillusionment over the Alliance for Progress grew, President Nixon in April, 1971, proposed some new approaches toward economic assistance. These emphasized playing a partnership, rather than a dominating role, relying on recipient countries to set their own priorities and plans, concentrating programs on selected sectors (agriculture, education, health), and coordinating plans with other assistance programs and multilateral institutions, such as the OAS and Inter-American Development Bank. These pronouncements were welcome but not sufficient to win Latin American acceptance of the United States as a partner. In the spring of 1973 the OAS established its own committee to study future U.S.–Latin American relationships and how the OAS should restructure itself. Impetus to this work was provided in September by Secretary Kissinger when he called for a new dialogue with Latin America. Then in the spring of 1974 he met twice with the Latin American foreign ministers and made three major speeches pledging consultation and action—not words—toward cooperative solutions of common problems. He also set new priorities for Latin American affairs within the Department. However, for various reasons, including the Secretary's preoccupation with the Middle East and other critical areas, it has been hard to see any real improvement in U.S.–Latin American relations.

NATO and Europe

Europe has developed several regional organizations that exercise great power and influence, and, to a large extent, American policy toward Europe is carried out through these channels. American involvement in European defense and economic progress dates especially from World War II, and the concept of the Atlantic Community, embracing Europe and North America, is the very foundation of the U.S. and European defense system, as formulated in the North Atlantic Treaty and its organization, NATO. This extraordinary alliance—made up of old allies, former enemies, and a once-isolationist nation—has maintained a military establishment under a unified command and based on evolving strategies of nuclear deterrance for the past twenty-five years. In recent years, with the fear that created the alliance diminishing, its spirit and cohesiveness have been under some strain. In 1967 NATO's own study of the problem (the Harmel Report) suggested that the organization extend its efforts into the political-social-cultural arena, and in 1969, the North Atlantic Council, as a result of American initiative, set up a Committee on the Challenges of Modern Society to stimulate collective action on environmental and social problems.

The conclusion of the four-power agreement on Berlin in 1971, the talks on strategic arms limitations early in 1972, and the Moscow summit agreement broke the log jam holding up progress on two pet NATO projects: negotiations on mutual and balanced force reductions in Europe and a conference on security and cooperation in Europe. The State Department, working with NATO, has been deeply involved in these negotiations, with its Bureau of European Affairs (EUR), the counselor of the Department, and the Department of Defense having prime responsibility for preparing U.S. positions and policies.

The United States favored the expansion of the European Common Market—more exactly, the European Economic Community (EEC)—with the consequent greater European integration, despite the impact of this move on the U.S. trading position. This policy was based on the conviction that an economically stronger Western Europe would strengthen Western diplomacy and that free and expanded trade would promote the prosperity of the Atlantic partners—views not shared by powerful protectionist interests in this country. State, particularly the EB and EUR bureaus, has upheld U.S. policy in this area in public forums, before congressional committees, and in interdepartmental meetings.

U.S. Relations with the European Common Market became more complicated in 1973 as the United States continued to put off clarifications of its own trade and economic policies. The American desire to associate Japan with the Atlantic community through a tripartite declaration on trade and economic matters did not evoke much enthusiasm either in Japan or in the EEC countries. For the first time since the disaffection of de Gaulle, the Atlantic Alliance itself was strained during the fall of 1973 by serious disagreement arising from American requirements to send military supplies to Israel, which involved drawing equipment from bases in Europe and using NATO facilities. Then, early in 1974 new strains were generated by the unwillingness of the EEC to take joint action with the United States in the face of the Arab oil embargo and the energy crisis. This situation among other things pointed up the fact that the United States must get used to treating its allies as partners and that it cannot automatically expect to dominate the regional organizations as it has in the past. This trend can only be abetted by the loss in power and prestige that the United States faces as a result of mounting economic and political problems at home.

X

The State Department in a Changing World

What the State Department of the future will look like, how it will develop and change, and the type of career opportunities it will offer, depend on future Presidents and on changing U.S. foreign relations. Inasmuch as the course of international affairs and the choice of future American Presidents are unpredictable, so are long-range predictions about the particulars of the State Department's future.

Herman Kahn, whose "think tank" has produced many long-range studies, admits that studies of international affairs projecting beyond five years are useless; they can do no more than speculate on trends, which are likely to take unexpected turns at any time. Kahn likes to recall that the most significant events in history have generally been unforeseen. Who, for example, could have predicted that the assassination of an Austrian archduke would start World War I? Who foresaw that the Austro-Hungarian Empire would collapse within four years and be carved up into the little nations of East and Central Europe or that both Czarist Russia and Imperial Germany would fall? The Bolshevik Revolution and its consequences were unexpected. The list goes on and on—all the cataclysmic events of wars and their consequences, all the key events of recent history—unpredicted, unplanned for. At any moment, the direction of U.S. foreign policy can be changed by unforeseen events, just as Pearl Harbor ended American isolationism and united the country in the war effort in 1941. Despite the best efforts of scholars, diplomats, statesmen, and soothsayers, the future of international relations is not likely to be much different. The employees of the U.S. State Department's Civil Service and Foreign Service can only be described as subject to the unexpected.

A few things can be said about the *immediate* future of the State Department if we assume the absence of a new world war, and the continuation of the present world order and current power relationships.

As modern technology pulls peoples together, the interrelation of nations will be more evident than ever in the future, and the conduct of official relations between countries or through multinational institutions can scarcely become less active or important. Numerous agencies of the U.S. Government will continue to be active abroad, but the delicacy and pitfalls of pursuing American objectives in a foreign country will continue to require the State Department and its Foreign Service to try to see that all U.S. agencies abroad are operating in line with American policy, that they are not working at cross-purposes or otherwise doing damage to the United States's long-range international objectives. Abroad, this is mainly the responsibility of ambassadors and their staffs. Their effectiveness in this role depends upon the extent to which they are backed up by a strong Secretary of State. The influence of American ambassadors in foreign capitals and of the State Department in Washington among the agencies concerned with foreign affairs is also determined to a great extent by the degree of support the Secretary of State gets from the President. After sinking to a low ebb, the influence of the Department appears to have revived to a considerable extent under the strengthened leadership given it in September 1973 by the appointment of Dr. Kissinger as Secretary of State. Yet nothing is certain. What happens to the influence of the Secretary of State and his Department if the power and prestige of the President collapses? This contingency until late in 1973 seemed too remote a possibility to mention. Despite the strains of Watergate and President Nixon's resignation, the Department has continued to grow in stature under Secretary Kissinger's leadership.

One thing that can be taken for granted is that the Department's structure and operations will continue to change. Since 1946, there have been so many internal reorganizations of the State Department and the Foreign Service that the announcement of a new one is received rather cynically by seasoned officers, who philosophically remark *"plus ça change, plus c'est la même chose."* That remark is more than a *bon mot* because one can cite so many innovations that are basically restorations of former organization patterns or procedures. What happens is that new methods are tried but found less satisfactory than the old.

Changes often reflect the personal views of a President, a Secretary of State, or a deputy under secretary for Administration and last only as long as that person's term in office. Thus, the innovations made under President Johnson in creating the interdepartmental group system were scrapped less than three years later by President Nixon, who resurrected and reorganized the National Security Council of Eisenhower days. This in turn was launched with great fanfare as the paragon of decision-making systems. Then after a few years of intensive activity it became less and less important. The machinery goes round and round but no longer seems indispensable to decision-making.

One of the casualties of the centering of power in the National Security Adviser in 1969 was the Department's Policy Planning Council; it was however restored in 1974 after Kissinger moved to the State Department. Secretary Rusk abolished office directors in 1966; they were restored in 1972. The emphasis on language and area specialization in the Foreign Service, which has been the name of the game for years, was "discovered" by Kissinger early in 1974 to produce officers lacking in the kind of versatility and adaptability that broader experience may create. This discovery led to a crash program to revitalize the service by immediately assigning large numbers of specialists outside of the areas with which they were identified—a rationale that, without the sense of urgency, had actually been personnel policy for years before the recent change.

Many of the more important reorganizations in the Department were, however, responses to the new responsibilities that the United States assumed as it emerged as a great power after World

War II. The Department found it necessary to set up new functional bureaus, for example, to handle politico-military affairs, educational and cultural affairs, scientific and technological affairs, and relations with international organizations. Numerous special assistants to the Secretary were appointed to advise and coordinate U.S. participation in international programs to cope with problems of labor, population, fisheries and wildlife, narcotics, the environment, and refugees. The addition of the Arms Control and Disarmament Agency, the succession of foreign economic assistance agencies under the Department's wing, and the close collaboration with the U.S. Information Agency are further examples of the expansion of the Department's role and influence in the foreign affairs community. The years ahead will probably see additional organizational changes as the Department adjusts to external developments, domestic pressures, reassessed priorities, and new policies.

Significant organizational changes relating not only to the State Department but to all agencies involved in foreign affairs, such as the CIA and the USIA, could emerge from the work of the Joint Presidential-Congressional Commission (Murphy Commission) that was activated in 1973 to study how to improve the system for the conduct of international relations in the U.S. Government. The Commission is reviewing such fields as Presidential responsibility on interagency coordination of foreign policy, seeking to determine the adequacy of the existing system to handle anticipated American involvement in future international crises. Its findings—to be reported to the President and Congress by June 30, 1975,* are expected to include some drastic proposals.

In considering the future role of the Foreign Service the Commission will undoubtedly examine such basic options as (1) a service that would serve the entire foreign affairs community but operate directly under the President; (2) amalgamating the Foreign Service into the civil service, with the State Department and posts abroad completely staffed by civil service personnel; (3) retaining

---

* The Murphy Commission's Refund was issued on June 27, 1975. Its impact, as measured by press reviews, was not as great as had been anticipated. See Appendix B for a summary of the Report.

the Foreign Service through Class 3 just as it is, but creating at the top a pool of executives drawn from several agencies available for the most important foreign affairs assignments at home or abroad; or (4) no drastic changes in the Foreign Service, with modifications as necessary being made under the Foreign Service Act.

The Murphy Commission's task and the examples previously cited relate almost exclusively to the perennial quest to devise revisions in the organizational structure that will assist the bureaucracies in the foreign affairs community to do a better job, as dealt with in chapters II and III of this book. It is well to stress once again, however, that important as the bureaucracies are, the effectiveness of American diplomacy over the years depends far more on the authority, leadership, and capability of the American Presidents and Secretaries of State, cabinet members and Congressional leaders, and the professional diplomats who work at home and abroad.

RELATIONS WITH COMMUNIST COUNTRIES

The future development of U.S. relations with the Soviet Union, China, and the rest of the communist world depend largely on the extent to which a relaxation of tensions serves the latter's interests. The policy of détente, being mainly a tactic, will have its ups and downs. In fact, serious setbacks can be expected, stemming from differences over domestic policies, such as Soviet handling of Jewish emigration, and over foreign policy, as in the Arab-Israeli conflict. In view of the precarious state of détente one can only say that as long as that describes East-West relationships, the State Department will be actively assisting Americans to take advantage of the opportunities to expand trade, investments, and cultural and other contacts with the Soviet Union, Eastern Europe, and China. The Department is not likely to favor risking détente by supporting the passage of laws that can be interpreted as interfering with the internal affairs of the Soviet Union. However, American principles upholding human rights throughout the world can be as strong in influencing American policies as communist ideology can be in determining communist courses of action. When public opinion and the U.S. Congress are sufficiently affronted by repressive actions of other nations, their influence on American foreign policy can be overriding.

In the background of Soviet-American relations there is always the thermonuclear stalemate, with neither country enjoying a preponderance of power and each one maintaining adequate power to destroy the other. Frightening as this stand-off is, it seems to leave room for very risky confrontations that look all too much like the terrible game of "chicken." The State Department can play a moderating role in support of policies designed to avoid dangerous confrontations if the views of its professionals are sought and listened to by the top policy-makers.

In the case of China, there is a vast amount of fact-finding, information gathering, and catching up on the years when the United States was out of touch, which must be done if Americans are to develop the necessary understanding and knowledge of that huge subcontinent of a nation that comprises one-sixth of the world's population. The State Department is still handicapped by the brutal, heavy-handed slashing of its knowledgeable body of professional experts on China during the (Senator Joe) McCarthy era. The long-range effects of this action can still be felt and point a warning finger toward the shortsightedness of cutting off all relations with any country in moments of national pique—and having to spend years to rebuild them later. Nevertheless, considerable progress has been made in two years of renewed contacts with China and it can only be to the good for this process to continue in a moderate way—economically, culturally, and politically. But whether anything approaching normal relations will be possible depends on many factors over which the United States has little control, such as Chinese-Russian relations and internal Chinese developments.

GEOGRAPHIC AREAS

The new relationships with the communist world that were set in motion in 1972 will continue to affect U.S. relations with virtually all the other nations of the globe as they adapt to the new situation. Nothing is static in international affairs. The fuel crisis exploited by the oil-producing countries set in motion political tensions felt round the world. Strong American leadership with competent assistance from the Department's geographic bureaus and Foreign Service will be more necessary than ever.

Europe surely will continue to be a priority area as the United States pursues a series of negotiations connected with East-West relationships, as competition with European Common Market countries increases, and as NATO re-evaluates its role. The United States is learning the hard way that it can no longer take for granted its relationships with Western European nations or the permanency of the Atlantic idea.

U.S. relations and problems with the Far East will also command much attention in the future. This includes relations with China and also with Japan, Korea, and Southeast Asia, for whose security the United States will continue to exercise varying degrees of responsibility.

The renewal of Arab-Israeli fighting in the Yom Kippur war of October 1973, with the ever-present danger of US-USSR involvement, and the alarming new problems caused by the Arab oil embargo of the consumer countries, whose inability to act together made them especially vulnerable, brought on a period of intensive U.S. diplomatic activity in the Middle East to try to end the fighting and obtain a peace settlement. Since the problems involved are not such as to be quickly solved, the prospect is that the United States is now indefinitely committed to play an active role in promoting and maintaining peace in the area.*

A hijacking treaty with Cuba early in 1973 was hailed as possibly paving the way for normalized relations with Cuba, but during that year no progress in that direction occurred. Pressures for such a change are, nevertheless, likely to continue and could well produce results in the not too distant future. Secretary Kissinger's offer of a "new dialogue" with Latin America and his meetings with Latin American foreign ministers early in 1974 indicated his inten-

---

* Secretary Kissinger's "shuttle diplomacy" is the most current example, with its initial failure and subsequent (September 1975) historic success in negotiating an agreement between Israel and Egypt.

tion to pay more attention to the problems of this area. Yet even if the times were more propitious for U.S. initiatives, the problems of Latin America, including the effects of the population explosion, make it hard to be optimistic regarding the future of its countries, with the possible exception of Brazil, whose economic development is progressing by leaps and bounds.

INTERNATIONAL ECONOMIC AFFAIRS

Both the White House and the State Department anticipated giving high priority to economic affairs in President Nixon's second term. Perhaps, it was thought, political-military-security issues would not require so much attention in the future and it would be possible to give more attention to the pressing economic issues. At any rate, international economic problems had become increasingly urgent for the country and, as has always been the case, there were many domestic and foreign interests ready with plenty of conflicting ideas as to how to handle the problems.

Improved relations with the Soviet Union following the 1972 summit meeting in Moscow and the new relationship with mainland China both were heavily influenced by economic factors, especially the need of the communist nations for trade and Western technology. It seemed that East-West trade would be given a big boost. But although Dr. Kissinger, when he became Secretary of State in September 1973, pledged full support for the international economic program, he almost at once became enmeshed in the efforts to end the Arab-Israeli war, which together with congressional failure to pass the long-awaited trade bill led to serious strains on U.S. détente with the Soviet Union. As was mentioned (page 172), Congress stood firm in refusing to write into its trade bill provision for nondiscriminatory (most-favored-nation) treatment of trade with the Soviet Union unless the restrictions on the emigration of Russian Jews from their homeland were relaxed. This situation reflects basic conflicting national goals and ideologies, which no amount of lip service to détente will dissipate. The improved political climate of détente with China in 1972 and 1973 bolstered trade between the United States and China to a moderate degree, but no startling changes in the future pattern of the China trade are anticipated.

The biggest economic and trade problems facing the United States are those with Japan and the countries of the European Common Market. Competition with these friends undoubtedly will lead to intensified U.S. Government activity in support of trade and investment abroad, including the development of U.S. policies acceptable to both the executive and legislative branches, and high-level negotiations with foreign governments on both bilateral and multilateral levels. Pressures from special interests on both the executive and the legislative branches, especially when trade and monetary policies are concerned, often constitute a test of statesmanship for public officials whose duty it is to try to do what is best for the nation as a whole. It is precisely here that the State Department's participation can be helpful; the Department has no special clientele and no axe to grind and is therefore uniquely qualified to provide the long view in the framework of international relations. This is especially true in an era when other countries are less inclined than in the recent past to follow the American line and skillful diplomacy rather than beating heads is the only effective approach.

With the changes in Treasury Department leadership and authority in April 1974, the State Department regained some of its former influence in international economic affairs through the leadership of dynamic business-oriented economic experts strongly backed by Secretary Kissinger. In the light of the rapidly escalating domestic and international economic and financial problems that this country and most of the world face in the last quarter of this century, the State Department will continue to need the very best leadership available for the conduct of international economic affairs.

MILITARY AND ECONOMIC ASSISTANCE

The Department supports economic and military assistance programs as useful adjuncts of diplomacy, but current trends and congressional attitudes point toward a reduction in the scale of these programs. In the event of a sizable reduction in U.S. participation in bilateral military and economic assistance programs and in the American military presence abroad, there may be some reduction in the work of the Department's Bureau of Politico-Military Affairs and of the Agency for International Development or its successor. There will, however, be continuing need for close liaison between the Department and the Pentagon at several levels, which will keep the PM personnel busy for years to come.

ARMS CONTROL AND DISARMAMENT

The future of arms control and disarmament depends on the continuing acceptance of a détente policy by the superpowers. Another way of putting this is to say that the arms control and disarmament responsibilities of ACDA and of the Bureau of Politico-Military Affairs can be expected to increase in the future, as long as the mutual dangers of the armaments race in the thermonuclear age continue to stimulate efforts to reach more effective international agreements. Involved are some of the most important political questions in US-USSR relations and equally serious questions relating to U.S. security. Therefore, policies are likely to be set out at the highest levels, by the President and the Secretaries of State and Defense, with ACDA furnishing technical advice. Relations between State and Defense on disarmament policy can be crucial because it takes strong State leadership (not always forthcoming) to stand up against fairly predictable Defense views.

MULTILATERAL DIPLOMACY

It is not unreasonable to expect some expansion in the Department's work with international organizations, especially with respect to the anticipated increase in international activity to cope with some of the global problems affecting the quality of life on this planet.

Multilateral diplomacy will be increasingly important, and the State Department should continue to play the central role in coordinating American participation. Much of this activity falls within the U.N. system, which the United States cannot afford not to support. From time to time U.S. support does waver. In the face of irresponsible resolutions pushed through the General Assembly by an irresponsible majority, it may well do so again—though it is fervently to be hoped that the U.S. Government will have the statesmanship, maturity, and vision to rise above petty irritations in the United Nations and act in a way that is consistent with its status as a great power. Congressional pressures for better or worse may complicate the State Department's task of developing policy and steering this country's representatives in the United Nations.

The United States will continue to participate in several regional organizations in the future, but, as the mainly military rationale for several of them loses some of its validity, changes in their purposes and programs are bound to take place. The United States is less likely to play a dominating role than it was in the past. Its alliance system will be reappraised periodically, not only to reflect revised American strategic thinking but to reflect changing relations with allies.

POLICY PLANNING

Pending a more effective international system, some equilibrium in power relationships has to be maintained despite its being more complicated and difficult to achieve than ever. The United States no longer has a preponderance of military power, nor an unlimited surplus of food, oil, and other resources at its disposal, and although it has obligations of one sort or another virtually everywhere, can only give limited support for limited involvement in any military situation. In its relations with the communist nations the United States pursues a détente policy, seeking to avoid confrontations that could lead to a major war, and the Secretary of State rushes about trying to put out fires as they flare up. But improved long-term policy planning and other studies of the problems of conducting foreign relations in this new environment are urgently needed. What should U.S. strategy be? If military power remains basically bipolar, what about political and economic power relationships? What about the five-power balance that Dr. Kissinger talks about? How realistic is the policy of inducing Japan to participate in some way in the Atlantic concept, at least as far as trade is concerned? What is the answer to the Arab use of oil as a political weapon?

The State Department's long-term planning functions have had a spotty history. Secretaries of State have tended to pull the planners away from their crystal balls to assist in day-to-day operations, especially during periods of crisis. Yet at no time since 1947 has there been greater need for analysis and study of the future course of American diplomacy. One reason for this is the low point the Department's policy planning reached during the first four and a half years of the Nixon Administration. This changed when Kissinger, at his first press conference as Secretary of State, on October 12, 1973, indicated his intention to strengthen policy planning. It was on this occasion that he announced the appointment of a new director for Planning and Coordination, a former Foreign Service officer who had been one of Kissinger's most trusted assistants in the White House. Several very competent Department and Foreign Service officers were recruited for the Policy Planning Staff, and that body has largely regained its former position of influence. The fact that its director, like several of his more influential predecessors, is frequently consulted by the Secretary on current problems augments rather than diminishes the reputation and effectiveness of the policy planners.

THE SECRETARY OF STATE AND THE WHITE HOUSE

It has already been said that the future role of the State Department depends in large measure on the caliber of its leadership— the man the President selects as Secretary of State, the kind of job the President wants him to undertake, and the men who are chosen as his key assistants in the Department. The Secretary's relations with the White House, with the other members of the Cabinet, with Congress, and with the public are vital factors. So is his management of the State Department and its civil service and U.S. Foreign Service personnel. The system does not work very well when the President and his own special adviser and White House staff try to handle all the important crises and foreign policy problems, as was the situation from 1961 to mid-1973. Neither the State Department nor the Secretary of State were properly utilized during that period. No one can criticize the President for taking charge of major crises affecting the security of the nation, as well as other critical foreign policy problems, but neither can anyone justify the President's ignoring his Secretary of State and the experts in the State Department, especially during times of crisis. Something is radically wrong with the organization of foreign affairs decision-making when this is the case.

Each President must, of course, find and utilize a system that works for him. The system President Nixon and Dr. Kissinger created produced some remarkable diplomatic successes. The President tried a similar system for about a year in 1973 and 1974 with respect to international economic policy, with the Secretary of the Treasury playing the lead role in that field. But the questionable if not wholly dangerous system of Cabinet officers serving also as Presidential assistants with offices in the White House was on the way out by April 1974.

When Dr. Kissinger became Secretary of State in September 1973 the system of White House control was at first maintained through the National Security Adviser-NSC apparatus. The National Security Adviser (Kissinger) even addressed memoranda of instructions to the Secretary of State (Kissinger). The situation was a built-in subject for jokes. For example, when a newspaper correspondent asked what the National Security Adviser thought of the new Secretary of State, Dr. Kissinger replied with a straight face that he considered the latter eminently qualified. Yet, from the State Department point of view it was an entirely new ball game: The man with the power had become Secretary of State, and State Department career officers, many of them Kissinger's own selections, became part of the inner circle of policy advisers. Kissinger more and more functioned as a strong Secretary of State and less and less as a Presidential assistant, a position that indeed appears to be gradually phasing out.*

* One of the remarkable aspects of the transition of power from President Nixon to President Ford in August 1974 was the smoothness of

THE STATE OF STATE: NOWHERE TO GO BUT UP?

Long one of the most prestigious of U.S. Government departments, the State Department has survived numerous batterings at
various times from various domestic sources. In recent years, in
common with the Defense Department, the CIA, and the White
House, it has suffered a loss of prestige as a result of the tragic
war in Vietnam. Nonetheless, the Department's reputation for
integrity and professional competence has remained high. It stacks
up well compared to any other foreign ministry and diplomatic
service in the world. However, during the time of weak leadership
(1969–73) when major foreign policy problems were handled
elsewhere, and the Department's best people were being ignored,
the Department's reputation, prestige, and influence understandably
sank to a low point. Foreign ambassadors preferred to consult with
the National Security Adviser rather than the Secretary of State;
there was a decrease in the influence of American ambassadors
abroad and of the State Department's representatives on the NSC;
there was also a loss of morale among State Department professionals, even those whose day-to-day work was not directly
affected. An example of this could be seen in the secret visit of
the President's National Security Adviser to Moscow to prepare
for the 1972 Moscow summit. The American Ambassador to the
Soviet Union first learned of Dr. Kissinger's visit three days after
his arrival; Dr. Kissinger stayed in accommodations provided by
the Russians. When he met with Brezhnev and Gromyko, the
Soviet Ambassador to the United States was at their side. The
American Ambassador had not been asked to accompany Dr.
Kissinger to the meeting. His role and influence in Moscow were
accordingly diminished. Nor did the State Department in Washington participate in the planning or the negotiations.

When the talents of a body of highly trained professionals are
not put to the best use, the result is bound to undermine such
basic attributes of a strong organization as pride, dedication,

---

the changeover in the foreign affairs area. This can be attributed to the
fact that Dr. Kissinger continued in office with much the same authority.
A potentially dangerous situation was thereby happily avoided.

loyalty, morale, and *esprit de corps*. There is also an adverse effect upon performance and recruitment.

Fortunately, the low state of State as of the summer of 1973 began to improve shortly after it acquired the dynamic Dr. Kissinger as Secretary. The new Secretary of State was immediately swept up in the same sort of crisis management he had been doing as National Security Adviser but with the difference that his team of close co-workers was largely a State Department–Foreign Service team. Spirits rose in the Department.

However, even though the increased isolation of the President placed still heavier responsibility on Kissinger's shoulders, it did not change his habit of transacting delicate diplomatic business with the utmost secrecy and with the fewest possible people. In fact, with Kissinger insisting on making all the important decisions, many decisions simply had to be postponed until the Secretary himself had time to consider them. The assistant secretaries who headed the bureaus reported more often than not to one of Kissinger's group of top officials on the Seventh Floor, but even a Helmut Sonnenfeld or a Joseph Sisco is unable to take key decisions on SALT negotiations or Middle East questions when the Secretary is concentrating on something else.

THE ROLE OF TOMORROW'S AMBASSADOR

Modern communications and jet air travel have made it possible for the White House and the State Department to participate directly in diplomatic negotiations, leaving less and less responsibility to the American ambassadors abroad. Instant messages can be exchanged between Washington and U.S. missions, and Washington "trouble shooters" are sent out to assist or temporarily replace the regular ambassadors.

These developments raise questions. What will be the role of the ambassador of tomorrow? Is he to become merely a messenger boy? Will he have any voice at all in policy-making? Will his management function be less difficult if there is the anticipated retrenchment in bilateral assistance programs? What are the prospects for Foreign Service officers to make their way up the career ladder to an ambassadorship?

Washington will certainly increasingly utilize modern communications to direct American activities abroad, inevitably restricting ambassadorial latitude to take action and to make decisions on the spot. The ambassador will still, however, have plenty of room left in which to exercise strong leadership. One must take into account what an American ambassador does after he receives an instruction from Washington: His personal influence with the officials of the country, their confidence in him, his tactics, style, approach, timing, and his interpretation of instructions can make all the difference between success and failure. Ambassadors will continue to take initiatives in emergency situations, and their reports back to Washington on trends and developments, with observations, analysis, and appropriate recommendations will always be a valuable contribution to the policy-makers in the capital. The burden of proof is on the Washington decision-makers to come up with a better alternative than that proposed by the President's representative in the field; not always, but more often than not, it is the field recommendation that is accepted.

The Ambassador's executive responsibilities as head of the official American family in a foreign country will also remain a big job, even if they are somewhat reduced in those countries where there is a large-scale decrease in military and economic assistance programs or in the American military presence.

No doubt Washington will continue to send out high-powered special ambassadors to "assist" resident ambassadors to handle special problems. Because Secretary Kissinger has engaged in so many negotiations abroad, it is not unlikely, however, that a number of foreign ministers will be reluctant to receive any special American emissary whose name is not Henry Kissinger.

THE FOREIGN SERVICE FUTURE

The morale of the Foreign Service and civil service personnel of the State Department suffered as a result of the reduced authority and influence of the Secretary of State and the State Department from 1969 to 1973, and as a result of personnel-administrative problems. Morale was given a lift by the appointment of the man with the real authority in foreign affairs as Secretary of State in September 1973 but is not helped by the continuation of pressures and inducements to early retirement of senior personnel. Nor is it lifted by the propensity of the White House to "sell" a certain number of diplomatic appointments to big campaign contributors—a hangover from the old "spoils system" long known about but brought out into the open when the scandals over political contributions to the re-election of the President in 1972 revealed several glaring examples of this practice. The ensuing publicity and the strongly critical congressional reaction may put a damper on the selling of ambassadorships for a while. Additionally, the American Foreign Service Association's officers have met several times with the Senate Foreign Relations Committee to help draft a list of criteria for the selection of ambassadors, and the Association has also called on Secretary Kissinger to urge the nomination of only the best-qualified individuals as ambassadors. These efforts are also no doubt helpful, but the White House has not accepted any such criteria, although there have been more appointments from the career service than usual in the first part of 1974.

Whether or not improvement is made in the system of appointing ambassadors, opportunities are still open for able diplomats to rise through the career Foreign Service to a wide range of responsible and challenging positions. Entrance is highly competitive. In 1972 over 7,400 took the written examination for the State Department, in 1973, there were 9,330, and in 1974 the number was 9,799. In 1974, to give the full picture, 1,525 passed the written test and about 200 passed the oral examination to compete for the 150 or so positions that were to be filled by the new Foreign Service officers. The figures for 1975 were expected to be comparable. Special provision is made for the recruitment and examination of minority group candidates, and the "Mustang" program is designed to encourage promotion from the ranks of those already employed in technical positions to commissioned officer status. (See Appendix B for details on recruitment.) Foreign affairs experts, economic and commercial officers, consular and administrative officers, and a host of technical and clerical specialists will continue to be needed to handle the international relations of the United States in the Department and in United States embassies and consular offices abroad. Only one-third of the staff jobs at State are filled by Foreign Service officers, the rest being civil service positions. But if the Foreign Service did not exist, something like it would have to be invented. Hence, regardless of how the Foreign Service may be reorganized in the future, it can be assumed that its work will continue to be performed by a professional body of foreign service experts.

A career in foreign affairs, regardless of position or the department or agency one represents, can be a rewarding experience. It is a career that places emphasis on service. It is not, however, a career without danger and sacrifice. In the course of American history members of the U.S. Foreign Service community have succumbed to disease or died in accidents or natural disasters abroad. More recently in Indochina, at least twenty are known to have been killed as a result of the hostilities or to have died in captivity; some were kept in prison camps for as long as seven years until released under the 1973 cease-fire agreement. Elsewhere in the world over the past few years at least fourteen civilian and military officers of the foreign affairs community have been kidnapped despite their diplomatic status, and ten have been brutally murdered —including Ambassador Cleo Noel and his deputy, G. Curtis Moore, in Khartoum in 1973.

The State Department and Foreign Service have come through a difficult time, largely as a result of a system that deliberately limited the role of the State Department for a considerable period. This was to a great extent corrected by returning the principal responsibility to the Secretary of State in 1973. On the basis of the experience of the recent past, it will probably be a long time before another President will follow the system inaugurated by Nixon in 1969. In a changing world, one prediction that can with confidence be made is this: Given the chance to show their skills and utilize their stored knowledge, the personnel of the Department of State and the Foreign Service of the United States can prove that they are indispensable to the effective carrying out of the American Government's responsibilities in foreign relations.

Appendix A: Summary of Principal Foreign Affairs Legislation

Basic Authority for the Department of State, Public Law 885, Eighty-fourth Congress, as amended.

P.L. 885 covers a large number of administrative and financial authorizations of a kind not generally accorded to other departments, and needed by the Secretary of State to operate a worldwide organization.

Foreign Service Act of 1946; P.L. 724, Seventy-ninth Congress, as amended.

This Act codified all prior laws relating to administration of the Foreign Service. The purpose of the Act was to enable the Foreign Service "effectively to serve abroad the interests of the United States"; to ensure that its officers and employees were "broadly representative of the American people," and were "aware of and fully informed in respect to current trends in American life"; to improve recruitment, training, and provide for promotions on the basis of merit; to authorize salaries, allowances and benefits to permit "the Foreign Service to draw its personnel from all walks of American life."

United States Information and Educational Exchange Act of 1948, P.L. 402, Eightieth Congress, as amended.

The "objectives of this Act are to enable the Government of the United States to promote a better understanding between the people of the United States and the people of other countries" primarily through the dissemination abroad of "information about the United States, its people, and policies promulgated by the Congress, the President, the Secretary of State and other responsible officials of Government having to do with matters affecting foreign affairs." The Act also provides for the interchange of persons, knowledge and skills (student/scholar exchanges, provision of books, periodicals and educational materials and sending abroad specialists having scientific or other technical or professional qualifications).

The Foreign Assistance Act of 1961, P.L. 87–195, September 4, 1961, as amended.

The purpose of this Act is to "assist the people of less developed countries in their efforts to acquire the knowledge and resources essential for development and to build the economic, political and social institutions which will meet their aspirations for a better life, with freedom, and in peace."

Executive Order No. 10973, November 3, 1961, as amended.

The President delegated to the Secretary of State the functions conferred upon the President by the Act. State Department Delegation of Authority No. 104, as amended, established in the Department the Agency for International Development.

Arms Control and Disarmament Act, P.L. 87–297, September 26, 1961, as amended.

It is the purpose of this Act to achieve the goal of the United States for "a world which is free from the scourge of war and the dangers and burdens of armaments, in which the use of force has been subordinated to the rule of law, and in which international adjustments to a changing world are achieved peacefully. The Act provides impetus toward the above goal "by creating a new agency of peace to deal with the problem of reduction and control of armaments looking toward ultimate world disarmament."

The Act establishes an agency to be known as the "United States Arms Control and Disarmament Agency" to be headed by a Director who serves as "the principal adviser to the Secretary of State and the President on arms control and disarmament matters." The Director carries out his duties under the direction of the Secretary of State.

The Peace Corps Act, P.L. 87–293, September 22, 1961, as amended.

Through this Act the Congress declared it is the policy of the United States and the purpose of the Act to promote world peace and friendship through a Peace Corps. The Peace Corps makes available to interested countries and areas men and women of the United States to help such countries meet their needs for trained manpower.

The Peace Corps was established as an agency in the Department of State by Executive Order and the Secretary redelegated certain powers to the Director of the Agency. When the Peace Corps was transferred from State to ACTION, the Secretary retained certain powers under Section 4 of the Act and by authority of Executive Order 11603, of June 30, 1971, particularly with respect to functions of negotiating, concluding and terminating international agreements under the Act, and functions with respect to the Foreign Service Act of 1946, among others.

The United Nations Participation Act of 1955, P.L. 264, Seventy-ninth Congress, as amended.

The Act authorizes the appointment of representatives of the United States in the organizations and agencies of the United Nations, and the participation of the United States in such organizations.

Appendix B: Summary of Report of the Commission on the Organization of the Government for the Conduct of Foreign Policy*

The Commission on the Organization of the Government for the Conduct of Foreign Policy, headed by Ambassador (ret.) Robert D. Murphy, submitted its report to the President and the Congress on June 27.

The 277-page report discusses the purposes of organization, the role of the President and the State Department, the conduct of foreign policy, and Congressional-Executive relations and the organization of Congress.

The report presents many wide-ranging recommendations of interest to the Department. Copies are available from the Superintendent of Documents, Washington, D.C. . . . Following are excerpts from the summary that relate to specific Department activities or organizational structures:

The State Department will continue to be the central point in the U.S. government for the conduct of foreign affairs. It should con-

* As published in Department of State *Newsletter* No. 70 (July 1975), pp. 8–9.

centrate upon three major functions, and adapt its personnel, organization and procedures to fulfill them. The Department should be the primary point in the government for assessing the overseas impact of proposed U.S. decisions and injecting international considerations into the national policy process. It should play a major part in the formulation of all U.S. policy having significant foreign implications, a responsibility which will require it to monitor, oversee, coordinate, and influence the foreign activities of other U.S. agencies. And it should continue to fill its responsibilities for the actual conduct of relations with other governments and international organizations.

The principal organizational changes proposed include the following:

—The position of Under Secretary of State for Political Affairs should be retitled Under Secretary for Political and Security Affairs, and become the focal point for strong State Department participation in Defense issues. The position of Under Secretary of State for Security Assistance should be abolished.

—The responsibilities of the Under Secretary for Economic Affairs should be broadened and his title changed to Under Secretary for Economic and Scientific Affairs.

—Functional responsibilities currently divided between the Bureau of Economic and Business Affairs and the Bureau of Oceans and International Environmental and Scientific Affairs should be divided among four bureaus all reporting directly to the Under Secretary for Economic and Scientific Affairs:

—Economic and Business Affairs
—Food, Population and Development Affairs
—Oceans, Environment and Scientific Affairs
—Transportation, Communication and Energy Affairs.

—A new Senior Officer for Policy Information should direct the press, public affairs and policy information functions currently assigned to the Department, and those to be transferred to State from the U.S. Information Agency. The Bureau of Cultural and

Educational Affairs should be transferred to the proposed Information and Cultural Affairs Agency (ICA).

—The current Deputy Under Secretary for Management would be upgraded to full Under Secretary status.

These proposals leave unchanged the number of positions at the Under Secretary level in the State Department. They transfer one bureau to another agency, carve two additional bureaus out of existing bureaus, and add one bureau of relatively small size. In addition, one office—that of Inspector General for Foreign Assistance—would be abolished.

The Department of State must significantly improve its capability to deal with the foreign policy aspects of economic, business, scientific, energy, transportation, food, population, development, and related issues.

To this end:

—More Ambassadors and Deputy Chiefs of Mission with economic expertise should be appointed.

—Personnel interchange among departments and agencies and between government and business should be expanded.

—Multiagency participation in policy negotiation and implementation abroad under State Department coordination should be increased.

—The Agency for International Development (AID) should remain the operating arm of the State Department for bilateral foreign assistance, with the Treasury Department having primary responsibility for supervision of U.S. commitments to international development institutions.

—The Federal Energy Administration (FEA) should provide leadership in carrying out the national energy policy, with the State Department responsible for continuing to bring foreign policy considerations to bear in the formulation of policy in that area.

—The Office of the President's Special Trade Representative should be transferred, following current trade negotiations, to the Department of State.

The State Department is inadequately equipped to deal with

political-military issues; a number of structural and personnel system changes are needed. These include, as indicated above, making the Under Secretary of State for Political Affairs (retitled the Under Secretary for Political and Security Affairs) directly responsible for State's expanded role in the Defense community. The Bureau of Politico-Military Affairs would report directly to him.

As foreign policy issues develop domestic ramifications, and radio and television bring world events into every home, public opinion will be an increasingly important determinant of foreign policy. The government will need to communicate more fully to the public, and in return develop a more accurate sense of public attitudes on policy matters. Procedures cannot substitute for receptiveness to what is being communicated, but improvements are possible. Important congressional foreign policy debates should be opened to television, more comprehensive public affairs programs should be developed, and programs for education in international affairs should be more fully funded. Policymakers can develop better information on the trends of public opinion through greater attention to polling, provision of more channels for interchange of views with members of the public, and inclusion in policymaking of officials familiar with public opinion.

Issues of humanitarian and human rights activities and sensitivity to ethical considerations in policymaking deserve greater attention. The new Office of Humanitarian Affairs in the Department of State should be upgraded, an Advisory Committee to the Secretary of State on Human Rights should be created, and a broader mandate given the U.S. Representative to the United Nations Human Rights Commission.

Bilateral Relationships. Three tasks should become the principal focus of posts and missions abroad: providing perceptive assessment of important foreign developments; supporting and overseeing the whole range of U.S. activities in each country; and furthering multilateral diplomacy through bilateral relationships.

The Ambassador must be the central representative abroad of

the United States and of the President; he must have greater control of communications and personnel in his mission. Foreign Service reporting requires substantial improvement. Officials at home and in the field should remain in closer touch to maintain a shared perspective toward their joint responsibilities. Modifications in the process of inspection of posts abroad would help provide more effective management.

Multilateral Relations. Multilateral channels of diplomacy will be increasingly important as more issues of global interdependence find their way into multilateral forums. Policymakers must decide when our national interests are best served by their use, and when other forms of diplomatic relations are more appropriate. Periodic review of our approach to these organizations should be undertaken.

No single unit or department of our government can take exclusive responsibility for U.S. participation in multilateral agencies. Lead responsibility should be assigned to the appropriate functional bureaus in the State Department. Delegations to multilateral organizations and conferences should be multiagency in composition; the Secretary of State should select heads of delegations from the best qualified individuals in or out of the government. Members of Congress can and should play a valuable part as members of delegations even if they are usually not voting members.

Public Diplomacy. Our information and cultural activities abroad have three separate aspects. First, the function of policy advocacy should be placed in the Department of State alongside the responsibility for policy itself. Second, the longer range functions of cultural communication and general information should be combined in a separate agency. Third, the Voice of America should be independent under a separate board made up of public and private members, taking guidance from the Department of State on all policy commentary. Personnel for public diplomacy should continue to be separate from the Foreign Service.

In the Department of State a strong Policy Planning Staff is also necessary. External expertise is vital to policy planning; to this end a planning Advisory Committee should be instituted, among other purposes to assist government planners to become more sensitive to newer methodologies and analytic techniques for forecasting and planning.

People may be the single most important element in successful foreign policy. The foreign affairs agencies of the government must provide a more systematic way of placing the right people in the right jobs, and particularly assuring that qualified people are placed in executive positions. Sustained attention to executive development and other major issues has been missing.

State Department's personnel capabilities must be improved by:

—raising the performance in functional specialties;
—emphasizing the specialty of diplomatic functions and particularly building Foreign Service assessment capabilities;
—improving management capabilities of the departmental and Foreign Service personnel;
—revising arrangements for employee-management relations, and
—instituting a strong Executive Development Program for both the State Department and the international activities of other government agencies.

In particular, the State Department's personnel management should be given a more professional basis by a single Director of Personnel, responsible for all personnel systems in the Department, and reporting directly to the proposed Under Secretary for Management. Job requirements should be matched more effectively with individual talents through comprehensive manpower planning. A Foreign Affairs Executive Service should be instituted under the leadership of the Department, utilizing the government-wide personnel systems, in order to provide for the development of broad-gauged executives for senior positions in all foreign affairs agencies, and in foreign posts and missions.

Appendix C: A Career in the Department of State

The Department of State employs American citizens in a wide variety of professional, technical, secretarial, and clerical positions both in the United States and at U.S. embassies, consular posts, and missions in foreign countries. Persons interested in serving only within the United States are employed under the civil service system. Professional positions include specialists in foreign affairs, research, education, management, library science, and similar categories requiring a degree in some general or specialized field. Technical positions include specialists in electronics (communications, computer operations, security), maintenance (electrical and mechanical equipment), and other activities calling for technical proficiency. There is considerable turnover in the secretarial field, and a good many openings generally exist. Clerical positions cover the usual civil service register openings for typists and mail room and messenger personnel. Security clearances are required.

Persons interested in serving either at home or abroad are employed under the Foreign Service system, which is entirely separate from the civil service. There are two broad categories—Foreign Service officer (FSO) personnel and Foreign Service Staff (FSS) personnel (including FSS officers as well as support personnel).

Applicants for the position of Foreign Service Officer should complete an official application form in order to take the written examination, which is given in December. The application form and announcement of the examination is contained in a booklet that is published each June and may be obtained by writing to the Board of Examiners, Department of State, Washington, D.C., 20520. Completed applications must be received by the Board of Examiners no later than the closing date specified in the announcement booklet, usually near the end of October.

Candidates must first pass a written and then an oral examination. Those who succeed in both are medically examined, and a background investigation is conducted. Finally, an evaluation is made of each candidate on the basis of all available information, and the names of those found fully qualified entered on a rank order register (waiting list), which becomes the basis for appointments made competitively as vacancies occur. Between 100 and 200 FSO class 7 or 8 officers (the rank depending on age, education, and experience) are usually appointed annually.

Candidates must be at least twenty-one—twenty if the junior year at college has been completed at the time the examination is given. In the past there was an upper age limit of thirty-one, but this has been rescinded. There are no specific educational requirements for appointment to the Foreign Service. However, a broad general knowledge is needed to pass the examinations.

Since 1971, FSO candidates have had to choose one of four functional fields ("cones" as they are called) in which to be examined and in which they will be expected to serve as junior and midcareer officers. These are: administration, commercial/economic affairs, consular affairs, and political affairs. Knowledge of a foreign language is not a requirement for appointment, but after appointment officers are expected to acquire an acceptable level of proficiency in at least one foreign language; junior officers are limited to no more than one promotion until they do so. Full-time training is provided as necessary.

The 1975 entering salary range for FSO-8 was $10,520 per year, for FSO-7, $12,285. At the senior level, the maximum salary for FSO-1 was $36,000. Promotions are based on recommendations of special boards that annually review the performance record of each officer. While officers are abroad their salaries are supplemented, depending on local conditions, by housing, cost-of-living, and hardship post allowances and educational allowances for children.

Foreign Service officers must be willing to serve at any post overseas, as required by the needs of the service. An officer's desire and qualifications for service in a given city, country, or region will be taken into account, but no assurance can be given that he or she will be assigned to the post or area of his or her choice. Assignments to a given office vary from eighteen months to five years (including time spent on home leave), depending on the officer's rank, work, and the nature of the post.

Foreign Service Staff Corps personnel may be appointed without examination to technical, secretarial, and clerical positions for which they are qualified. Entry is usually at the lower grades, but if the need exists, higher-level appointments may be made. The rules for service abroad apply equally to FSO and FSS personnel, and both categories receive the same types of allowances to supplement their salaries while serving overseas. Salaries for Foreign Service staff personnel in 1975 ranged from $7,596 to $27,221.

Information regarding civil service and Foreign Service *Staff Corps* employment may be obtained by writing to the Employment Division, Department of State, Washington, D.C., 20520.

STATISTICS ON DECEMBER 1974
FOREIGN SERVICE WRITTEN EXAMINATION

	Applied	Took	%	Passed	%
STATE	15,318	9,799	63.9	1,525	15.5
USIA	2,581	2,012	77.9	224	11.1
TOTAL	17,899	11,811	65.9	1,749	14.8

Appendix D: State Department Regulations

The regulations of the Department of State are contained in twelve Foreign Affairs manuals. They are listed below by title and with a brief explanation of the contents.

1 FAM—*ORGANIZATION AND FUNCTIONS*
Organizational structure of the Department of State; functions, responsibilities, and authorities of components of the Department and field organization.

2 FAM—*GENERAL*
Foreign Service Regulations: (1) Post management, (2) privileges and immunities (3) protocol, and (4) training.

Department Regulations: (1) issuance of regulatory material and publications, (2) action and clearance procedures, (3) committees and public relations, (4) inspection program, (5) protocol, and (6) opening and closing of Foreign Service posts.

3 FAM—*PERSONNEL*
Employment, compensation, allowances, leave, performance evaluation, conditions of service, separations, and discipline, local employees and consular agents, departmental training, and security of personnel.

4 FAM—*FINANCIAL MANAGEMENT*

Budgeting, disbursing, accounting procedures and financial management of the Department and overseas posts.

5 FAM—*COMMUNICATIONS AND RECORDS*

Authorized correspondence, communications with international agencies, preparation of correspondence, mails, pouches, couriers, media of correspondence, records management, and security of documents.

6 FAM—*GENERAL SERVICES*

Supplies and equipment, publications, language services, safety, space management, travel and transportation, storage of effects, property conservation and maintenance, disposition of property, loss or damage of property, printing and binding, commissary and recreation, safety program, office and residential quarters abroad, and miscellaneous services.

7 FAM—*SPECIAL CONSULAR SERVICES*

Shipping, seamen, notarials, protection and welfare, civil aviation, import controls, and protection of foreign interests.

8 FAM—*CITIZENSHIP AND PASSPORTS*

Laws, regulations, and procedures governing registration and issuance of passports to American citizens abroad.

9 FAM—*VISAS*

Laws, regulations, substantive and procedural notes governing the issuance of visas to aliens.

10 FAM—*ECONOMIC AFFAIRS*

11 FAM—*POLITICAL AFFAIRS* (Classified)

12 FAM—*EDUCATIONAL AND CULTURAL AFFAIRS*

Bibliography

Books

ACHESON, DEAN. *Present at the Creation.* New York: Norton, 1969.
BAILEY, THOMAS A. *A Diplomatic History of the American People.* New York: Appleton-Century-Crofts, 1958.
BARNES, WILLIAM, and JOHN HEATH MORGAN. *The Foreign Service of the United States.* Washington, D.C.: Government Printing Office, 1961.
BERDING, ANDREW. *Foreign Affairs and You!* New York: Doubleday, 1962.
BLANCKÉ, W. WENDELL. *The Foreign Service of the United States.* New York: Praeger, 1969.
CARROLL, HOLBERT N. *The House of Representatives and Foreign Affairs.* Boston: Little, Brown, 1966.
CLUBB, O. EDMUND. *China & Russia.* New York: Columbia University Press, 1971.
DAVIES, JOHN PATON, JR. *Dragon by the Tail.* New York: Norton, 1972.
DECONDE, ALEXANDER. *The American Secretary of State: An Interpretation.* New York: Praeger, 1962.
GORDON, KERMIT, ed. *Agenda for the Nation.* Washington, D.C.: Brookings Institution, 1968.
GRIFFITH, ERNEST S. *Congress, Its Contemporary Role.* New York: New York University Press, 1951.
HARTMANN, FREDERICK H. *The Relations of Nations.* New York: Macmillan, 1967.
————. *The New Age of American Foreign Policy.* New York: Macmillan, 1970.

HENDERSON, JOHN W. *The United States Information Agency*. New York: Praeger, 1969.

HERTER COMMITTEE. *Personnel for the New Diplomacy*. Washington, D.C.: Carnegie Endowment for International Peace, 1962.

Hoover Commission on Organization of the Executive Branch of the Government. *A Report*. Washington, D.C.: Government Printing Office, 1949.

JACKSON, HENRY M., ed. *The National Security Council*. New York: Praeger, 1965.

JONES, ARTHUR G. *The Evolution of Personnel Systems for U.S. Foreign Affairs*. New York: Carnegie Endowment for International Peace, 1965.

KISSINGER, HENRY A. *American Foreign Policy: Three Essays*. New York: Norton, 1969.

————. *The Necessity for Choice*. New York: Harper, 1961.

————. *Nuclear Weapons and Foreign Policy*. New York: Harper, 1957.

————, ed. *Problems of National Strategy*. New York: Praeger, 1965.

LEACACOS, JOHN P. *Fires in the In-Basket*. New York: World, 1968.

————. *Legislation on Foreign Relations*. Committee on Foreign Relations, United States Senate. Committee on Foreign Affairs, U.S. House of Representatives. Washington, D.C.: Government Printing Office, 1971.

MORGENTHAU, HANS J. *Politics Among Nations*. New York: Knopf, 1967.

MURPHY, ROBERT D. *Diplomat Among Warriors*. New York: Doubleday, 1964.

NIXON, RICHARD M. *U.S. Foreign Policy for the 1970's*. A Report to the Congress. Vols. I, II, III. Washington, D.C.: Government Printing Office, 1970, 1971, 1972.

PRICE, DON K., ed. *The Secretary of State*. The American Assembly, Columbia University. Englewood Cliffs: Prentice-Hall, 1960.

REISCHAUER, EDWIN O. *Beyond Vietnam: The United States and Asia*. New York: Knopf, 1968.

ROGERS, WILLIAM P. *United States Foreign Policy*. A Report of the Secretary of State. Department of State Publication 8575. Washington, D.C.: Government Printing Office, 1971.

SAPIN, BURTIN M. *The Making of United States Foreign Policy*. Washington, D.C.: Brookings Institution, 1966.

SIMPSON, SMITH. *Anatomy of the State Department*. Boston: Houghton Mifflin, 1967.

SORENSON, THEODORE S. *The Kennedy Legacy*. New York: Macmillan, 1969.

STUART, GRAHAM H. *The Department of State.* New York: Macmillan, 1949.

TRUMAN, MARGARET. *Harry S. Truman.* New York: William Morrow, 1973.

Wriston Committee. *Toward a Stronger Foreign Service.* Report of the Secretary of State's Public Committee on Personnel, June, 1954. Washington, D.C.: Government Printing Office, 1954.

―――. *United States Foreign Policy.* Study prepared at the request of the Committee on Foreign Relations, United States Senate, by the Brookings Institution, No. 9. Washington, D.C.: Government Printing Office, 1949.

Articles and Periodicals

ASTOR, GERALD. "Henry Kissinger—Strategist in the White House Basement," *Look,* August 12, 1969, 53.

BROOKS, PETER C. "Why Not a Foreign Service Career?" *The Readers Digest,* Vol. 64, October, 1956, 81.

CAMPBELL, JOHN FRANKLIN. "What Is to Be Done?" *Foreign Affairs,* Vol. 1, October, 1970, 81–99.

―――. "Diplomacy for the 70's." A Program of Management Reform for the Department of State. Department of State Publication 8551. Washington, D.C.: Government Printing Office, 1970.

―――. "Employee-Management Relations in the Foreign Service of the United States." Text and Analysis of Executive Order 11636. *Department of State Newsletter.* Special Supplement, January, 1972.

JAVITS, JACOB. "The Congressional Presence in Foreign Relations," *Foreign Affairs,* Vol. 48, No. 2, January, 1970, 221.

MACOMBER, WILLIAM B., JR. "Progress Report on the Management Reform Program," *Department of State Newsletter,* No. 123, July, 1971, 3–6.

―――. "Change in Foggy Bottom: An Anniversary Report," *Department of State Newsletter,* No. 130, Februrary, 1972, 2–5.

―――. "Reform of the U.S. Foreign Assistance Program." Message from President Nixon to the Congress, *The Department of State Bulletin,* Vol. 64, May 10, 1971, 614.

SIMPSON, SMITH, sp. ed. "Resources and Needs of American Diplomacy," *The Annals,* Vol. 380 November, 1968.

―――. "United States Foreign Policy in the Nixon Administration," *The New York Times,* January 18–24, 1971.

WILCOX, FRANCIS O. "President Nixon, the Congress and Foreign Policy," *Michigan Quarterly Review,* Vol. 9, No. 1, Winter, 1970, 37.

Serial Publications

AFSA Bulletin on Management Reform, published periodically, 1971–1972. Washington, D.C.: American Foreign Service Association.

Congressional Record, published daily when Congress is in session. Washington, D.C.: Government Printing Office.

The Department of State Bulletin, published weekly. Washington, D.C.: Government Printing Office.

The Foreign Service Journal, published monthly. Washington, D.C.: American Foreign Service Association.

Issues. Department of State Publication 8488. Washington, D.C.: Government Printing Office.

Library of Congress Information Bulletin. Washington, D.C.

Major Publications of the Department of State. An Annotated Bibliography. Historical Office, Division of Public Affairs. Department of State Publication 7843. Revised, September, 1971. Washington, D.C.: Government Printing Office.

Management Reform Bulletin, published periodically, 1971–1972. Department of State.

Newsletter, published monthly. Department of State.

Organization Manual. U.S. Department of State.

United States Government Organization Manual, published yearly. Office of the Federal Register, National Archives and Records Service, General Services Administration. Washington, D.C.: Government Printing Office.

Weekly Compilation of Presidential Documents, published weekly. Washington, D.C.: Government Printing Office.

Index